AF413060

AUTOMATION IN LIBRARY REFERENCE SERVICES

Recent Titles in
The Greenwood Library Management Collection

Strategic Marketing for Libraries: A Handbook
Elizabeth J. Wood with assistance from Victoria L. Young

The Smaller Academic Library: A Management Handbook
Gerard B. McCabe, editor

Operations Handbook for the Small Academic Library
Gerard B. McCabe, editor

Data Bases for Special Libraries: A Strategic Guide to Information Management
Lynda W. Moulton

Time Management Handbook for Librarians
J. Wesley Cochran

Academic Libraries in Urban and Metropolitan Areas: A Management
Handbook
Gerard B. McCabe, editor

Managing Institutional Archives: Foundational Principles and Practices
Richard J. Cox

Automated Information Retrieval in Libraries
Vicki Anders

Circulation Services in a Small Academic Library
Connie Battaile

Using Consultants in Libraries and Information Centers: A Management
Handbook
Edward D. Garten, editor

Automation in Library Reference Services

A Handbook

Robert Carande

GREENWOOD LIBRARY MANAGEMENT COLLECTION

Greenwood Press
WESTPORT, CONNECTICUT · LONDON

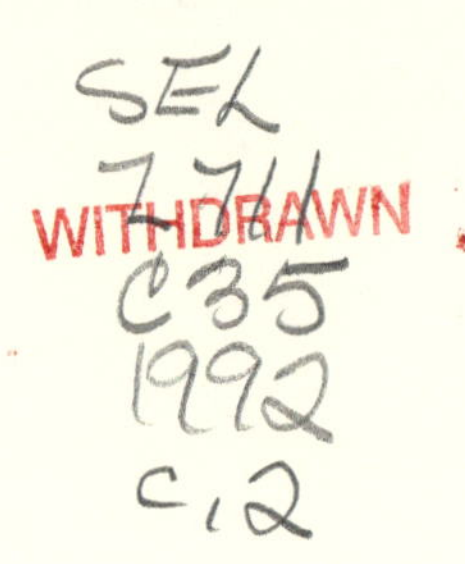
SEL
Z711
WITHDRAWN
C35
1992
c.2

Library of Congress Cataloging-in-Publication Data

Carande, Robert.
    Automation in library reference services : a handbook / Robert
Carande.
        p.   cm. — (Greenwood library management collection, ISSN
0894–2986)
    Includes bibliographical references and index.
    ISBN 0–313–27837–7 (alk. paper)
    1. Reference services (Libraries)—Automation—Management—
Handbooks, manuals, etc.   I. Title.   II. Series.
Z711.C35   1992
025.5′24—dc20   92–19417

British Library Cataloguing in Publication Data is available.

Copyright © 1992 by Robert Carande

All rights reserved. No portion of this book may be
reproduced, by any process or technique, without the
express written consent of the publisher.

Library of Congress Catalog Card Number: 92–19417
ISBN: 0–313–27837–7
ISSN: 0894–2986

First published in 1992

Greenwood Press, 88 Post Road West, Westport, CT 06881
An imprint of Greenwood Publishing Group, Inc.

Printed in the United States of America

The paper used in this book complies with the
Permanent Paper Standard issued by the National
Information Standards Organization (Z39.48–1984).

10 9 8 7 6 5 4 3 2 1

For Kathryn

Contents

Preface

This handbook identifies some of the main elements coming together to create the information environment of the near future. The objective is to involve the reader as a potential actor in these new technologies; consequently, emphasis will be placed on application, with practical considerations and public service advantages of these implementations highlighted.

The future of reference librarianship depends on developing a participatory, hands-on approach to automation. The locale of reference work will make a slow but irreversible migration from the physical confines of the reference desk to the screen and its cursor. In this environment, librarians will apply the concrete concept of information-as-an-organized-system to specific patron-centered information needs. Building this concept, however, means the librarian must play a role in the design of the tools used in its construction. This handbook will be a success if any of the computer-based implementations and challenges I describe inspire readers to become involved in creating reference automation tools.

Many people have made this book possible, not least my colleagues in the San Diego State University Library who have provided a supportive environment for many of my own explorations into automated reference services. I extend my appreciation in particular to Catherine Friedman,

Bruce Harley, Patricia Knobloch, Mike Perkins, Anne Turhollow, Wayne Shimoguchi, and Phillip White for their helpful suggestions and insightful discussions. I especially thank my wife, Kathryn, for her encouragement and feedback during the writing of this book. Whatever shortcomings this book has are solely my responsibility.

Introduction

The effects of automation continue to sweep over information resources and institutions, changing forever the ways and means by which information is collected, connected, stored, retrieved, and used.

Reference services perform several functions in the information-hungry setting of the contemporary world. First, reference work helps people to find specific pieces of information by explaining to them how to use a reference tool or providing the specific fact requested. Reference services also work to equip patrons with the general skills they need to traverse the information environment effectively, teaching patrons that a particular type of reference tool (index, handbook, thesaurus, etc.) exists across disciplines or teaching them what types of information can be found in what types of resources.

These reference functions presume a static series of connections: The routes to the facts will remain the same, the access tools will remain the same, and the demarcations between information will remain the same. Were this the case, automation eventually would eliminate the need for reference librarians. Information concerning any tool could be canned and programmed through a self-paced scroll of screens, and the facts could inevitably be linked together into one universal ready reference file accessible from an Online Public Access Catalog (OPAC) or any other interface.

Reference services do more than help people find information, however.

Another service, though more conceptual, also has a direct bearing on the practice of librarianship: the comprehension and understanding of the operative connections between and the routes to information. This grasp of the working whole, which is continually changing rapidly, requires an unrelenting exploration of and immersion within the world information matrix to maintain currency and knowledge. This knowledge not only consists of knowing what information is available, where it is available, how to find it, and how to retrieve it; it also consists of a series of broader elements: knowing how to find what information is available, knowing how to find where it is available, and so forth. This knowledge encompasses the myriad of burgeoning local resources, such as expert systems, local area networks, mounted data tapes, computer-aided instructional modules, and OPACs, as well as remote sources such as full text databases, anonymous ftp (file transfer protocol) sites (accounts set up on remote computers to allow "strangers" access), remote OPACs, electronic conferences, wide-area information servers, and a variety of interface front ends used as remote search platforms. The knowledge covers where and how resources are physically organized within the local building, as well as how remote resources are linked to one another across the world.

Immense exponential jumps in what is available and how it is available and the ever-shifting connectivity of resources stand as permanent features of the information landscape. The reference librarian's ability to recognize, anticipate, and manage such change so that patrons can be consistently provided with optimum access to information will become one of the defining characteristics of the profession.

This new world information matrix is by no means simply an objective web of resources; it also includes the psychological dimension that reference librarians have always encountered during negotiation: the patron's knowledge and model of how information is ordered. Taylor (1968), in his classic article on question negotiation, identified the contribution of the patron's understanding of how information is organized in the forging of the initial information query. Just as patrons recognized books and card catalogs and conjured up their own models of how to use the library and phrase questions, so too patrons notice CD-ROMs (Compact Disc-Read Only Memory), expert systems, and OPACs and develop a model of how the current configuration of information must be traversed and queried. The automation of reference resources has placed a whole new set of factors—and possible confusion—into the patron's understanding of how information is organized and how best to formulate queries. A full grasp of this world information matrix means a knowledge of how it affects and is understood by the patron and, most important, how it is reflected in the questions the patron asks. The often trumpeted human element of reference services has been amplified by the presence of automation since it introduces radical change and shifting connections into the mix.

This book is like a series of static snapshots of this expanding sphere of information. In many ways, each picture is similar to a hologram, with all other dimensions of information contained and reflected in the matter being examined. For instance, the Online Public Access Catalog appears to be a well-defined and discrete resource whose impact on reference services can and has been analyzed; it is a familiar-enough place to begin demarcating the boundaries of the current state of affairs. Yet this resource is far from stable. What is a straightforward OPAC one year becomes the platform for searching a variety of electronic resources the next year. And the year after, the OPAC can impose its own interface onto remote databases throughout the world. The electronic connections that weave all access points together indicate that there is no line of information that necessarily stands alone. No access resource in the new world of automation has a fixed, innate, inviolable identity. Parameters of every access point are arbitrarily fixed to accommodate local custom and tradition but are essentially wholly malleable. Yet there are still recognizable traditions or "customs" that can be separated out and that still function in librarianship as independent resources in accessing information. The chapters of this book probe those basic categories in terms of the general issues and the challenges raised for reference services and the specific implementations found in libraries.

Because the OPAC is one of the most important elements in the automation of reference services, it is a natural starting place. Chapter 1 provides a general overview of the conceptual roots of the OPAC. It examines the theoretical ideals developed by early pioneers in the light of the configurations found in most libraries today. Several important reference challenges of the OPAC as a dynamic information access platform are identified and evolutionary changes are discussed. The access point, which initially appeared as the computerized version of one of the library's most familiar and discrete resources (the card catalog), provided the technological impetus and platform for the expansion of access far beyond the traditional content of the card catalog. Special mention will be made of the Z39.50 ANSI (American National Standards Institute) standard, which will further enhance the power of "local" OPAC software to impose a common interface on the world's information resources.

Online searching, the subject of chapter 2, is another example of an access point that has evolved far beyond the meaning it had only a few years ago. Remaining within the traditional definition of online searching as access to fee-based vendor systems, several important issues identified in the literature are examined. Telecommunication software is listed, as well as new front-end and gateway technology. A bibliography of online directories found in recent books and journals is provided by major subject discipline.

Chapter 3 treats the explosion of CD-ROM–based reference tools. The factors that make CD-ROM an attractive information medium will remain regardless of future developments within optical disk technology. The idea of a "permanent" or read-only information medium does not rule out manipulation of that information. The linking of CD-ROM technology with the personal computer makes it a powerful reference resource whose contents can be selectively downloaded, reformatted, and smoothly integrated into further intellectual activity. The effect of this automation technology on the reference desk certainly belies the idea that automation will replace the librarian. In many libraries, CD-ROM technology generates the largest number of questions directed at the reference librarian and has been responsible for rapid increase in interlibrary loans. The exposure of students to CD-ROM products has spread the recognition of such automation tools throughout the patron population and has generated intense demand for additional automated resources.

The global networks of BITNET and the Internet comprise the most important development that will affect reference librarians in the rest of the 1990s and beyond. The networks are at the heart of the new interconnectivity, which will eventually make any resource available from any access point. Chapter 4, on networks, provides a general introduction to the major systems and their important reference capacities. Emphasis is placed on the Internet, specifically the telnet, ftp, and mail protocols. Providing access to approximately 300,000 computers throughout the world, the Internet protocols (TCP/IP) have become the structural skeleton upon which the world information net is draped. Listings of library-related conferences and bulletin boards are provided, as well as an information resource directory. The National Research and Education Network is described and its potential effects on librarianship briefly examined. Finally, some revolutionary Z39.50-based interface front ends, specifically the Wide Area Information Server (WAIS) from Thinking Machines, are defined as future super-reference resources.

Chapter 5 examines the place of expert systems in reference services. Expert systems, attempts to translate human skills into the performances of computer programs, provide the most successful application of artificial intelligence to library science in evidence. The idea of an expert system as made up of knowledge base and inference engine is stressed to spotlight the importance of knowledge representation. Specific expert systems are detailed in the categories of reference advisory systems and online search systems. Finally, major steps to be taken when researching and developing an expert system are analyzed.

Natural language processing or understanding, like expert systems, is a part of the discipline of artificial intelligence. Unlike expert systems, however, its presence in the immediate environment of reference automation is not as conspicuous. Nevertheless, the skills of reference librarians during question negotiation are seen as a primary resource for those interested in natural language understanding in terms of an interlocutionary context. Natural language processing as a potential reference automation is situated within the boundaries of a constrained discourse in Chapter 6. These constraints, shared by librarian and patron, make the reference environment an ideal one in which to design natural language interfaces. Several reference negotiation prototypical systems have taken advantage of just such characteristic constraints found in the typical reference discourse to create relatively resilient natural language interfaces.

Chapter 7 addresses the question of the relevance of programming languages to reference services. Certainly with the exponential growth of computer-based reference resources, the skills required to maximize the individual librarian's or library's control over the platform become valuable. Computer programming provides increased control over screen elements, screen sequences, and overall program execution. It also permanently transforms the computer into a more familiar and more hospitable technology. Factors to be considered in deciding whether to devote the time to learning a language include the range of programming projects envisioned and the institutional commitment to support such projects. The further question of whether there should be an "official" programming language for librarianship is considered. Various languages are described, and two, C and BASIC, are identified as possible standard languages.

The last few years have seen much discussion about object orientation, a major model for understanding and representing information processes; it will become the underlying paradigm for many of the important future information technologies and interfaces. Chapter 8 explores the central feature of this approach in terms of programming languages, information systems organization, and information interfaces. The importance of the object paradigm in current and future reference automation is highlighted with several examples. A simple reference discourse is included using turbo C++, providing some indication of how thinking in terms of objects helps organize thoughts about the process of reference negotiation and the transference of that process into computer code.

Chapter 9 discusses a technology that is now leaving the research laboratories. Virtual reality (VR) promises to create new ways through which to visualize information and relationships between information. Sometimes called cyberspace, VR is a three-dimensional environmental matrix in which reality is created by a computer; as such, it is wholly susceptible to human control. The notion of VR as a new information interface involves perceiving it as a possible representation of data and not just as a presentation of environmental objects. Several prominent projects within the virtual reality industry are described, including VR in which two or more individuals can simultaneously occupy the same manufactured reality. Potential roles for VR as an interface for information are being considered within the library and information science community.

The Appendix provides an index by implementation to the literature of reference automation. Attempts have been made to compile a selective index of practical uses of computers that provide automated reference services. Well-known applications such as OPACs and online searching have not been included unless they are connected to particularly novel implementations (natural language front-end online searching, graphic user interface OPAC front ends, etc.). I hope that this index will serve as a source for both practical ideas and concrete methods of application.

The automation of information manipulation in terms of storage, classification, retrieval, and integration into intellectual activity is only a few decades old. The momentum continues to grow, bringing the fruits of automation into new areas, as well as reconstituting and replacing old forms of automation with new. The isolated, discrete resource entities of the traditional library find themselves interconnected through telecommunications nets. Expertise that was formerly personalized and resident within the mind is now objectified and available for continuous public use. Access points that were once unforgiving and forced their interfaces on the patron are slowly becoming malleable and more accommodating to patrons' needs. Patron activities that were once separated, such as information searching and writing, are now being brought together to form an efficient, seamless research environment. Still, with all of this momentum melding together the realm of information, there is created such continuous change and realignment that sometimes it seems to border on chaos. In this milieu, the reference librarian's skill at perceiving the overall shape of the information matrix, its temporary configuration of pathways and connections, and the relative value of its myriad resources to any query is the essential function of reference services. The application of a conceptual grasp of information-as-system to specific patron-centered information needs will remain the central reference skill.

1

The OPAC Concept

The selection, implementation, maintenance, and evaluation of the Online Public Access Catalog in a variety of library settings has been thoroughly documented. Since the early 1970s over 1,000 articles have appeared in both library and computer science journals covering a multitude of OPAC issues. This literature has become so voluminous that by the early 1990s citation analyses have appeared dealing with the referencing patterns and evolutionary trends within this one genre of literature alone (Efthimiadis, 1990b). Recently, several extensive bibliographies covering the literature of the OPAC have been published: Dale (1989) organizes the literature on subject access; Elsbernd, Campbell, and Wesley (1990) selectively provide a bibliography of OPAC instruction; Pask (1990) supplies a selected bibliography on patron education for online systems covering the years 1970–1988. And each month *Library Literature* continues to index several dozen citations on OPAC-related topics.

The extent of this literature and its vitality reflect not only the importance of the OPAC in the contemporary library but also the continued evolution of a central access tool. This presents a dilemma when analyzing the impact that OPACs have had on reference services. A detailed analysis would fill several volumes and be out of date before publication. A broad overview, on the other hand, would be equally problematic since it would depend upon generalizations derived from implementations and scenarios that reflect expedience, not conceptual essence.

The objective of this chapter is to develop a conceptual description of the way OPACs have affected reference services. This is distinguishable from a general description based solely on generalization of details. The conceptual approach involves moving back from the myriad of facts surrounding OPAC implementations. The OPAC is examined in a more speculative manner, using early influential notions of the OPAC to fuel the analysis. The regulatory ideals present in the early, "pretechnical" visions of the OPAC will be seen to have had tremendous influence as ideal forms of access toward which actual implementations strive. The reference challenges that result from the attempted realization of these idealized forms of access will then be examined.

SOME ORIGINAL VISIONS

OPACs have become common reference resources in all kinds of libraries; there can be few librarians who have not been touched by this medium. Indeed, a significant number of librarians have pivotal roles in the sometimes-grueling OPAC implementation process. Much of this process demands a nuts-and-bolts, detailed, and scrupulous interlacing of the library's needs with the software's capacities. This concentration on complex detail precedes either final selection or, in the case of larger state institutions, the composition of an RFP (request for proposal), and becomes even more focused as the library's information resources are reconstituted through the OPAC. Everyone involved is intensely aware that decisions made during implementation will be lived with day-in and day-out for years to come.

To the extent that the profession as a whole is still engrossed in the details of implementing the first generation of OPACs, it may be instructive and helpful to step back and consider the broad underlying concepts behind the OPAC as originally envisioned in the literature. There are times prior to the facticity of practical implementation when the broad and sweeping outlines of a promising future technological possibility can be clearly seen. This vision can be obscured and lost during the detailed attempt to design and promulgate such a technology. The application of computer technology to library information retrieval, specifically to the card catalog, was one such promising technological possibility in the 1960s. During this period several very broad principles and objectives concerning the application of computer technology to the card catalog were clarified by librarians and information scientists. These practitioners were well informed about the practical considerations of information retrieval and unfettered by today's plethora of facts concerning library automation. Their speculations are of great value in grasping the long-term significance of the OPAC to reference services.

Kilgour's External Memory

Writing about the situation of computers in the library during the late 1960s, Kilgour (1970), then the director of the Ohio College Library Center (OCLC), began by identifying the library as an external formation of human memory. Hitherto, the instruments that fed the data of this external memory into the creative activities of individual minds had been cumbersome and imprecise. Although this had been necessary considering the state of information technology, it was nevertheless unfortunate. Ideally this external memory should "transfer data to the human mind with as great speed as possible to prevent hindrance of thought that admits distraction" (2). Kilgour realized that this organic immediacy lay beyond the foreseeable future. And yet, "in the meantime it is entirely feasible to strive for simulation of human memory with speedy recall of bibliographic information" (2).

There was no more important bibliographic resource to automate than the card catalog. The automation of such a process is only the beginning step, however. The OPAC is the initial phase in the construction of what will eventually be a kind of artificial substructure of information underlying and directly accessible to each and every mental act. The emphasis on speed of transmission in terms of the rapidity by which relevant information would be appropriated mentally, and not just transferred from one site to another as a file, has become a key ingredient in critical thinking about OPACs. Kilgour's belief that the "bibliographic" dimension of information would be the first to find its way onto computer has been borne out.

Writing about the objectives of OCLC, Kilgour (1972) states that the database represents only the "first major computerized break-out of classical librarianship" (217). The future development includes the ability to "supply users with textual information when and where they need it" (217). While OCLC was geared primarily for catalogers and was far from being an OPAC, Kilgour saw the computerization of the bibliographic dimension of information as an instance of the automation of any information. The OPAC as part of an ongoing process of broader and broader information access coupled with more precise search and retrieval options is a model that permits the current configuration of the OPAC to be seen as part of a historical evolution. Such a view of the evolving character of the OPAC makes it not just a computerized version of the card catalog but, rather, a platform for future large-scale automation of both "local" and "remote" resources.

Licklider's Procognition System

Another exploration of the library catalog comes from J. C. R. Licklider. Writing in the early 1960s, Licklider (1965) conceived of information as being totally distinct from the material in which it was found (i.e., books). He blamed many of the inefficiencies that then plagued information retrieval on the need to convey information through the transmission of matter. "When information is stored in books," he wrote, "there is no practical way to transfer the information from the store to the user without physically moving the book or the reader or both" (5). Thus, the searching and retrieval of information cannot escape the physical limitations of the medium. The computer offers the possibility of separating information from turgid materiality. Licklider attempted to construct speculatively what he called a "new schema" of the library in which information is communicated to the user without the transmission of matter. Furthermore, he envisioned a situation in which the fund of knowledge held in this new library, or "procognition system" as he called it (40), functions not only as a storage facility but also as a kind of extended organ of intelligence that researchers can access when examining a topic or the results of empirical experiments. This procognition system filters new information through the fund of collective human knowledge to derive significances and relevancies not immediately apparent to the individual researcher. The library thus acts as a kind of resonator, amplifying the meaning of a piece of information until its true and ultimate import is recognized.

The most realistic beginning point in the development of the procognition system is the automation of the card catalog. "As soon as it is feasible, . . . multiple computer console systems should be brought into contact with libraries. Perhaps they should be connected first to the Card Catalogs. Then they should be used in the development of descriptor-based retrieval systems" (Licklider, 69). The OPAC as an initial component in an intelligence and knowledge amplification scheme again situates the technology of the OPAC within the broader context of an evolutionary progression of information automation.

Grignetti's Automated Card Catalog

Licklider identified one of the key steps on the road to a full procognition system as the development of an automated card catalog. He referred to the promising efforts of Grignetti, whose work in the early 1960s had resulted in a completely screen-based (oscilloscope) interactive computer catalog capable of supporting a sophisticated Boolean logic.

In a 1963 report for Bolt, Beranek and Newman, Grignetti described an automated card catalog (ACC) running on a state-of-the-art PDP-1 computer. Ordinary card catalogs do not provide the indexing precision required to facilitate exacting search queries. Users are forced to wade through many irrelevant hits within a single subject heading in a quest for the few that focus on the right issue. Grignetti's solution to the problem of index imprecision was the ACC, providing computerized access to a database stored on magnetic tape. Such access includes full multiterm Boolean searching. The ACC even contains a robust spell checker that runs every term through a "sound index" containing the "phonemic content of the word" (8). If a word is spelled incorrectly but "sounds" correct, the ACC queries the user concerning the spelling. "Cards" fulfilling the Boolean query conditions are displayed on an oscilloscope screen for the user to inspect.

Grignetti's ACC was more than just an idea. Approximately twenty-five years before the OPAC became a common library fixture, the ACC had all the basic structures that have become essential to OPAC configuration: visual displays, indexed fields, and some means of effecting a Boolean search. Regarding this last structure, the ACC equipped with operators AND, OR, and NOT still exceeds the Boolean precision possible using most large OPAC software. Of course, the ACC was not equipped to deal with the number of multiple users currently supported by OPACs, but in theory additional "ports" could be wired.

Grignetti's main concern, retrieval precision, was shared by other information scientists of the time. The Boolean operations permitted by the ACC focused the search onto just those card records that were relevant. Users of single-index search systems such as card catalogs achieved high levels of recall (relevant records retrieved over total relevant records in the catalog) only be accepting low levels of precision (relevant records out of all records actually "hit"). The ACC, and subsequent automated catalogs, made certain that relevancy was not so adversely dependent on low levels of precision.

Swanson's Console Model

Another speculative description of the possibilities of the computerized catalog is found in Don Swanson's 1964 article, "Dialogues with a Catalog." Swanson took an operative approach and set about imagining the "ideal intellectual interaction between the library user and the bibliographic tools of the library" (113). The key development would be that of the console, a "machine operated directly by the user which communicates with automated bibliographic tools" (113). The console would consist of a keyboard, a cathode ray tube display, and some means of creating a hard copy of the resultant bibliography. Access to digitally stored bibliographic data would be supplemented with microfilm images (on demand) of tables of contents, title pages, and key passages of any work desired. In addition to title and author searches, the console would be able to engage the database to construct subject-related bibliographies. After limiting the "programmed interrogation" to a specific discipline field, natural language input or key-word association would be accepted. Thereafter, a discipline-related thesaurus, replete with a rich associative internal structure, would be applied to all the natural language key words, basically performing a Boolean AND operation to all terms translated into "authorized" headings. The console would also deliver "reprints of a group of specific articles bound together in a single package," creating what the author calls "custom built journals" (120). Under a "browse" option, all bibliographic entries would be linked with bibliographies of books on related subjects. Thus, after procuring a specific bibliography on a given subject or by a particular author, the user could choose a citation and summon up other citations to documents with similar subjects. Swanson also suggested the ability of the console to store and link individual users' evaluative notes to specific bibliographic items, providing a kind of personal hypertext information reservoir.

Swanson's console model empowered individual users by bringing as much information to them as possible. The console acted as both an information search engine and a retrieval mechanism for citation, text, and personal notations. It not only allowed users to see what was in the database but also let them directly integrate the information into their creative intellectual enterprise. Just like the current attempts at developing sophisticated OPAC front ends that contain word processors and citation formatters, the console configured the link between bibliographic data and intellectual research within a single interface.

Heilprin and the Coming Information Crisis

In the early 1960s, at a time of technological competition with the Soviet Union, information scientists and librarians became concerned with the exponential growth and pattern of information. Their concern arose from two different problems: the physical difficulty of storing and making room for the growing body of literature and the difficulty of retrieving the precise documents required to fulfill a complex information need.

L. B. Heilprin of the Council on Library Resources saw disaster in the offing: "What we face is a breakdown in the established system of communication of recorded knowledge. The systems of the past are being saturated" (Heilprin, 1961, 7). Seeing great promise in the advent of machine indexing and abstracting, Heilprin sought to sketch out a national (or international) network of finely meshed association matrices between units of information that would make accessing the growing body of knowledge more precise and quicker. "The extent to which the mind can search for messages external to itself," he wrote, "is determined by the extent of the bibliographic (to use one word for all aspects of the process) connections between messages" (8).

The classification and indexing of knowledge would be done by machines simulating human mental processes. After reviewing the Perceptron and Heinz von Foerster's early "biological-type computers" as offering promise for the simulation of human discrimination, Heilprin emphasized the importance and feasibility of then current text-reading devices for making broad, automatic categorial classifications of format type. Robust machines capable of indexing and abstracting would follow in the future.

The human retrieval of knowledge would be assisted by "teaching machines," which, in Heilprin's description, act like a hybrid expert system and OPAC. Organized by specific disciplines, all major topics and primary materials would be accessible directly through a rich set of associated index terms. When desiring bibliographic information on secondary material and more detailed data, the user would be led by the computer through a series of questions and answers, narrowing the topic further and further through a variety of possible association paths, until the final bibliographic objective was found. Searches, then, would not be dependent on brute string matching of input terms to authority terms but on the knowledge structure of the discipline itself. The linking of discipline intelligence and retrieval precision presupposed by such a system would require a national effort to support and would need constant attention and updating.

Heilprin believed that the mechanical basis for the solution to the "information problem" already existed. Further development in the capacity of computers to simulate mental activity, chiefly associative, was only a matter of time. The chief obstacle he saw was the ignorance of the public to the looming information crisis.

Griffin's Library of Tomorrow

Heilprin was somewhat hesitant about the eventual ability of computers to perform outright deductive and inductive reasoning; Marjorie Griffin (1962), however, was fully convinced that such powers would make the library of the late 1970s almost purely machine mediated in all its major functions. Documents would be scanned into machine-readable form and indexed, abstracted, and analyzed for content "on the basis of word frequency, phrase frequency and word relationships" (1555). Stored electronically, such documents would be searchable from remote locations.

Information access would again involve a hybrid of reference negotiation simulation systems and what today passes as an OPAC: "The reference function will be expanded to involve an heuristic querying system between the user and the machine. This will supersede the librarian's interrogation at a reference desk" (Griffin, 1962, 1556). Card catalog and reference desk would be combined to form an intelligent dialogue, complete with feedback loops to ensure resiliency of response. The result would be a bibliography of titles and abstracts or even full documents. A browsing machine would also be available "with an associative memory" encouraging serendipity in the user's interaction with the database. Griffin predicted that the "library of tomorrow is a library filled with people and not with books" (1557).

REGULATORY IDEAS UNDERLYING THE VISION

Numerous other visionary outlines from the 1960s and early 1970s influenced the general direction of practical OPAC research and development. These ideal objectives are still with us as regulatory ideals influencing the direction in which public access catalogs advance. They include: precision of the search engine, including a full array of Boolean operators and proximity locators; speed of information access; intelligent feedback concerning search strategy and results through a dialogue design; automatic search strategy enhancement; integration with other kinds of bibliographic and non-bibliographic information, such as union catalogs, periodical indexes, full text, and personal files; a workstation-like environment letting the user "process" and "link" together OPAC information with other pieces of information; and the capacity (of the OPAC) to identify other significant items not directly found by the search but that ought to be of interest. Overarching all other ideals is the notion that the OPAC is a component in an evolutionary process of automation in the library. Nevertheless, because of the commercialization of OPAC technology, such ideals are difficult to discern clearly as realistic objectives in the evolutionary development of OPACs.

The regulatory ideals underlying and guiding OPAC implementations are in various stages of realization. Clearly any contemporary configuration of the OPAC is best seen as a snapshot of an ongoing developmental process that possesses greater and greater momentum over time. The complete realization of these "ideals" can be boiled down to a single screen whose cursor is infinitely three-dimensional. To the extent that the cursor represents the volitional power of the patron, the evolution of the OPAC is an evolution of the patron's power to choose. Enhancement of the available choices for the patron, not to mention the multiplicity of interfaces, command structures and navigational possibilities, and the very revolutionary change implicit in screen-based searching itself, promises to be an ongoing challenge to reference services. The configuration most common today, though a momentary phenomenon soon to change, already holds the basic dimensions of this challenge.

EFFECTS ON REFERENCE SERVICE

The late 1980s and early 1990s have seen a significant evolution in the OPAC as it changes from a public access catalog to a public access information gateway to locally and remotely mounted data and knowledge bases. The ideals enumerated above are slowly being realized. This results in several pervasive phenomena whose impacts on reference service have challenged traditional methods of providing public service: dispersal of access points, homogeneity of information shape, and proliferation of different interfaces summonable to the same screen.

Dispersal of Access

A computerized catalog transforms the whole concept of location. A card catalog had a physical location and distinct boundary in space and time; an OPAC's "location" is less obvious. In some ways it is more realistic to represent or think of the OPAC's location as a node on a communication grid rather than as a physical point in Euclidean space. The paradigm of proximity is replaced by that of connectivity. That patrons themselves grasp the connotations of this new paradigm is revealed by the strong and immediate demand for remote access the moment computer terminals appear in place of the card catalog. A national online survey (Matthews, Lawrence, & Ferguson, 1983) found that 34.9 percent of the respondents requested availability of terminals outside the library (228). Within the library itself, apart from issues of remote access, the establishment of an OPAC multiplies access points. Although most libraries continue to cluster terminals around reference service points, terminals are also dispersed throughout various floors and can be found in remote locations within the library. Since the OPAC exists wherever a screen is capable of summoning up the catalog, the "location" of the catalog depends more on the connectivity of the telecommunication system than on the availability of physical space.

Multiplication of access points and the transformation of the physically based card catalog into the telecommunication-based computerized catalog has challenged the ability of public services to provide assistance with and instruction for this central reference resource. With the card catalog, access was restricted to one locale, which in the case of most libraries was near the reference desk. Instruction on conducting author, title, and subject searches could be efficiently offered. Both proactive approaches on the part of public services and requests from patrons physically proximate to those services made high standards of instruction expected and possible.

When the catalog became a telepresence whose location ceased being fundamentally physical and whose access points came to include terminals both near to and far from the reference desk, the physical conditions upon which traditional catalog instruction rested disappeared. While the catalog has become telepresent, no similar systematic transformation regarding instruction on search strategy formulation, application of authority names and uniform titles, and other expertise has taken place on the public services side. The need for a non–locale-based bibliographic instruction for OPAC use is pressing. The extensive list of user problems summarized by Yee (1991) in a review of recent literature is a good indication of the extent of the need. Yee identified the following categories of major patron problems in the use of OPACs:

Finding subject terms,
Enlarging search results,
Overspecification, too many search terms,
Key word versus phrase searching relevance,
Misinterpretation of error messages,
Narrowing search results,
Problems with stoplist,
Viewing long displays,
Infrequent use of system,
Typos and spelling errors,
Use of control vocabulary,
Confusion with various files, indexes, and record fields,
Abbreviations and initialisms,
Wrong first word when phrase searching,
Word spacing and hyphenization,
Remembering correct system commands,
Scope of catalog,
Failure to use relevant features (truncation),
Understanding display codes and abbreviations,
Display too brief,
Help screen confusing,
Difficulty with Boolean logic. (93–94)

OPAC vendors permit some freedom in the design of help aids. Typically these help screens are context free and contain lists of commands or brief descriptions of OPAC contents. Some systems permit the summoning of specific help files organized around important commands and accessed by some syntax like HELP followed by SUBJECT. The MELVYL system at the University of California is often mentioned as an example of an online catalog with context-sensitive help screens. Each menu screen prompts the user for one of a series of possible commands. The HELP command brings a further description of the kind of decision required by the user. The HELP screens themselves are enhanced by a series of EXPLAIN options that provide even greater detail concerning specific commands and options. The MELVYL HELP and EXPLAIN utilities are good at providing navigational clarity and determining the meaning and function of system commands, but even such a clear, powerful, and mutually reinforcing system of instructions provides no guidance in formulating search strategy or in the interpretation and evaluation of search results. Most of the categories Yee enumerated remain untouched.

With a few notable exceptions, most sophisticated help utilities are unable to focus instruction on the patron's specific objective, and only a few base their instructions on even the simplest multiple user models (beginner, intermediate, etc.). Systems such as the Okapi catalog at the Polytechnic of Central London and the Mirlyn system at the University of Michigan provide transparent help in which the user strategy is followed and supplemented by the catalog without the user necessarily knowing what the catalog has done (Drabenstott, 1990). To the extent that help is contextual, it is aimed primarily at successfully completing a given search strategy. But little interactive instruction is offered (Drabenstott, 1990). Even if a given search is enhanced, no similar augmentation occurs in the user's skills. Furthermore, since the help is transparent, the user does not know when the enhancement is provided, leading to the possibility that mediocre search habits, which were successful because they were enhanced, will be reinforced.

Commonality of Information Shape

The fully fleshed-out OPAC provides another set of reference challenges, possibly less intractable, based on the homogeneity of information shape it enforces. The concept of information shape designates the distinctive physically based graphic features inherent in whatever medium is used to convey, store, and display information. In the case of the card catalog, the catalog card, with its identifiable 3- by 5-inch shape, black typeface library elite font, bibliographically describing one item, has a distinctive information shape. The typical periodical index, which is a multivolume work consisting of citations grouped by subject and listed in columns, has another distinctive shape. Furthermore, these shapes have specific spatiotemporal locations that are more or less self-evident; an 8½- by 11-inch periodical index will not fit into a catalog drawer, nor are book shelves likely depositories for catalog cards.

With the current OPAC, all information possesses the same shape: glowing electroluminescent ASCII characters. This exacerbates certain tendencies toward misinterpretation, especially when the OPAC screen offers, as is more and more becoming the case, access to periodical indexes and other locally mounted information resources. Common information shape makes it very easy for patrons to conflate the bibliographic description of one type of item with that of another. Books are confused with periodicals, and periodical article citations with books. Furthermore, patrons, accustomed to finding a multiplicity of source kinds with the same shape on a given system, may expect the same coverage from other computerized bibliographic resources and not immediately (visually) recognize that this is not the case.

The problem of shape commonality can be remedied by instruction or by using more sophisticated terminal graphics that renders each different source type using different fonts and colors. Currently, this approach is costly. State-of-the-art GUI (graphic user interfaces) desktops, which act as intuitive front ends, go some distance in sorting out information shape by demarcating distinctive launch points (so too, for that matter, does any carefully crafted text-based main menu). Once the user is in the file, however, the omnipresent "shape" reasserts itself. In addition to cost, the thorough presentation of differing kinds of sources through differing graphics and font media requires and awaits some standardization, since the OPAC increasingly will be a springboard to remote systems.

That leaves the method of instruction from reference librarians to instill sensitivity in the patron to information format (book, journal, etc.). Since the OPAC is quickly transforming itself into a gateway through which periodical indexes, near and far, can be accessed, commonality of information shape will become an even more pronounced problem, creating greater time demands on reference staff.

Diversity of Interface

The converse of the difficulty that arises through the homogeneity of information shape occurs when the user is lulled into expecting similarity in interface. The interface that mediates between user and catalog may be entirely different from that which mediates between user and locally mounted index files despite the fact they are accessed through the same screen. It will not be apparent to the user that there will be a difference or should be a difference. Particular difficulties arise when the same screen that accesses the OPAC also accesses a local area network (LAN) with CD-ROM products from different vendors. The interfaces in such cases can proliferate, creating difficulties for information retrieval and placing further demands on the reference desk's instructional resources. Resolving this problem has become a concern for many in the library community who have turned their interests to developing user-friendly front ends that provide a single, consistent interface. The front end translates the patron's requests into the proper query language automatically, freeing the patron to concentrate on information retrieval rather than the appropriate command language. Several producers of OPAC software "massage" vendor-specific periodical indexes so that they are searchable using a single front end, typically identical to the OPAC interface. A working example of such a vendor-supplied front end exists in the Colorado Alliance of Research Libraries (CARL), available through the Internet. There one can use the same commands to search over a number of different OPACs, periodical indexes, and full-text files.

This confusing diversity of interface, particularly within the realm of bibliographic databases such as online catalogs and vendor-mounted periodical indexes, may be mitigated somewhat by the development of standardized query procedures such as the common command language. In addition, the "Information Retrieval Service Definition and Protocol Specifications for Library Applications," more commonly referred to as the NISO Z39.50 standard, permits a "local" computer to perform search retrieval at a distant database using the "local" computer's familiar interface options. The implementation of such a protocol is now underway at several institutions. Both OCLC and RLIN (Research Libraries Information Network) are developing Z39.50 servers, and Thinking Machines has developed the Wide Area Information Server (WAIS) for use on Dow Jones databases. Data Research Associates (DRA) has invested heavily in creating networking software based on Z39.50. It is working with the University of California's MELVYL system to permit extension of the MELVYL search interface onto circulation record files. The idea of an underlying standard that will permit the familiar "local" search interface to project itself onto "remote" or "foreign" databases is one of the more exciting possibilities in the development of the OPAC.

CONCLUSION

The OPAC is a process, an ever-expanding opportunity, not a static unchanging resource. One month a patron finds no way of looking up specific articles on an OPAC; the next month, this capability has been added to the system. Bibliographic instruction aimed at the catalog needs to be continuous and flexible. The epoch of discrete reference tools is coming to an end. Patrons require awareness not just of the surface features of the information landscape but of the internal infrastructure. This will permit the patron to understand that the rapid changes taking place are not the result of arbitrary whim but of stages in a development toward a single, infinitely deep and broad, screen of access.

The online public access catalog inaugurated a new epoch in information retrieval. It rationalized and made bibliographic access more efficient, and it increased flexibility of search strategy and the number of access options (author, title, subject, key word, call number, etc.). Perhaps the most important result of this computerization is the fact that it meant the installation within libraries of an adaptable infrastructure that could be extended outward and linked to more and more information resources. This effort has just begun, and at times problems of standardization seem overwhelming. Yet the realization of a single screen possessed of an infinitely extended cursor linked to the entire universe of information will owe much to this period of OPAC implementation.

2

Online Searching

Online searching was the first modern automation technology that directly influenced the way reference services were conducted in libraries of all types. It forever changed librarians' range of effectiveness and self-image. Valuable reference skills, such as knowledge of resources, negotiating sensitivity, and the ability to link an information need with the proper resource, were supplemented by the logical manipulation of sets, applied algebras of relevance versus recall, and the mastery of a relatively complex software command interface. The distinction between information science as a theoretical discipline and librarianship as an applied practice began blurring as search strategies and assessments conducted at the reference desk began using the logic of Boolean operators, the results of citation analysis, and the categories and terminology of information retrieval. The traditional skills of the librarian had to be melded with those of the information scientist. Many library programs, realizing the need to expand the curriculum to include information science, changed their names to indicate this new reality.

For the library as an institution, the advent of online searching was the first step in a continuing process of expanding information access and information dematerialization. The egalitarian aspects of this information expansion were obscured initially because of the high expense of conducting comprehensive searches and the complexity of the powerful command systems provided by major vendors. Yet there was something reassuring in a technology that permitted the smallest libraries to jump beyond their confined physical collections out into the relatively unrestricted universe of bibliographic data. That the reality was, and has been, less than the dream is of little consequence compared to the expectations it has fostered. Such expectations are among the most important forces guiding the profession toward a completely rationalized open system.

The phrases "online searching," "online reference services," and "database searching" have come to include many different search environments. Among the reference activities that now fall under these rubrics are searching of remote databases, locally mounted databases, and CD-ROM–based indexes on LANs. To the extent that all these activities are some kind of computerized information query, dependent on some kind of telecommunications, they might loosely be described as online. To complicate the issue, running through all these various "online" environments is the division between end user and mediated search approaches. And, of course, an OPAC is literally an "online" public access catalog. Consequently, "online reference services" has become a vague and indefinite descriptor for a whole cluster of computer-enhanced reference activities. In academic libraries, a clear reflection of this rapid growth and dissolution of functional boundaries can be seen in the name changes for committees overseeing "online" activities. Names such as "Online Computer Search Committee" or "Computer Searching Committee" have been replaced by "Electronic Reference Services Committee" and "Committee for Automation," indicating the wide diversity of computerized "online" offerings found in most libraries.

This chapter defines online searching in its traditional sense: the searching of remote databases, usually bibliographic, typically Dialog, Bibliographic Retrieval Services (BRS), and Scientific and Technical Information Network (STN) through the public telecommunication network. Because of the expense and complexity of the search strategies employed, such searching is usually done or overseen by a trained librarian intermediary. CD-ROM, OPACs, online ready reference, and searching the various networks such as Internet and BITNET, though closely related, are treated in separate chapters.

Despite the fact that the definition of online service has grown to encompass more and more activities, the librarian-mediated search is still an identifiable, and extremely important, component of the services offered by most reference departments. Without ignoring the considerable progress in the development of expert systems for online searching, research indicates that librarian-mediated online searching will remain vital into the foreseeable future (Cornick, 1989; Bernal & Renner, 1990).

There was a time in the 1970s when online searching was considered practically synonymous with reference automation or computerized reference service in general. Arguably, it is the most studied element of reference automation and finds its roots in the early machine-searchable inverted indexes of the 1950s and 1960s. The initial objective of this chapter is to identify the perennial issues and their respective bibliographies that have emerged during two decades of mediated online searching. Surprisingly, considering the computerized basis of this new access point, the most important of these issues has been neither technical nor practical but political. Three issues are examined: Who pays? When does the patron search? Which librarians search? The current telecommunication and front-end software is then described, and a brief directory of manufacturers is offered. The chapter ends with a bibliography of selected online directories, organized by subject, published since 1986.

WHO PAYS?

During the late 1970s, lively debate occurred over competing approaches to funding online search services. One side argued that in an environment of finite budgets, the only way of offering this new, expensive technology was to introduce a fee schedule. The inability to predict demand, and thereby cost, to any great degree also made the service difficult to integrate into a line item budget cycle, and therefore a pay-as-you-go policy seemed inevitable, if not always ideal. Proponents of "free access" attacked fee-based proposals, claiming they would create inequities in information access based on socioeconomic status, anathema to the American tradition of open access.

This economically and politically based issue has not disappeared. As late as 1986, a survey of academic librarians (McKinney & Mosbey, 1986) cited the charging/financial issue as the chief unresolved problem in online search services. At least one researcher (Meglio, 1987) declared that any charge is a "barrier," and the issue is never far from discussion of the proposed National Research and Education Network (NREN).

There is clear evidence that fees are an impediment to searching. Several experiments in totally free search services resulted in an upsurge in online searching, experimentation, and patron satisfaction (Diodata, 1986). Such free access is extremely rare, however. In 1981, prior to the advent of CD-ROM, a survey (Lamb, 1981) of academic libraries identified only two of forty-six as describing their fee schedule as "free" (79). The majority listed either straight cost recovery or cost-plus-surcharge as descriptive of their fee schedule. A later study (McKinney & Mosbey, 1986) found that 84 percent of academic libraries charged a fee.

The belief that online services are too costly to permit a library to offer them without charge has come under attack from several directions. Quint (1987), supporting greater accessibility of online services, believes that the "too expensive" argument masks a conscious prioritizing of library objectives, which she finds suspect. In arguing for a new system of priorities, with emphasis on provision of a patron-centered information service, she questions the monies currently spent on technical services, administration, and library physical design. A new system of priorities, with user access playing a prominent part, would find online availability at the beginning of the list. Nielsen (1987) conducted empirical research to determine whether librarians are more responsive to patron needs in a fee-based or no-charge environment. The study found that while certain measures of responsiveness increased in a fee-based context, the fee-based approach "distorts the overall allocation of service provided in a general reference department" (36) because it increases significantly the time professionals spend on clerical work (maintaining search logs, payment records, billing, etc.) and impairs the underlying reference ethic of unrestrained access. Similarly, Cooper and DeWath (1977) found that fee-based services some-times *increase* the costs to the institution, not only by added clerical re-sponsibilities but by increasing the amount of professional time spent in preparation for and explaining the search.

By the early 1990s, the issue had lost some of its polemical edge and philosophical urgency due to the rise of CD-ROMs, locally mounted da-tabases, and LAN-based CD-ROM systems, whose costs were predictable and therefore amenable to fiscal planning. Nevertheless, even in libraries that have invested heavily in the new technologies, there are many times when a mediated online search is still the best strategy. In most academic and public libraries, it is not surprising to find the Wilson Indexes, Eric, PsychLIT, or Medline up and running on CD-ROM stand-alones, LANs, or locally mounted databases. More expensive resources, however, are less in evidence. In many libraries, products such as INSPEC, Compendex, and important business databases are available only as computerized op-tions through the various online services. This leaves many areas (computer science, mathematics, physics, astronomy, and chemistry) still dependent on the traditional online options for comprehensive access. And, finally, in an ironic twist, access to CD-ROM in some institutions (Schloman, Gatten, & Byerly, 1990) is being offered on a pay-for-information basis. It is premature to put the pay-access versus free-access to computerized information issue to rest yet.

WHO SEARCHES?

Libraries have struggled with the issue of end user searching since the beginning of online database availability. It seems a reasonable goal to have systems that are friendly enough to accommodate direct user access and patrons skilled enough to take advantage of the opportunity. Direct (skilled) user access frees the librarian from the role of mediator, which is both time-consuming and intrusive to all concerned. This objective, however, has not been easy to achieve. Primary obstacles include complexity of online database indexes (Baker, 1981; Hunter, 1983; Peischl & Montgomery, 1986) and their expense (Arnold, 1987). However, even with the advent of user-friendly CD-ROM products, which sidestep considerations of online time expense, patrons frequently need the assistance of a professional intermediary to cast and pursue an effective search strategy (Miller, Kirby, & Templeton, 1988). Cornick's (1989) research at the University of North Carolina shows that many potential patrons of end user searching prefer the fee-based mediated search over its free end user–based counterpart because of the mediator's perceived "expertise." Furthermore, case studies of the superior effectiveness of trained online searchers over self-taught end users (Fjallbrant, Kihlen, & Malmgren 1983; Hurt, 1983) indicate that many end users not asking for assistance might nonetheless benefit from such intervention. The question of the place of the end user in online reference services ultimately boils down to the question of end user education, the ability of the reference staff to provide such education, and the continued accessibility of "expertise" to which the end user can turn. The division between end user searching and mediated searching may be a false one: optimum end user searching may be achievable only in an environment where the search expertise of the librarian is available.

A number of related issues circle around the topic of end user education: Who trains end users? How are end users trained? How can end users' search strategies and results be evaluated in terms of effectiveness and efficiency?

Proponents of direct end user searching can point to the advent of user-friendly services such as Dialog's Knowledge Index and BRS's After Dark as minimizing the need for formal training. Front-end systems such as EasyNet also offer simple menu-driven access to a variety of vendor systems. The eventual commercial release of artificial intelligence front ends promises to create an end user searching interface capable of accommodating natural language requests and question-negotiation dialogues. Although making no claims for artificial intelligence, some software, such as Symantics Q/A, already provides restricted natural language querying of a database (see chapter 6 for further details on commercially available natural language interfaces). Others advocate full-scale formal training of end users within a variety of curriculum contexts. However, even with the most detailed elaborate training, end users are likely to become competent practitioners only if they subsequently conduct online searches frequently and regularly. Even the expertise of a highly skilled online searcher soon suffers from infrequent use.

How online searching is taught to the end user depends on the institutional context (Elias, Vaupel, & Lingwood, 1980; Linder et al., 1986; Tatalias, 1985), databases searched (Janke, 1984), the overall level of competence desired (Faibisoff & Hurych, 1981; Steffen 1986), and cost/equipment availability factors (Bodtke-Roberts, 1983; Lucia & Roysdon, 1984; Roberts & Jensen, 1986). The literature indicates certain phenomena that seem to be relevant across contexts.

1. Not surprisingly, training seems to be best accomplished on a one-to-one basis. Gordon (1983) emphasizes its importance in education, and Linder and colleagues (1986) identify the same technique as crucial to the education of medical physician searchers. Even with user-friendly BRS After Dark, Simon (1986) found the one-on-one presearch aid was effective in guaranteeing a successful search. Speaking of CD-ROM products, Miller, Kirby, and Templeton (1988) concluded, as Simon did, that only rigorous one-on-one training ensures improved end user search strategies.

2. Access to a written manual is vital to continued search effectiveness, even after rigorous training. Hutchins, Anders, and Jaros (1987) compared a slide/tape program and a CAI (computer aided instruction) to a printed training manual and preferred the latter due to its ease of use, updating, and accessibility. In a related context, Friend (1990) suggests providing end users with information in several formats, including a training packet.

3. Search effectiveness is enhanced if the trained end user can depend on the intervention of a professional librarian when necessary (Hartely, Keen, Large & Tedd, 1990).

4. Information self-interest is the most effective motivation for end users in training. Elias, Vaupel, and Lingwood (1980) showed the importance of stressing concrete information objectives in holding end user interest across educational, student, and managerial groups.

5. Some researchers have found that truly superior end user training, on databases as they are currently configured, is too expensive for institutions to sustain (Gordon, 1983).

Batt (1988) provides an excellent annotated bibliography on end user searching, and the issue of end user education is also treated in Pask's annotated bibliography (1990). Of importance as an indication of both policy and ideological commitment is the American Library Association's Reference and Adult Services Division's guidelines for the use of online systems by end users. These guidelines appeared in the Winter 1985 issue of *RQ*.

In addition to the end user issue, there is another dimension to the question, Who searches? Specifically, who will conduct the intermediate search? In a reference setting, what are the principles governing the division of online responsibilities? This is an important question even to institutions that seek to support an end user approach, since end user searching is most successful when conducted in an environment that permits the end user access to a trained online professional. In settings where end user CD-ROM and free, mediated online searches are available, mediated searching invariably rises, indicating that end user activity fosters reliance on the skills of trained intermediaries (Bernal & Renner, 1990).

The manner in which the responsibilities are divided depends upon institutional setting, but there are at least three common ways of dividing the work among librarians:

1. Online search responsibilities evenly divided throughout staff irrespective of bibliographic responsibilities.
2. Online search responsibilities determined by bibliographic specialization throughout the entire staff.
3. A subset of staff chosen as online specialists.

The first two configurations are similar in their emphasis on total professional staff participation in the area of online responsibility. Apart from arguments based on broad conceptions of fairness, such a division of responsibilities has some powerful justifications. All reference librarians should be competent with using important technologically based access points to information. To restrict some reference librarians from conducting or advising online searching is to deprive them of what could be considered a professional right to exercise and strengthen those skills that constitute their livelihood. As a kind of resource, the electronic information medium has more similarities to paper/manual than differences. Adopting a policy that mandates a restricted number of searchers places those outside this group in the precarious position of not being able to aid patrons with a number of important resources. Ultimately, online databases are information access points, and familiarity and facility with them is just as important to professional reference service as is competence with the paper resources. Most important, electronic access points will play a greater and greater part in the future of reference services, and to skew the division of online responsibilities could be the beginning of a serious disparity and imbalance within the institution's reference service. With electronic access as an important future paradigm, those restricted from online searching, by either administrative fiat or their own discomfort with computer technology, may find themselves in greater difficulty in being able to provide needed information as OPACS, networks, expert systems, and CD-ROMs proliferate.

Expertise in online searching is also required to provide state-of-the-art ready reference, and there exists research (Hitchingham, Titus & Pettengill, 1984) suggesting that restricting reference librarians from intermediate searching adversely affects their ready-reference contributions at the desk. Versatility and efficacy at handling the variety of questions that arise at a busy reference desk depend on the ability to determine quickly which questions lend themselves to rapid online solutions.

On the other side, the creation of online specialists as a subset of the professional staff also musters strong arguments in its favor. Everyone has certain strengths and weaknesses. Why force those with no special talents in online searching to take on a responsibility they cannot do well? Training and the requisite continuing education require great expense and investments of time by the institution and should be spent only on those who show promise (Riechel, 1989). To believe that any reference librarian is just as good as any other in providing online searching and advice defies experience. The conception of fairness can now be turned to the patron: Why should patrons get poor or even fair online service when they could consistently receive excellent service from specialists who have a knack for manipulating electronic databases? Furthermore, in institutions where the demand for online searching is small, not creating an online search specialist almost guarantees the service will consistently be inferior since no searcher will have frequent, regular experience upon which to draw.

While differing institutional environments, patron expectations, and reference service missions are factors that will influence the division of online search responsibilities, all things being equal, the arguments for total staff involvement seem strongest. In particular, the growing interdependency of traditional reference desk service with online gateways to local information networks and OPACS, national commercial vendor systems, and large international systems (Internet, BITNET) make versatility in electronic resources a central skill of the reference librarian. Whatever benefits will be derived through selectively identifying the "best" online searchers and scheduling all mediated searches through them will be lost later at the reference desk when the untrained librarians find themselves in an electronic environment. Despite the recent concern over the "human" characteristics of reference desk interaction, the effectiveness of such humanness increasingly will be dependent on the librarian's facility at using computer tools.

THE FUTURE OF ONLINE SEARCHING

The mediated online search will remain a mainstay of reference services into the rest of the 1990s. The evidence indicates that although CD-ROMs and front ends make end user searching an attractive and popular alternative, users still ask for library-assisted search alternatives. Furthermore, the skills required to conduct a mediated online search will still be called upon by end users who find themselves stymied at the CD-ROM. Equally important, online ready reference is an expanding service, and reference librarians will spend a great deal of time providing it. One of the reasons for the expansion is the ever-increasing number of inexpensive electronic information resources available. Although the week-by-week numbers of full-scale mediated searches may fall with the addition of CD-ROM and friendly front ends, the overall exposure of librarians to a variety of online systems should remain frequent and recurrent.

TELECOMMUNICATION SOFTWARE

Many librarians resist the use of online searching, particularly for ready-reference services, because of the welter of differing log-in protocols and passwords. Properly installed and configured, most popular telecommunication packages can take much of the tedium and confusion out of logging onto a remote system. A typical telecommunications program permits users to construct macros consisting of all the procedural steps, including passwords, that are required to log on and search a vendor system. Instead of inputting a half-dozen or more key sequences, the user chooses a vendor system, and the telecommunication software dials the number and inputs the necessary data automatically. Some telecommunications software also allows users to design the specific search strategy offline so that precious online time is not spent keying in the search steps. This can account for considerable savings in many instances. Packages such as DialogLink are actually full-blown front-end systems that shield the user from the most unforgiving elements of the system. The following list identifies the tele-communications software most popular among online searchers (entries provide the names of the required operating system):

Crosstalk (CPM, DOS, Apple)
  DCA/Crosstalk Communications
  1000 Holcomb Woods Pkwy., Suite 440
  Roswell, GA 30076
  404–998–3998

DialogLink (DOS)
  Dialog Information Services
  3460 Hillview Ave.
  Palo Alto, CA 94304
  800–334–2564

Microphone II (Apple)
  Software Ventures
  2907 Claremont Ave., Suite 220
  Berkeley, CA 94705
  415–644–3232

PC-Talk (DOS)
  P.O. Box 8
  Tiburon, CA 94920
  415–435–0770

Procomm/PC Plus (DOS)
  Datastorm Technologies Inc.
  1621 Towne Dr., Suite G

P.O. Box 1471
Columbia, MO 65205
314–474–8461

Prosearch (DOS)
Personal Bibliographic Software
P.O. Box 4250
Ann Arbor, MI 48106
313–996–1580

Red Ryder (Apple)
Free Software Co.
150 Hickory Dr.
Beaver Falls, PA 15010
412–846–2700

Smartcom (DOS, Apple)
Hayes Microcomputer Co.
705 Westech
Norcross, GA 30092
404–449–8791

STN Express
STN International
c/o Chemical Abstracts Service
P.O. Box 3012
Columbus, OH 43210
614–447–3600

VersaTerm (Apple)
Synergy Software
2457 Perkiomen Ave.
Reading, PA 19606
215–779–0522

FRONT ENDS AND GATEWAYS FOR ONLINE SEARCHING

Commercially available front ends for online searching (sometimes called interfaces or intermediate systems) provide a user-friendly gateway to one or more systems, mediating between natural user input and the formal query language of the system as far as possible. The objective of such software is to make the complex mechanics of the search engine totally transparent to the user. Chengren Hu (1989) uses the acronym MGIFI (micro-based gateway, interface, front-end, and intermediate system) and identifies four types by function: (1) auto-communication packages permitting auto dial-up and log-on/off, (2) friendly front-end interfaces that provide a more intuitive search environment for the user, permitting menu or modified command query options, (3) gateway systems, used to access more than one online system, and (4) intelligent interfaces that involve the application of artificial intelligence techniques. (Advances in artificial intelligence components to online front ends are examined in chapter 5.) Items in Hu's first category have been treated under the rubric of straight telecommunications packages. This section will consider commercially available products falling into Hu's second and third function categories. The division between telecommunications packages and front ends is a reasonable distinction and is still relevant, though more and more software on the market successfully delivers both functions. The following list identifies popular front ends and combinations.

Front Ends and Gateways

EasyNet
    Telebase Systems Inc.
    763 West Lancaster Ave.
    Bryn Mawr, PA 19010
    215–296–2800
    800–421–7616

Grateful Med
    Department of Health and Human Services
    Public Health Service, National Institutes of Health,
    National Library of Medicine
    8600 Rockville Pike
    Bethesda, MD 20894
    301–496–6193
    800–638–8480

OCLC FirstSearch
    OCLC
    6565 Frantz Rd.
    Dublin, OH 43017–3395
    614–764–6000
    800–848–5878

Pro Search
    Personal Bibliographic Software Inc.
    P.O. Box 4250
    Ann Arbor, MI 48106
    313–996–1580

Search Helper
    Information Access Company
    11 David Dr.
    Belmont, CA 94002
    415–378–5000
    800–227–8431

Searchworks
    Online Research Systems

2901 Broadway, Suite 154
New York, NY 10025
212–408–3311

WilSearch
H. W. Wilson Co.
950 University Ave.
Bronx, NY 10452
800–367–6770

BIBLIOGRAPHY OF ONLINE DIRECTORIES

This section contains recently published articles and books containing compilations of online databases relevant to specific subjects or disciplines. Articles concentrating on a single vendor database have been excluded. Full bibliographic descriptions can be found in the master bibliography at the end of this book.

General Directories

Computer-readable databases: A directory and data sourcebook (semiannual). Detroit: Gale Research.

Directory of online databases (semiannual). Santa Monica, CA: Cuadra/Elsevier.

Subject Directories

Agriculture
Frank, R. C. (1987)
Weintraub, I. (1986)

AIDS
DuPont, G., and Dutcher G. A. (1990)

Anthropology
Kibbee, J. Z. (1991)

Artificial Intelligence
Stern, H. D. (1990)

Astronomy
Albrecht, M. A., and Egret, D. (1991)
Stern, D. (1991)

Automobile Industry
Ojala, M. (1991c)

Botany
Davis, E. B. (1987)

Business (see also Commerce and Investments)
Ackerman, K. (1987)

Ball, S. (1989)
Cropley, J. (1989)
Freed, M. N., Diodato, V. P., and Rouse, D. A. (1991)
Guy, R. F., and Large, J. A. (1989)
Monk, J. T., Landis K. M., and Monk S. S. (1988a)
Robinson, M. L. (1990)
Scanlan, J. M., de Stricker, U., and Fernald, A. (1989)
Walsh, B. P., et al. (1987)

Business Credit Reports
Ojala, M. (1991a)

Cancer
Van Camp, A. J. (1990)

CD-ROM
King, A. (1991)

Ceramics (see also Materials Science)
Dueltgen, R. R. (1990)

Chemistry
Barnard, J. M. (1989)
Wiggins, G. (1990)

Commerce and Investments (see also Business)
Chadwick, T. B. (1990a, 1990b)

Communications and Mass Media
Block, E. S., and Bracken, J. K. (1991)

Company Information (see also Business; Competitive Intelligence)
Ojala, M. (1990e, 1990f)

Competitive Intelligence
Combs, R., and Moorhead, J. (1990)

Country Profiles
Kelly, N. (1991)

Cross-Border Business Deals
Bell, S. J., and Halperin, M. (1991)

Demography
Crispell, D. (1987)

Earth Sciences
McKay, D. J., and O'Donoghue, M. (1989)

Eastern Europe, Business
Ojala, M. (1991b)

Economy
Woggon, M. (1987)

Education
  Buttlar, L. (1989)
  Freed, M. N., Hess, R. K., and Ryan J. M. (1989)

Engineering (see also Science and Technology)
  Anderson, V. N. (1987)

Entomology
  Gilbert, P., and Hamilton, C. J. (1990)

Environment
  Alston, P. G. (1991)
  Stoss, F. W. (1991)

Export Information (see also International Trade)
  Chadwick, T. B. (1990a, 1990b)

Foreign Exchange Rates
  Pagell, R. A. (1990)

Geology (see also Earth Sciences)
  Le Bas, M. J., and Durham, J. (1989)

Gerontology
  Wasserman, P., Koehler, B., and Lev, Y. (1987)

Hispanic Americans
  Guerena, S. (1990)

History
  Fritze, R. H., Coutts, B. E., and Vyhnanek, L. A. (1990)

Humanities
  Walker, G. (1990)

Insurance Industry
  Ojala, M. (1990c)

International Trade (see also Export Information)
  Monk J. T., Landis, K. M., and Monk, S. S. (1988b)

Japanese Technical Information
  Dueltgen, R. R. (1991)
  Talbot, D. E. (1991)

Linguistics
  DeMiller, A. L. (1991)
  Sano, H. (1988)

Materials Science (see also Ceramics)
  Hightower, C., and Schwarzwalder, R. (1991)

Medicine and Health
  Haselbauer, K. J. (1987)
  Nixon, J. M. (1989)

3

CD-ROMs

CD-ROMs have come to play an increasingly important role in the provision of reference services throughout academic, public, and special libraries. Small and large libraries alike have profited from the optical revolution in storage media. Since 1985 the number of databases available on CD-ROM has grown exponentially, from fewer than a dozen to well over a thousand (Chen, 1991). Both commercially available databases and in-house creations are finding their way onto the medium in increasing numbers. One survey found that 68 percent of a random sample of 121 college and university libraries possessed some kind of CD-ROM technology (Salomon, 1988). Another survey (Chen, 1991) indicated that 58.6 percent and 56.5 percent of academic and public libraries, respectively, possessed some kind of optical product.

In addition to the reference arena, the technology has affected technical services, particularly as a storage medium for small- to medium-size library catalogs (Chen, 1991, p. 37). CD-ROM packages of *Books in Print* and other selection tools have become important bibliographic resources for acquisitions. Public service units such as InterLibrary Loan find that having periodical indexes on CD-ROM dramatically increases their workloads by providing an efficient and effective method by which patrons can amass citations. CD-ROM has also made it possible for libraries to predict the financial costs of computerized resources, something that is not possible with demand and fee-based online vendor systems.

This chapter focuses on the primary effect CD-ROMs have had, are having, and will have on the provision of reference services. Attention will be devoted to CD-ROM used to house popular print indexes and abstracts, with occasional attention paid to CD-ROM–based encyclopedias and multimedia applications.

FACTORS IN CD-ROM's RELEVANCE TO LIBRARIANS

CD-ROM technology has been quickly accepted as an essential part of reference services for a variety of reasons. These reasons revolve around the physical attributes resident in both parts of the acronym—CD (compact disk) and ROM (read-only memory)—and promise to make the medium popular among reference librarians far into the future. These physical attributes provide the material foundation for the realization of several essential information concepts at the heart of CD-ROM. Three factors in particular are significant: unidirectional flow of data, portability and multiplicity of access settings, and technological simplicity of access.

Flow of Data

All storage media have been susceptible to revision. Even the stone carving of early civilizations could be modified and erased. All monumental references to Aton, for example, were obliterated by the revisionist Amonists during the immediate post-IhknanAton period in Egypt. The names of former royal houses were frequently expunged from the Mayan stele by jealous successors. Vellum, parchment, and paper storage media throughout the last two millennia have also been malleable to read-write data revisions. These revisions could be appropriate, as in the elimination of copying errors or the recording of changes over time, or inappropriate, as in the selective censoring of cultural products that accompanied the political expansions of many economies. CD-ROM is perhaps the first storage medium (with the exception of vinyl sound albums) that eliminates the bidirectional flow of data that is characteristic of traditional media. Information streams in one direction only: out to the user. Once cast, the information forever remains the same.

This unidirectionality makes CD-ROM the model storage environment for retrieval in numerous kinds of library reference settings. The read-only memory ensures integrity and inviolability of data in heavily trafficked areas where patrons might accidentally or purposefully erase or change the contents of a more flexible medium. While some see the advent of read-write CD as "progress," the "backwardness" of CD-ROM in this respect becomes an attractive feature to librarians interested in providing unlimited access to accurate and well-organized information. Far from making CD-ROM a transient technology, its factual permanency makes it the ideal storage candidate for a completely open information system. The sine qua non of unlimited, unconditional public access to information being the elimination of all write opportunities, CD-ROM becomes the obvious storage medium.

An unconditionally open system depending on a read-only medium does not necessarily preclude the operation of mediating agents linking and rearranging the information retrieved from storage. Claiming CD-ROM is "retrograde" because it excludes "writing" confuses its read-only characteristic with immovability. In fact, lack of manipulation is in no way a consequence of a read-only storage environment. What is read-only is not the database as a single entity but the information out of which it is comprised. For instance, all current CD-ROM bibliographic databases provide some kind of search engine through which the searcher imposes relevancy on the citations. Citations can be selected, linked with one another, stored in separate files, downloaded to a floppy, or undergo any number of other manipulations. The picture can be arranged and rearranged, but its elements cannot be obliterated. Various nonbibliographic multimedia read-only environments encourage creativity and interaction on the part of the user. The information "atoms" can be connected to form any number of patterns significant to individual users.

Portability

The compact disk (CD) is but one possible implementation of an underlying concept that could be described as "information portability" or "access portability." The concept is an ancient one. Its most popular and successful implementation has been the printed book, which affords easy conveyance, a high degree of random access, and breadth of information. The CD increases that breadth of information tremendously and adds a highly sophisticated indexing system to rationalize random access. And as a storage medium, it possesses an even lighter physicality than almost any book.

CD-ROM can store an extensive database file on a highly portable platform. This physical portability is sustained by the widespread dispersal of the technological means of access: the personal computer. Portability, then, is of two mutually supporting kinds: physical and accessible. The CD can be physically transported with ease, and its accessibility exists wherever a personal computer, supporting software, and CD-ROM drive can be found.

Proliferation of CD-ROM players, their incorporation within the personal computer milieu, and the physical transportability of the optical disk make this medium a great asset in a number of library-related areas. The physical similarities of optical disk to magnetic floppy disk reinforce the belief that CD-ROM is merely an extension of a very familiar, accepted, and widely available information technology. Among other things, the technical environment of the personal computer makes updating and maintaining bibliographic currency an achievable objective. Because CD-ROM is coupled with the well-known personal computer environment, replacing the old CD with a newer version is an understandable process involving familiar equipment.

Contrast this with the often praised locally mounted database. The updating of data tapes, the dumping of large files onto mainframes or minicomputers, is not something about which the average librarian is likely to be well versed. Although portability of access is possible through the locally mounted database, its technical underpinning is too esoteric for simple updating and maintenance from within most reference departments.

When coupled with the modest logistical requirements of a stand-alone workstation, portability becomes important by accommodating variations and changes in the physical layout of reference services as a whole. CD-ROMs and other computer systems necessitate a continuous rearrangement of the physical design of the reference service points. The stand-alone workstation does not require significant space and can accommodate multiple CDs either at once (using a jukebox player system) or consecutively, so that once the space is committed for the workstation, the portable nature of the CDs permits expansion of database options without requiring the expansion of space.

The fact that CD-ROM is portable in the two senses (physical and accessible) is important for those interested in an unrestrained and unregulated flow of information. The CD-ROM–personal computer (PC) dyad is the technical embodiment of a decentralized information infrastructure. The mounted database may provide access to the same information and may be numerically as widely dispersed as the PC–CD-ROM dyad due to the proliferation of modems, but all access flows through and is controlled by a central nucleus. The locally mounted database places the information at the center and harnesses all access points to itself. It is really one system of myriad nodes with all real power (deciding who gets access when and for what reasons) centralized. The dyadic nature of the CD-ROM–PC is wholly redundant; there is no unique essential component or nucleus through which all other access points filter. This situation disperses not only access to information but also control of access. The number of different scenarios under which access to CD-ROM–based information can take place is maximized, and power remains local.

In contrast, the natural vulnerability of centralized information systems invites and even necessitates controls over access. The heightened and completely justified concern over Internet "security" after the notorious virus infection of November 1988 is but one example. The Internet was forced to reexamine the philosophy of openness and unrestricted access in an effort to head off future viral attacks. Another political problem with centralized networks is reflected in censorship issues raised by Prodigy's editorial control over electronic discussion groups. Prodigy defines itself as "family oriented" and refuses to allow postings dealing with controversial sexual and political issues it deems offensive to that idealized constituency. While bibliographic databases are essentially "inert" and it is hard to imagine an "offensive" search strategy, the mentality of control linked with the actual power to intercede and impose barriers is a design feature built into the administration of centralized networks, including database vendor systems, electronic mail, and interactive conference systems. A technology like CD-ROM, which provides both access and physical portability and can potentially spread to every household across the land, should be of interest to anyone desirous of maintaining maximum openness to large bodies of information.

Technical Autonomy

Portability touches on another feature that makes CD-ROM a popular publishing instrument: the technological simplicity and relative autonomy of the medium. The disk is a mere 4.75 inches in diameter and can be loaded into a CD-ROM player with the push of a button. The reference librarian typically is not dependent on any other institutional unit to provide support or aid—certainly not to the extent necessary when dealing with locally mounted data tapes. Obviously, with the rise of LAN-based CD-ROMs, certain advantages of simplicity and independence have to be weighed against other efficiencies, but as a general rule the technology of CD-ROM is simple and easy to grasp, and it does not set up a technical barrier between the information and the quick and open provision of reference services.

The significance of this portability and technological simplicity may not be apparent to libraries set in large universities with sophisticated computer centers and the skilled personnel to sustain a more multifaceted and robust information infrastructure. In smaller libraries, however, or those with less technical and financial resources, such attributes have great import. And recently there has been much effort and study concerning the appropriateness of CD-ROM in providing developing countries with access to information (Ali, 1990). Of more significance in this regard is the closely allied WORM technology (write once ready many), which retains portability, increases technical complexity slightly, and empowers academics and knowledge workers in developing countries by permitting bibliographic control, full text recording, and mass storage dissemination of indigenous information.

CD-ROM AND REFERENCE SERVICE

Although many believe CD-ROM is essentially a transitional format, soon to be replaced by networked locally mounted databases, the interconnected attributes of unidirectional information flow, portability, and technological simplicity that characterize CD-ROM provide it with considerable staying power. Various estimates are that (Chen, 1991) 90 to 100 percent of academic libraries now have CD-ROMs. Many of these CD-ROMs exist on stand-alone workstations, although there is a strong trend toward using LANs to provide multiuser access (Carey & Massey-Burzio, 1989; Akeroyd, 1991). This explosive growth has come in a relatively short span of years; in 1986 less than 10 percent of academic libraries used any form of optical technology (Chen, 1991).

The addition of CD-ROM technology has had a number of significant effects within the typical reference unit, regardless of whether such a unit is located in an academic, public, or special library setting. Predictably, this is most apparent at the reference desk itself, where patron questions concerning CD-ROM swell the numbers of reference queries. Reese (1990) has identified CD-ROM–related questions as the largest category of reference negotiation at the Education Library of Vanderbilt University. In the estimation of selected academic and special librarians, the problems patrons encounter in learning CD-ROM interfaces are the single greatest disadvantage of CD-ROM (Chen, 1991). Not only do CD-ROMs have a significant impact on the number of reference negotiations, there is evidence suggesting that the length of reference negotiation is longer for instruction on CD-ROM than for paper periodical indexes (Reese, 1990; Moore, 1990; MacDonald, Maskell & Auer, 1990). This is of extraordinary importance considering that a user study (Reese, 1990) on patrons' CD-ROM knowledge found that 68.5 percent of the patrons received initial instruction primarily from reference librarians staffing the desk. Another study (Steffey & Meyer, 1989) revealed that 72 percent of users learned to use available CD-ROM from instruction by the library staff. These statistics are in line with the perception that the most effective way to instruct is at the point of use (Whitaker, 1990, p. 31; Stewart, 1990, p. 10). In addition there are indications that regardless of familiarity with CD-ROM technology, a patron conducting a search requiring a sophisticated strategy almost always involves the on-duty reference librarian (Moore, 1990). Case studies from several universities make frequent mention of individual librarians who are specifically responsible for providing CD-ROM help during peak hours at the reference desk (Whitaker, 1990). At my own university library, the addition of four CD-ROM workstations in 1989 housing PsychLit and ERIC required the addition of another librarian at the reference desk several hours a day whose duty was to aid users of the CD-ROM.

Some institutions have found it necessary to distance the CD-ROMs from the reference desk. According to Glitz and Yokote (1990), CD-ROMs had to be removed from the immediate vicinity of the reference desk at UCLA's Biomedical Library, since staff were being overwhelmed with CD-

ROM–related questions and equipment difficulties. In fact, the issue of "equipment" is a whole new dimension to reference tool upkeep. Rarely in the past, with the exception of some large indexes available on microfiche (such as Biological Abstracts), did librarians have to worry about mechanical problems of reference tools. Workstations, however, are a different story. Recurring time-consuming problems include printer foul-ups, system freezes, and accidental (or intentional) system crashes, not to mention regular upkeep chores such as paper and ink cartridge replacement.

The increase in desk-based instruction is amplified by extreme variations in vendor-specific interface formats (Rosen, 1990). From the standpoint of reference instruction, this lack of a common interface throughout all available CD-ROMs can be frustrating for both librarian and user. Although few librarians complain about the lack of a common manual "interface" as far as printed indexes are concerned, the added time necessary to instruct novices in CD-ROM use makes many librarians wish for standardization. This lack of standardization is particularly acute when LANs are used to access a variety of vendor-distinct CD-ROMs. Patrons are not easily convinced of the necessity or logic of having multiple command and menu systems appearing on the same screen. Moreover, it is unreasonable to expect the unwary user to anticipate the varied interfaces poised and waiting behind the common opening menu screen. LANs in which Silver Platter, Dialog, and UMI CD-ROMs are available can produce frustration and apprehension in patrons who feel their hard-won mastery over Silver Platter ERIC should count for something when searching UMI's ABI Inform. In fact, the emotive atmosphere surrounding CD-ROM workstations can reach a pitch seldom seen around even the most intransigent print reference tools, especially when the patron is new to the particular CD-ROM interface or had expected it to perform like "the other ones." Such frustration is predictable.

The patron's ultimate objective is to find information on a particular subject. But after being directed to a CD-ROM, he or she must sublimate this ultimate objective and the planned steps to achieve it and instead focus on the intermediate objective of mastering an electronic reference tool. Unlike the print indexes, which are relatively quick to master but slow to employ, the CD-ROMs demand a great deal of conceptual energy and intellectual motivation from the start. A patron new to the particular CD-ROM interface can easily perceive such an additional requirement as a barrier toward the ultimate information objective: whatever time and energy is spent learning the interface is not spent acquiring the desired information. So instead of being ready to work on realizing their ultimate goal, which is psychologically what they had come prepared to do, patrons discover they are still a considerable distance from taking even the first step. And if, in addition to mastering the interface, they must also step back even further and master written instructions, it is not surprising that patrons learning a new interface feel and express great frustration. Instead of moving forward toward the information objective, patrons believe they are moving away from it and becoming mired in complexities far beyond their needs or expectations. This can result in strident appeals for detailed and labor-intensive one-on-one help.

The circumstance of multiple user interfaces makes it impossible to teach patrons how to use CD-ROM per se. Rather, patrons must be instructed on how to use a particular interface. Consequently, not only does CD-ROM retrieval power and variation in search options and strategies impose greater time investments in training, but lack of common interface structures across products substantially increases the efforts and patience required on the part of both reference librarian and patron.

To what extent this teaching of interfaces becomes a substitute for and distraction from teaching about the content of the resource is an interesting question. The conceptual evaluation and construction of a search strategy may become secondary to concentrating on the mechanical features of its input, especially when it is precisely those mechanical features about which the patron feels flustered. It is already difficult to convince patrons of the importance and utility of thesauri, authority lists, and presearch conceptualization in a technologically less stressful environment. Too often the conceptual bases of a sound and successful search strategy are ignored or given short shrift in exchange for mastery of an interface usurping the patron's immediate concentration.

My own institution's CD-ROM network is illustrative of this skewed emphasis. San Diego State University Library's CD-ROM network has two separate types of help sheets. One provides hints for developing search strategy, and the other provides a sample search, complete with correct function keys and menu options to press. The first is primarily conceptual (how to think through a search strategy); the second is primarily mechanical (how to input the search strategy). The mechanical help sheet is heavily used and soon disappears; the conceptual help sheet is rarely examined and more often serves as a scratch pad. This use reflects not a lack of conceptual acumen on the part of the students but a realistic recognition of the immediate barrier to be overcome.

CD-ROM's effect on formal class-based bibliographic instruction has been documented (Schloman, Gatten & Byerly, 1990; Starr, 1990). In the course of such bibliographic instruction, librarians must reserve time for detailed explanations of CD-ROM tools. Among the topics to be examined should be the mechanics of searching and the place of CD-ROM resources in a patron's overall search strategy. The lack of interface standardization complicates and extends greatly the bibliographic instruction effort required to educate patrons adequately. In addition, distinguishing CD-ROM from remote online databases, locally mounted OPACs, and other computer facilities is both necessary and difficult to communicate to first-time users. Even within a single resource, such as Medline, it is often difficult to convince patrons that the various online and CD-ROM options are all, more or less, providing access to the same database.

The presence of CD-ROM not only influences the content of bibliographic instruction; it is also often the prompt that instigates instruction requests in the first place. At the San Diego State University Library, no fewer than twenty-two forms recording bibliographic instructional requests from teaching faculty during the spring 1990 semester mention training and introduction to CD-ROMs as desired instructional objectives. Although there is no indication that the requests for instruction would not have been made without the CD-ROMs, several authors (Moore 1990; Dickinson, 1990) attribute the increased demand for bibliographic instruction classes at their institutions to the arrival of CD-ROMs. Some institutions have developed multiclass course sequences to introduce patrons to the use of CD-ROM in research (Raimondo, 1990; Plutchak, 1990). Clearly the presence of CD-ROMs as a reference tool has increased both point-of-need instruction and formally planned bibliographic instruction.

Finally, the maintenance demanded by some configurations of CD-ROM creates additional time constraints. Stand-alone workstations equipped with single CD-ROM players frequently require the swapping of disks. Consider, as an example, the Medline available from Dialog. Currently each disk holds six months' worth of citations and abstracts. For information prior to 1988 Dialog has compressed one year onto one disk. In 1992, a search covering five years required eight disks; a search covering three years required six. Unless the library accepts the risk of permitting patrons to load and unload disks, staff will be kept busy providing new disks. The rapidity at which this demand arises can be particularly irksome when the topic being searched is obscure and few, if any, hits are found on any given disk.

Various workstation configurations can help to reduce the time spent on maintenance. Workstations with CD jukeboxes can eliminate loading and unloading, but even they need to be booted in the morning, rebooted throughout the day in response to system "hitches" monitored from time to time for security purposes, and finally turned off and "closed" at the end of the day. Such disk-drive configurations provide no relief from printer and paper demands, on which a not inconsiderable amount of time is spent by professional staff (Salomon, 1988). To what extent reference librarians feel the imposition of equipment technician responsibilities to be a threat to their sense of professional identity is an open question, but one might surmise that more than a little stress is generated by such demands.

LANs, which permit the user to access CD-ROMs resident in a centrally located "tower," go far in placing maintenance outside the immediate confines of the reference services area. For the library as a whole, however, the LAN still demands great amounts of time and expert technical personnel capable of maintaining and updating the network. The software and hardware configurations involved in networking CD-ROMs are mastered only after careful study, and the current "networking" capability and compatibility of many products leaves a lot to be desired, especially when products from different vendors occupy the same LAN.

CD-ROMs have made substantial demands on reference librarians in terms of both desk- and class-based instruction, as well as maintenance. What are the compensations that justify such expenditures of time and effort? Compensation can be found in two places: increases in patron access to relevant information or substantial decreases in other reference duties (without adversely affecting quality of reference services).

REFERENCE BENEFIT OF CD-ROM

Search Efficiency

What evidence is there that CD-ROMs increase patron access to relevant information? While it seems intuitively obvious that a tool providing multiterm subject entrance to computerized files covering many years is more access efficient than a paper version that must be searched year by year and subject heading by subject heading, the question is nevertheless an empirical one and demands an empirical answer. It may be obvious that CD-ROM permits quicker access than paper to information, but does it provide quick enough access (in terms of compensating for increased instructional and maintenance obligations) to relevant information?

Apparently users are convinced that CD-ROMs are efficient and successful. Stewart and Olsen (1988) found that of a select group of students who had participated in a comparison of ERIC print and CD-ROMs, 92.1 percent would select ERIC on CD-ROM exclusively for future research. A survey of CD-ROM users at Vanderbilt University (Steffey & Meyer, 1989) found that 40.4 percent of users rated the value of retrieved citations as "very valuable," 38.4 percent as valuable, and only 1.6 percent as "unusable." More germane to my question, 40 percent of users spent "15 minutes or less on their search" (p. 42), and an additional 33 percent spent between fifteen and thirty minutes. When asked how long they would need to do the identical search using the printed version, only 16 percent replied less than fifteen minutes, and approximately 4 percent replied between fifteen and thirty minutes. Steffey and Meyer identify this latter evaluation as "the most subjective measurement on the survey"; it is, nevertheless, an accurate reflection of patron impressions and a good indication of patron satisfaction with the electronic medium.

Is there any solid evidence in the literature that similar information objectives are more efficiently reached with CD-ROM than with paper? Distinct from the relative ability of the competing media to accommodate various search strategies is the question of screen versus paper as presentation media. Does screen text provide any specific processing problems for the reader?

As far as comprehension and understanding is concerned, studies comparing the use of monochrome text-filled screens versus paper lead Dillon, McKnight, and Richardson (1988) to observe that "it seems comprehension of material is not affected by presentation medium" (p. 459). With the presentational issue resolved, under what circumstances will search strategies be more fruitful when carried out on CD-ROM? Research by Stewart and Olsen (1988) at the Albert R. Mann Library (Cornell University) addresses the hypothesis that "students using ERIC on SilverPlatter will outperform students searching the same topics in the ERIC printed indexes. By outperform, we mean they will find a greater number of relevant references and they will spend less time finding each relevant reference" (p. 48). Comparing groups that received formal training using CD-ROMs (fifty-minute session) with groups that received formal training using the print index, (thirty-minute session), the authors found the former groups to average 16.6 relevant references, while the latter averaged only 8.4. Time spent per relevant reference was even more lopsided: 2.8 minutes for the CD-ROM users versus 16.5 for the print indexes. Clearly, in this case, CD-ROM provided for a more efficient method of searching than its print counterpart.

Yet, when asked to identify the chief impacts of optical products on libraries in 1987, only 4.7 percent of respondents from academic libraries responded with "more information access" (Chen, 1991, p. 40). However, when asked to rank the key "advantages" of CD-ROM, the categories of "faster searching" and "more sophisticated search[ing]" were frequently mentioned by academic, public, and special librarians.

The evidence concerning the ultimate superiority of CD-ROM in retrieving relevant information over the paper version is suggestive but inconclusive. There are a few worrisome elements regarding end user computer information retrieval that are relevant in this context. The greatest danger in using CD-ROM is not "no answer" but "an answer." It is not uncommon for users to interpret computer results as being unambiguously "the result." Patrons tend to shift locus of control over to the computer in a way that cannot occur using a printed index. "An answer" gets accepted as the reflection of the best possible circumstance. Indeed, it is easy to attribute some significant contribution in terms of search effectiveness to a process that occurs within a "black box" and to suppose that if there were more information, the computer would certainly divulge it. Anecdotal reports (Youngkin, McCloskey, Dougherty & Peay, 1990) even indicate that some patrons put a high degree of faith in the computer to perform in accordance with their information needs even if they know the database they are searching does not adequately cover their required disciplines.

CD-ROM versus Online Searching

Decreases in other areas of reference obligation may be considered as further justification to embrace CD-ROM technology. The area most likely to see an impact is online searching, particularly where costs for such searching are passed onto the patron. Chen (1991) reports that American librarians believe that optical products are easier (20.3 percent) and faster (19.7 percent) to use, than online sources. This, coupled with the typically open end–user free access of CD-ROMs, would augur dramatic decreases in demand for paid intermediate online searching.

Despite compelling logic behind the expectation, the facts concerning diminished demand for online services in a library with CD-ROM are ambiguous. Reese (1990) reports significant drops for fee-based mediated online searching after the advent of CD-ROM (ERIC, PsycLIT, and Dissertation Abstracts) in the Education Library of Vanderbilt University. At Central Michigan University, Moore (1990) found a precipitous decline in overall online statistics with the addition of ERIC and PsycLIT CD-ROM. San Diego State University Library statistics for fee-based mediated Medline searches for semesters preceding and subsequent to installation of a single Medline CD-ROM terminal also reveal a sharp drop in demand. Use of online Medline fell from $1,432.43 during the 1989/90 academic year to $754.24 during 1990/91, a decrease of approximately 50 percent. In addition, Anders and Jackson (1988) found that the installation of CD-ROM ERIC, PsychLIT, Agricola, and Dissertation Abstracts considerably decreased fee-based mediated online usage of these same databases. However, Brahmi (1989), addressing the effect of Medline CD-ROM availability on paid mediated searching at a high-volume university medical school library, found no discernible decrease in mediated searching of the online Medline. In fact, overall annual numbers increased.

Reese, Moore, and the case of San Diego State University are comparisons of free CD-ROM access and fee-based online database searching. Anders and Jackson is a mixed case in which the institution normally allowed one free mediated online search on those databases not available at the library on CD-ROM. Bernal and Renner (1990) report on a different scenario when cost is not involved in either CD-ROM or mediated online searching. Immediately after the availability of CD-ROM, the number of mediated searches dipped by one-third. However, several months later, the number of free online mediated searches began to rebound, until they were about at the same level as before the arrival of the CD-ROM. Meanwhile, CD-ROM searching continued to grow, indicating that "other factors, besides cost, contribute to the popularity of CD-ROM" (p. 25). Other research (Rapp, Siegel, Woodsmall & Lyon-Hartmann, 1990) has discovered that the presence of a variety of CD-ROM–based Medline products spread over a number of institutional test sites across the country produced no appreciable diminution in the use of the fee-based online Medline except for one location. "Study results suggest that CD-ROM appears to be finding its own niche and generally does not detract from online searching of Medline" (p. 182).

The various studies appear to show an inconsistency in online savings:

Study	Resource	Result
Moore	ERIC/PsychLIT	Decrease
Reese	ERIC/PsychInfo/Dissertation Abstracts	Decrease
Brahmi	Medline (NLM)	No change
Anders/Jackson	ERIC/PsychLIT/Dissertation Abstracts/ Agricola	Decrease
SDSU	Medline	Decrease
Rapp et al.	Various Medlines	No change
Bernal	Medline	No change

Bernal's result (no change) is a special case since it compares CD-ROM Medline usage to free, mediated online Medline searching. The others compare CD-ROM–based usage to fee-based mediated searching. Both Rapp and associates and Brahmi compared CD-ROM usage to searching Medline on the National Library of Medicine, an inexpensive network. Brahmi estimates most online searching at his institution to cost between $5.00 and $10.00 (p. 53), not a considerable financial burden, especially for patrons in a highly motivated research environment seeking optimum access to information. Furthermore, Rapp and coworkers' and Brahmi's patrons were in large part experienced with online services and sensitive to the advantages of having an expert mediator conducting the search. These factors may help explain why usage statistics for online searching remain stable even after the appearance of CD-ROM workstations. Another phenomenon documented by Rapp and associates and Anders and Jackson to consider is that free CD-ROMs alert the user to the availability of computerized databases for searching. The presence of a conspicuous CD-ROM workstation leads patrons to ask whether other databases are available. Many of these will be available online only, possibly resulting in increased demand for mediated searching of the inexpensive online databases. As more patrons become accustomed to computer-based information resources, these "flowback" patrons may make substantial impacts on fee-based mediated searching.

It is far from clear that the availability of CD-ROM workstations decreases usage of fee-based mediated online searching. However, reference staff can adopt certain strategies that eliminate inappropriate use of mediated online searching and, for that matter, unnecessary use of instruction-intensive CD-ROM.

A certain percentage of mediated online searching on databases already available at the same library on CD-ROM occurs because the patron is either unwilling to learn how to use the particular CD-ROM product or is intimidated by computers in general. To what extent is such unwillingness and intimidation to be accommodated? It can be argued that since such anxieties exist in the patron population, they should be respected: mediated online searching should be done under such circumstances since the primary objective of the librarian is to fulfill the patron's information need. But consider to what extent reference librarians would (and should) aid patrons who repeatedly request staff to search several years of *Biological Abstracts* manually for them because they found the resource confusing and difficult to master. What about patrons who politely refuse to listen to instructions on how to use the *Science Citation Index* and instead request that reference staff manually search the resource because of its stressful nature? The point is not to denigrate people who find such resources confusing, stressful, or intimidating but to emphasize that reference librarians must and already do make decisions about the kind and level of aid that will be provided patrons. In the context of computerized information retrieval, the librarian does no real ultimate service by retarding the patron's acceptance of the computer as a personal information option. In the future, computer interfaces will become even more omnipresent as information conduits both inside and outside the library setting. It is a losing battle to try to insulate patrons from the rigors of computerized information retrieval.

One way of guaranteeing that flowback patrons can be accommodated without substantial addition to time spent on fee-based mediating searching is to make as much of this demand as possible self-sufficient. This depends on purchasing CD-ROM databases produced by either online vendors (such as Dialog or Wilson) or those that use the vendor's command software. High-use CD-ROM patrons can be identified and instructed to use the command-search option on the CD-ROM interface instead of the more user-friendly menu-search option. CD-ROM users would thus be equipped with knowledge of the interface structure found on the online vendor system. A broader approach still is to orient all instruction and help sheets to the command search mode from the very beginning so that all patrons using the CD-ROMs become familiar with the command language of a major online vendor system. Many users who inquire about online databases will then have the rudimentary skills necessary to conduct their own search if they have the opportunity.

CD-ROM versus Print

Is it possible that CD-ROM will ever completely replace its paper analog? Several reasons have been offered to explain why total substitution will not take place. One is that a single workstation devoted to a specific CD-ROM allows only one patron access to the database. The paper analog, with each year typically spread through several volumes, accommodates multiple use. This advantage quickly disappears, however, with the introduction of networked CD-ROM. With the rise in numbers of various configurations of CD-ROM networks, this advantage of paper will cease.

Arguments that speak to the lack of historical depth in the CD-ROM alternative provide no solid reason for continued subscription to current paper versions. Many publishers lower the subscription rates for CD-ROMs to libraries that also subscribe to the paper counterpart, but this is rarely enough of a financial incentive by itself to motivate continued acquisition.

The most important reason for maintaining print versions of acquired CD-ROM is the medium's minimum dependency on technology. The low-tech nature of the method of information access (access methodology) becomes a valuable feature of the printed medium. This value rests on two factors. First, books are extremely robust physical objects. They can be dropped, turned upside down, left open on a table for days, or ignored on the shelves for months at a time without incurring any damage. Certainly the CD-ROM disk itself is also a hardy physical medium, but its access methodology is not. Problems with the disk drive, hard disk, the memory, printer, screen, or any other number of internal workstation components essential to data acquisition can render the CD-ROM inaccessible. Second, the access methodology essential in reading books is not likely to change for millennia to come. Humanity would have to evolve a new visual physiology before the access methodology of the printed book became obsolete. Not so the CD-ROM technology of today. With the current rate of change, it would be naive not to doubt whether the read technology twenty years hence will be able to access the information on today's CD-ROMs. The fate of the microcard technology of the 1950s is a case in point. Quickly surpassed by microfilm and microfiche, the hundreds of thousands of pages found on microcard are today almost inaccessible to patrons. The microcards are in good condition, but the microcard readers are breaking down; manufacturers no longer service them or dropped out of business long ago. Since the access methodology of the CD-ROM revolution is so embedded in technology, it becomes vulnerable to changes in that technology. Because that technology is changing rapidly, few institutions are willing to rely on the CD-ROM industry to make all future technology changes compatible with the past. The precise strength of print media rests on this low-tech modality and the consequent vigor and survivability of its access methodology.

Despite the hardiness of print as a storage medium and the durability of its access methodology, CD-ROMs are frequently perceived as total replacements for their print analogs. Because CD-ROM provides more powerful search options, both librarians and patrons can rely on it exclusively, causing the print version to fall out of the referral loop and into disuse (Whitaker, 1990). Research (Steffey & Meyer, 1989) indicates that the more aware that patrons are of the availability of CD-ROM, the less likely they are to use print indexes, coming to rely almost entirely on available CD-ROM format. Whitaker (1990) found much the same results from her research. Wall, Haney, and Griffin (1990) discovered in a survey of 741 libraries that of those institutions that actually cancelled print versions of databases available on CD-ROM or online, only 4.2 percent of respondents felt "the users were dissatisfied to some degree" with the cancellation (p. 274).

Despite this perception, CD-ROMs are not always superior to their printed counterparts. Putting aside issues of workstation accessibility and the low-tech advantages of the access methodology, certain types of searching are much more easily accommodated in the printed realm. Needs that are singular in topic can be satisfied quickly by a printed version of a periodical index. This is the case regardless of whether the topic is specific ("I want articles on Kevlar steel") or broad ("I need to do a report on materials and want to see what materials and articles are out there"). Of course, many of these "single" topics quickly evolve into candidates for complex Boolean searching and are more appropriately realized using CD-ROM, but this can be decided during the reference negotiation. There are also many times when patrons need to find a few articles on one subject out of a range of possible topics. When the criteria of satisfaction are very broad and the number of required hits small, the paper version is more appropriate. Salomon (1988) refers to the ease with which the printed version abets browsing. Here again, the simplicity of the access methodology figures prominently, with CD-ROM browsing requiring use of eyes, hands, and conceptual model of the software command options. Paper browsing primarily calls for use of the eyes and interferes less with the natural serendipity of browsing.

CD-ROM and Government Documents

Special note should be taken of CD-ROM in federal depository libraries. Numerous agencies of the U.S. government are mandated to collect, produce, and disseminate information on a regular basis. The decennial census is one of the most notable and important of these collections and serves as an excellent case study of how CD-ROM format has facilitated the dissemination of government data through the depository system.

While most commercially available databases, such as Index Medicus, Psychological Abstracts, or ERIC, have three or four competing companies providing CD-ROM format and access software, the census data, dispersed in CD-ROM format without cost to the depository library, lacks competition. This has adversely affected the quality control of the product, especially regarding access software. For census data solely available on CD-ROM, the lack of user-friendly, sophisticated access software is particularly acute. Furthermore, the dissemination of such data solely on CD-ROM makes any access to it dependent upon owning a workstation. For some CD-ROMs, there is no access software produced by the government. Such significant CD-ROM resources as the TIGER/Line files, containing digitized geographic data, come bundled with no access software, leaving depository libraries dependent upon expensive commercially produced search engines. Thus, by producing important data exclusively on CD-ROM and ignoring the software and workstation requirements for access, the government imposes a tremendous burden on librarians, whose mission is to make these data available to the citizenry at large. Considering the many interests that take advantage of the census information—business, public health, environmental planning, and transportation—there can be no doubt that exclusive dependence on CD-ROM databases for the dissemination of such data has an impact on every public services unit within the library.

Conclusion

There exists much anecdotal and commonsense-based perceptions that CD-ROM, when bundled with an adequate search engine, provides faster access to more relevant information than analog print-based resources. A limited number of empirical tests (surprisingly few) bear this hypothesis out. The diminution of online searching with the advent of CD-ROM, though equally as plausible, is not so straightforward, and several factors have been identified that militate against any inverse relationship between the two approaches. Print remains a viable storage medium, and in those contexts where the print versions have disappeared, to be replaced exclusively by CD-ROM (such as in some areas of government documents), problems of access have arisen.

While it is true that, on the whole, CD-ROM has made for more precise and timely patron access to information, it has also become the component in the contemporary configuration of reference services that demands the greatest investments of time from reference librarians.

FUTURE DEVELOPMENTS

Optical storage technology promises to become the future platform of choice, hosting a plethora of multimedia information experiences. There are a variety of format species competing within the CD genus. Some are in direct competition, while others provide supplemental features whose advantages are relative to the specific information objectives of the undertaking.

Compact Disk Interactive (CDI) manipulates several media, such as audio, text, graphics, animation, and video, through a unitary digital platform. At their current capacity CDI disks can hold approximately 650 megabytes of information (1,000 floppy disks). Championed by electronics giants SONY and Phillips, CDI provides an interactive environment that can be used to author and present various configurations of information through interconnected media (Desmarais, 1989a). Conceptually, it is a hypertext facility expanded to encompass nontext media organized around a specific topic, so that comprehension of the topic can take advantage of a variety of presentational modes.

According to Morris and Zimmerman (1989), Digitial Video Interactive (DVI), the direct competitor of CDI, rests on four building blocks: full motion video, still imagery, graphics (including text), and audio. Sponsored by Intel, DVI is currently available to run on 286 or higher computers (though other literature from Intel claims a 8088 PC will run DVI with proper hardware additions) equipped with special DVI boards (available from Intel) and a SONY CD-ROM player.

Palenque is an example of a DVI program already available. The user is able to walk through the ruins of an ancient Mayan city, deciding which roads to traverse and which pathways to explore. Every possible alley, street, room, and hall is digitally recorded and summoned up to provide a seamless video experience in response to the user's direction. DVI can hold approximately 40,000 video stills and can quickly manipulate them to verge upon real-time interactivity.

CD-I and DVI promise to be of interest to librarians. Such formats as the general and specialized encyclopedias or history textbooks are some of the more obvious resources that will find their way onto such a medium. The production of DVI also promises to be available at reasonable prices to end users such as librarians before too long. Considerable advantage can be taken of DVI's superior video quality in the production of bibliographic instruction interactive videos. Just as in Palenque, where the user gets to decide what street to walk down, so in a DVI instructional CD, the librarian-author provides the user with a multitude of interactive instructional episodes all accompanied with video, providing even "walking maps" to where a particular resource is located . Video tours of the library and reference sources could be subject sensitive, selecting and concentrating on resources especially important to the user's discipline area. Such a DVI workstation would be based on one single storage medium whose "information" could be experienced and ordered from numerous perspectives.

The impact of WORM (Write Once Read Many times) technology is already affecting the library profession. The chief current use and probably the future use of the WORM technology is to provide custom-made databases without abandoning the inviolability of data inherent in ROM. Currently two sizes, 12 inch and 5.25 inch, dominate the market. The 5.25 disks hold 600 megabytes and the larger 12-inch disk between 1 and 6 gigabytes. (Ranade 1990). Examples of WORM applications can already be found in the broad library setting. Recent implementations of a newspaper cutting collection in a public library, the archiving of radiological imagery, a suspect identification system, and a full text database for a consortium of libraries (Eaton, MacDonald & Saule, 1989) are some of the many ways WORM technology can be made to facilitate local information storage needs.

INFORMATION RESOURCES

Like the transportation of print data into online databases that occurred in the 1970s and early 1980s, the creation of CD-ROM products is now occurring at such a pace as to be almost untrackable. New databases are appearing on CD-ROM daily, and many are being issued by competing vendors. CD-ROMs that never made it are also disappearing daily (though at a slower rate). A list of CD-ROM subject directories published in journals would surely be out of date by the time it was printed. Nevertheless, in this tumultuous field, a number of literature resources, directories, and periodicals can be recommended based on their recurring or comprehensive nature.

The Directory of Portable Databases published by Cuadra/Elsevier and structured very much after the *Directory of Online Databases,* is a semiannual compilation of all available CD-ROMs. Types of databases covered include bibliographic, numeric, and full text. The *CD-ROM Yearbook* from Microsoft Press is an annual almanac of CD-ROM–related events, which includes informative narrative overviews of various concepts and products, as well as a directory of available CD-ROMs organized by subject. *CD-ROM Information Products: An Evaluative Guide and Directory,* edited by C. J. Armstrong and J. A. Large, is a multivolume, in-depth description of CD-ROMs with evaluative assessments. Desmarais's *CD-ROMS in Print 1991* is a yearly publication from Meckler that covers information-based CD-ROM, as well as entertainment-based offerings. A timely literature guide can be found in M. R. Gabriel's *A Guide to the Literature of Elec-*

tronic Publishing: CD-ROMs, Desktop Publishing, Electronic Mail, Books and Journals, available from JAI Press.

The topic of networked CD-ROMs is treated in *CD-ROM Local Area Networks: A User's Guide,* edited by Norman Desmarais. The book examines network software, hardware, management issues, LAN alternatives, future considerations, and licensing and copyright issues.

A series of case studies of CD-ROMs in a variety of academic, public, and special libraries is contained in *Public Access CD-ROMs in Libraries: Case Studies,* edited by L. Stewart, Katherine Chiang, and Bill Coons. Attention is paid to goals and roles, funding, user training, reference impact, and issues of access. This book provides a good opportunity to perform comparisons across institutional environments.

The statistical results of questionnaires distributed to American and European libraries in 1987 and 1988 are analyzed by Ching-chih Chen in *Optical Discs in Libraries: Use and Trends.* Graphics are put to instructive use in forty data tables and forty-three charts. The second part of the book, "Information Sources on CD-ROM Products and Their Uses in Libraries," contains an extensive annotated bibliography. A helpful subject classification of various articles in the area of CD-ROM implementation and evaluations of specific products is also included.

In addition to *Online* and *Online Review*, journals either wholly or in great part devoted to CD-ROM products, are *Laserdisk Professional, Optical Information Systems, CD-ROM End User, CD-ROM Librarian,* and *CD-ROM Review*.

4

Networks

No single technology will affect reference services within the next ten years with such intensity as the burgeoning international communication system. An international communication network consists of individual computers, typically mainframes and minicomputers, linked together by a common communication protocol. Networks such as Internet, BITNET, and the NREN (National Research and Education Network) promise to multiply information resources and opportunities quantitatively and qualitatively. Such networks will create reference centers capable of immediately reaching information resources anywhere on the globe, to tap the past and current collective expertise of humanity. Networks may also become the means by which individual librarians will share their own expertise and knowledge with the rest of the profession, enabling the world to access "locally" constructed knowledge bases, computer-aided instruction, and reference advisory systems.

The initial advantages of the international networks have accrued to academic and select special and public libraries set up to access one or more of the available systems. However, the near future promises the advent of large-scale government financing of computer communications, specifically the NREN. The NREN will bring widely distributed information resources into libraries across the institutional spectrum, from large academic facilities to small elementary school media rooms.

Consider the information resources and utilities of interest to reference librarians that are already available on the Internet, the most developed of the international networks:

1. Access to approximately 200 online library catalogs at leading universities. The numbers are growing weekly and often include access to special subsidiary databases mounted on the specific university's mainframe. For instance, the online union catalog of the Colorado Alliance of Research Libraries (CARL) includes a contents index to over 10,000 journals, Grolier's multimedia *Academic American Encyclopedia*, book reviews from *Choice* magazine, and several other databases containing data on Colorado. Although most of the university OPACs are based in the United States, systems in Israel, Europe, Australia, Latin America, and Asia are also accessible.

2. The opportunity to participate in thousands of electronic discussion and news groups on either USENET or BITNET covering practically every aspect of knowledge and attracting members from all over the world. Among library-related discussion groups are PACS-L ("an international computer conference that deals with all computer systems that libraries make available to their patrons"), the BI-L (bibliographic instruction list), GOVDOC-L (government documents list), and about two dozen more. Also available are conferences closely related to library and information science covering such fields as artificial intelligence and expert systems, hypermedia, hypertext, search logic, and OPAC systems. Many of these conferences archive the resulting discussion, providing a permanent, searchable resource of library-specific information.

3. The ability to send and receive messages throughout the world using electronic mail (e-mail). Messages can be sent to specific individuals or a group requesting help and information on appropriate topics. This informal network of relationships can be utilized in finding and providing the most recent information possible.

4. The capacity to send and receive immense text files throughout the Internet using the file transfer protocol (ftp), available on all computers using the ubiquitous transmission control protocol/internet protocol (TCP/IP) suite of communication protocols. Most news groups and electronic conferences compile extensive bibliographies and text files on their respective topics, which are kept in files on the home computer. Such files can be accessed and downloaded to "local" computers (on a PC on ethernet) and then either transferred to a stand-alone PC on the reference desk or printed offline. There is also a growing body of electronic texts and journals that can be obtained via ftp from various sources.

COMMUNICATION NETWORKS: A BRIEF HISTORY

Several generic, inclusive terms have been coined to describe the latticework of hosts and links comprising the international networks; the

Matrix, *Infosphere*, and *metanet* have all been used to refer to this loose conglomeration. Quarterman's (1990) term, the *Matrix*, will be used when referring to the various communication networks as a single conceptual phenomenon.

The two most important international networks comprising the Matrix are the BITNET and Internet. They should be considered essentially two webs of affiliated computers distinguished by the communications protocols employed by each. Administratively, in fact, huge chunks of the Internet (such as the component network known as CSNET) are actually part of the corporation that manages BITNET, the Corporation for Research and Education Networking (CREN). However, because the communication protocols of the two webs are so different, they function and should be conceived of as two distinct networks. The Internet functions under the TCP/IP. The BITNET protocol is the Remote Spooling and Communications Subsystem (RSCS) from IBM. TCP/IP provides a suite of protocols for mailing, remote access (telnet), and file transfer (ftp). RSCS provides for mailing but has no remote access facility.

The origins of the current Internet go back to 1968 with the formation of a project sponsored by the Advanced Research Projects Agency (ARPA). The central objective of the ARPA Network (ARPANET) was to develop a communication infrastructure supportive of resource sharing among defense and academic researchers (Quarterman & Hoskins, 1986, p. 943). Basing this infastructure on "packet switching," which permits the amount of information routed between nodes to be increased dramatically, ARPANET grew from a four-node network (University of California at Los Angeles, University of California at Santa Barbara, Stanford University and University of Utah) to a true national network in a matter of years. By 1975 approximately forty institutions (academic and military) were linked together (Cerf & Kann, 1990). The set of communication protocols that had come to be accepted were destined to become the de facto standard of all interfacing between Internet hosts, the TCP/IP. The TCP/IP were eventually promulgated by the Department of Defense (DoD) as the official communication protocols of the ARPANET (Quarterman & Hoskins, 1986). As other networks and their myriad "midlevel" networks developed, they were also based on the TCP/IP protocols and could therefore "talk" to one another. This interlocking web of networks became known as the Internet, a geographically diffuse, loosely coupled set of communication systems and hosts over which users could meander, explore, interact with one another, and upload and download files.

BITNET is a relative newcomer to the national network scene having its beginning in 1981 with a connection between City University of New York, and Yale University campuses (Arms, 1990a). Its name, derived from "Because-It's-Time Network," is indicative of the objectives the founders had in mind: an open access network connecting university campuses with minimal restrictions and no fees. The only requirement was that each host serve as a linkway to a single other BITNET node (Quarterman & Hoskins, 1986). IBM's RSCS was the initial communication protocol used by hosts in supporting mail and file transference. Emulation software, however, has been developed so that computing centers need not use IBM environments. The BITNET has several non-U.S. geographic sections, such as NETNORTH (Canada's BITNET), AsiaNet, and EARN (Europe).

While the initial idea of BITNET was to remain free of user fees, the realities of financing a central administration with even minimal support created the need to institute a membership fee. In 1989 the BITNET, along with the large Internet mid-level CSNET, became the Corporation for Research and Educational Networking (CREN). But while these two major networks are administratively linked, their differing communication protocols make them functionally discrete systems.

BASIC CONCEPTS

The current networks seem to be anything but user friendly, especially to novices who see their vast geographies clouded in a forbidding haze of acronyms. And yet despite the jigsaw puzzle impression of the Matrix, mastery of a few simple concepts, and the purging of other misleading ones, can eliminate a great deal of initial confusion and trepidation.

Carolyn Arms (1990a) has suggested thinking of a network as a highway over which various services and information travel. Another helpful analogy is that of a railway system. On the rail system one finds numerous items, most of them unrelated to one another, being moved to and fro. Trains of various lengths and powers, comprising many types and shapes of freight and passenger cars, ply the tracks. However, they must all repose on a wheel carriage sharing the same gauge as the track. This common gauge is the communication protocol to which all pieces of information flowing along the network must conform. Without adhering to this common gauge, the information cannot move over the system.

A common communication protocol should not be confused with a common command software found on database vendor systems like Dialog and BRS. A communication protocol guarantees only that nodes on the system can communicate with one another, not that they share the same search capacities (if any) or utilities. Communication "systems" such as BITNET and the Internet are functionally distinct from the well-known vendor systems (although many of these vendor systems can be reached through the Internet). The information contents and software capacities found on various host computers around the Matrix cover a wide range of possible options. Some contain databases, some online public access catalogs; some hold lists of electronic addresses (servers), online interactive conferences, numeric resources, local news and information banks, electronic mail systems, communication networks, gateways to other networks, and/or various operating systems such as UNIX. And although the Internet and BITNET have central administrative offices, there is no central information center exhaustively listing everything available on the networks. Whereas the typical commercial vendor system provides complete documentation to all its databases and leaves no stone unturned in alerting the new subscriber to its information resources, neither the Internet nor BITNET provides any single centralized table of contents. This is because both are concerned primarily with the linkages between hosts, not with the content resident on hosts. What is found or not found on a given host computer is basically a "local" concern, as is the willingness to advertise the content to the rest of the Matrix.

The simplest conceptual relationship that characterizes the national networks is of a communication link between three separate nodes. There are six items in this relation: the three nodes, (A, B, C) and various physical connections (d, e, f). A sends messages to B or C over d or e, and B and C use the appropriate channel to send their missives. Consider the conditions under which communication is possible in this simple system. First, both sender and receiver must agree on a communication format; they must possess the means to send a message using a medium the other can "decode." A communication standard or protocol must be adopted. Furthermore, the sender must know where the receiver is so that the correct route is taken. A must contain the fact that "If the address of the message is B, send content over d." If the message is a request for information, then the receiving node must also know the address of and route to the sender to effect a reply. Hence, every node on this small network must "know" the address of and route to every other node on the network.

Now imagine that another network, including nodes X, Y, and Z, using the same communication protocol, also has C as one of its nodes. There are now two of these systems "linked" at C (C is a member of both systems). Since X is not a node on the first system, A does not contain its address. But A can still shuttle a message to X through C, since C does possess X's address and knows the correct route. C then becomes known as the gateway to the respective "other" system or as the host that contains the correct addresses and routing information for both systems. Now suppose that a group of researchers, Q, wishes to create a link between nodes whose primary research efforts fall under electrical engineering. Both B and Y are interested; they apply for passwords and are thereby linked through Q ("electronet"). B can then interface with Y, either going through the C gateway or directly through the electronet. Imagine another interrelated system of equal size linking to the described configuration at B. This new addition is also a loosely linked dyad with one special interest "net" linking nodes involved in computer engineering ("compunet"). Add to this a node that specializes in utilities such as addresses or lists of special interest "subnets" and is located on some specified node of the system available to anyone who happens to know the address.

From simple beginnings, a large, sprawling, decentralized network comes into existence held together by various gateways and comprising single nodes and groups of nodes and crisscrossed by special interest networks. In no time at all, the conceptual simplicity of the building blocks is replaced by a complexity of access points, subnetworks, passwords, names, and acronyms, over which no single node has complete control or knowledge. The only character they share in common is a communication protocol. The current national networks are such multidimensional systems. Cerf and Kann (1990) have collected a set of ARPANET maps from 1969 through 1990 that diagrams the actual growth of the proto-Internet and is an instructive visual representation of how a multifaceted network can quickly develop from a simple, straightforward connection between two computers.

A SAMPLE EXPLORATION

The easiest way to communicate the power of the national networks is to take an excursion through them. In the sample search of the Internet that follows, each stop and its "locale" in the "space" of the system will be explained. (For a bibliography of texts that provide full treatments of the Internet see the "Information Resources" section in this chapter.)

A "local" university is proposing to develop a new B.A. degree in physics and wants to examine the online catalog of Princeton University, which has a renowned subject collection in plasma physics, because this information will be helpful in collection development. What recent acquisitions has Princeton made in the area of popular, lower-division books on string theory?

Using the telecommunication software Procomm, a call is placed via modem to the local university network (SDSUNET). SDSUNET is a communications network specific to San Diego State University campus, which runs on a campus-wide ethernet. (Most academic campuses, research installations, and large corporations have such a network.) This type of system provides personal computers with access to mainframes and facilitates the high-speed transfer of data between discrete mainframes within the same institution. SDSUNET runs the standard protocol TCP/IP, which means that all host computers at San Diego State University must have that protocol available to participate on and utilize SDSUNET as a communications backbone. From SDSUNET, a specific local computer, the ELXSI, is called and at the UNIX operating system prompt (%), the telnet utility is summoned. Telnet, one of the more important protocols within the TCP/IP, permits remote access to any computer for which an address is known. This means that from the telnet prompt, an operator can access any other computer running the TCP/IP protocols providing its address is known. The "remote" computer at Princeton University that houses the online catalog has the address PUCABLE.PRINCETON.EDU. At the telnet prompt, "open PUCABLE.PRINCETON.EDU" is entered. A second or two later, access to the Princeton OPAC is achieved.

This OPAC includes the library of the Physics Plasma Laboratory. At this point, the personal computer on the searcher's desk two feet away is linked to the Princeton computer three thousand miles away. Search commands entered "locally" are instantly carried out "remotely." The heading "String Models" is searched and the results perused. Likely entries are printed off on the printer next to the local PC. The Princeton PAC is asked to display the MARC record for several entries so the subject search can be enlarged by using other headings. After a sufficient number of records has been found, the connection with Princeton is broken. The user is again at the telnet prompt.

From the telnet prompt, a connection is established with CARL, and the online *CHOICE* reviews option is selected. This database carries the full text of all *CHOICE* reviews published during the previous three years. A search for "Introduction to String Theory," one of the more interesting titles found at Princeton, is conducted and a review is identified, which is then printed. After the user is finished with the *CHOICE* review, the connection with CARL is broken, returning the user to the familiar telnet prompt.

At this point, it would be helpful to get in touch with the reviewer for further bibliographic suggestions. The reviewer is Barry Smith at Idaho State University (this information is in the *CHOICE* full text file). Now the searcher wants to know if Smith has an electronic address reachable through the Internet. Various address and name directories strewn around the Internet (see the "Network Help Services" section in this chapter) are available as a kind of hit-or-miss white pages. The address of the Knowbot Information Service (KIS) is entered and a connection made with this master address list. KIS provides a common interface to several major address/name directories on the Internet, which are searched automatically by the KIS software. A search for Smith, however, turns up nothing. This is not surprising, since probably 90 percent of the personal address/names are not in these large directories. What about an institutional address? Typically the directories are much better when it comes to this kind of address. Is there an address for the entire Idaho State University that can then be called via telnet to find whether Smith has a mailbox? An organization search on KIS finds several addresses for various hosts located at the Idaho State University. Exiting KIS, the user calls two of these addresses via the telnet protocol. The hope is that one or more of the remote sites has an anonymous log-on account along with a "local" mail address list, allowing "strangers" access to the computer files at the Idaho site. All sites, however, require passwords so an alternative, more chancey option, is chosen: an e-mail message to Smith will be sent to both sites using the address SMITH@IDAHO-SITE-1 and SMITH@IDAHO-SITE-2, in the hopes that he has an account on one of these computers.

After the user mails the messages to Smith, a connection is made with two of the many news groups on the USENET section of the Internet. USENET consists of several thousand news conferences organized around distinct issues and disciplines. Sci.phys, a discussion group about physics, is opened, and a string search for the word "bibliography" is conducted. Approximately three hundred unread messages are searched for the term. There are several messages that speak about various bibliographies, and one refers to a bibliography of currently popular books in physics. The author of the message provides the address of the computer (in New Jersey) and the name of the directory on which this extensive bibliography resides. This message is saved to a file on the ELXSI for later use, and the second news group, sci.astro, is opened. A string search reveals no mention of the term "bibliography" so contact is terminated and the telnet utility is quit, bringing the cursor back to the familiar % prompt.

The next objective of the session is to transfer the bibliography from the computer in New Jersey to the "local" personal computer so that it can be formatted by the resident word processor and printed out. While the telnet utility permits remote log-on, another important TCP/IP protocol, ftp, allows the transfer of large files across the Internet. The ftp utility is called by typing "ftp" at the % prompt. At the ftp> prompt, the full address of the remote computer is used to establish a link. The computer has an anonymous ftp account that allows "strangers" to log on using the log-on "anonymous." The specific directory is found and the specified file transferred (for full details on commands, see Anderson, Costales, & Henderson, 1991) to the ELXSI computer across campus. The link is broken with the New Jersey computer and the bibliography file on the ELXSI transferred to the arms-length PC using the Kermit file transfer utility. Kermit is a software program that makes error-free transmission of data possible using the telephone system. Using an ethernet-based LAN, it is also possible to have the local PC linked directly to the campus mainframe, bypassing the telephone system and speeding up the rate of data transmission by a number of magnitudes.

At most of the previous steps, alternative methods of achieving the same objective are available. Instead of sending an e-mail message to the reviewer, the telephone might have been used. It might have been more efficient to search the OCLC database instead of the single library system at Princeton or to have examined recent printed issues of *Science/Technology Publications*. The most significant feature of the exploration, however, was the ability to engage in a multidimensional, multiple-task information endeavor from a single screen prompt. It is this linking-together of information resources to a single screen point that makes the fledgling Internet a potent harbinger of the future computerized reference environment.

Internet is a large, loosely coupled system whose contents, utilities, and users remain uncoordinated and whose features are mastered only after great effort. Each month it increases in scope and depth, and the mechanisms by which it can become a completely self-reflexive information access environment take form. Chief among these mechanisms are the information directories that provide some control over the content of the Internet and its subsidiary groups. (These directories are treated more fully in the section "Network Help Services.") Also, the openness of the Internet spurs local development of many attempts at rationalization of access. For instance, the ELXSI computer on SDSUNET contains a telecommunication program called "libtel" (this program contains the St. George list of library OPACs and can be found on a number of Internet hosts), which can be called up from the UNIX prompt and provides a menu-driven interface for accessing remote OPACs. The program eliminates having to remember the syntax involved with telnet protocol and a multitude of specific addresses: the user selects the specific state or country and the specific library from a subsequent submenu. Since the ELXSI is part of the Internet, anyone logging on remotely can access the libtel facility (if they are aware of its presence).

The development of searching agents that traverse the many byways of the Internet looking for information that fits the patron's custom-made request also enhances the network's accessibility.

NETWORKS AND REFERENCE SERVICES

Because there is no single file or series of files that fully reflects the current content of the Internet or BITNET, there can be no final word on the utility of such systems at the reference desk. The creation of many library-related electronic bulletin boards provides a central clearinghouse for relevant reference information, yet exploration and initiative on the part of individual librarians is still necessary to bring the networks' reference resources into focus. There are several general parameters that describe the reference utility of the networks.

Electronic Mail

In addition to eliminating the vexations of telephone tag with distant colleagues, e-mail via the Internet and BITNET can play a supportive part in the provision of reference services (Delfino, 1990). Complicated bibliographic verification that evades online searching (for instance, the place of a specific graph or table in a book or the volume in which the topic "Cancer" falls in a multivolume encyclopedia) can be successfully provided by drawing on a colleague's proximity to an information source. Used in tandem with fax, e-mail creates a quick informal interlibrary loan that can be of immense value. The various bulletin boards can also be used to "advertise" a reference query along with the sender's e-mail address, thereby tapping into the combined reference expertise of several thousand librarians (the LIBREF board is an example of this pragmatic welding together of e-mail and the BITNET bulletin board structure).

The mail program has the capacity to send the same message to all addresses on a prescribed list, so networks can be used to circulate regular reference division "newsletters" to interested parties. This is a powerful method for accentuating the library's visibility and relevance among institutions whose members are geographically dispersed throughout various campus, branch, or corporate sights. According to postings on the PACS-L electronic conference, several institutions have even experimented with providing reference services through the e-mail. Questions are sent by e-mail to the library's address and routed to the appropriate librarian, who can either respond directly or negotiate the question further with the patron over e-mail.

OPAC

Currently, there are two sources for up-to-date "authorized" lists of OPAC. Art St. George (University of New Mexico) and Ronald Larsen (University of Maryland) maintain a list, and Billy Barron (University of North Texas) compiles another. They basically contain the same institutions, although the organization of the information differs. The Barron list can be procured via anonymous ftp from VAX.ACS.UNT.EDU (directory is "library"), and the St. George and Larson list can be acquired by sending the message "get internet library" to the LISTSERV@UNMVM.BITNET. Such lists can also be found as part of the "information files" (publicly accessible directories usually identified with the term "info" in the directory name) on many state and regional networks and have appeared in several published articles (Raeder & Andrews, 1990).

A recent version of the St. George list is divided into the following sections:

1. Catalogs and Databases Accessible Without Charge, listed by state.
2. Catalogs and Databases Accessible With Charge.
3. International Catalogs.
4. Dial-up Libraries and Catalogs.

5. Other Online Resources (bulletin boards).

6. Campus-wide Information Systems.

Everything but the fourth and fifth categories are available directly through the Internet. Billy Barron's list, originating at the University of North Texas, contains:

1. An alphabetical listing of catalogs by institutional location.

2. A series of appendixes providing instruction on several popular OPAC interfaces such as Innovative, GEAC, and NOTIS.

3. A bibliography of Internet resources.

A typical entry in either list furnishes the correct address and log-on required to access the relevant OPAC.

Quantitatively the Internet-accessible OPACs are still a long distance from the OCLC or RLIN databases. However, it is important to understand that through the Internet, one directly accesses the OPAC and not a virtual construct of institutional holdings, as in the bibliographic utilities. Consequently, circulation and acquisition information are also available, as well as any other locally mounted data files or knowledge bases accessible through the OPAC. Remote access to locally mounted data tapes from Wilson and other database vendors through national networks brings up knotty problems of licensing and copyright. Typically such remote access is restricted to on-campus use.

Locally crafted OPAC-accessible knowledge resources such as expert reference advisory systems, intelligent computer-aided instruction, and multimedia information platforms have begun to proliferate. In the future, these ancillary resources will make searching Internet-accessible OPACs even more rewarding. Consider the rich network of information now available through CARL. Some of the OPAC available through CARL include Colorado University at Boulder, the Colorado University Law Library, University of Wyoming, Regins College, and Colorado Health Sciences Libraries. In addition there is a government documents index covering federal and Colorado state documents deposited at the University of Colorado and the Denver Public Library. CARL also permits linkage to a periodical union catalog of a Massachusetts consortium of libraries including Brandeis, Boston College, Wellesley College, MIT, and other major collections. Users paying for a special account with CARL can search a huge current contents index of over 10,000 periodicals across all disciplines.

Bulletin Boards

Bulletin boards and discussion lists on the national networks serve to bring together people scattered across the world who share common interests. There are several dozen BBSs (bulletin board systems) dealing with varying aspects of librarianship (a complete list can be found below). The PACS-L (Public Access Computer Systems) Bulletin Board is one of them. The majority of postings on PACS-L are directly relevant to applied computer technology in library public services. There are approximately 1,500 members from around the United States and abroad. On any day, messages are sent to the PACS-L and distributed to all subscribers; typically three or four ongoing issues are being discussed. Some of these topics flicker for a day or two; others evolve and develop into weeks of long, interactive discussions, which are then bundled together in a special file and mailed to subscribers. Frequently messages are sent providing information concerning a new piece of software or computer application or asking for aid with it. Conference announcements, the Internet/BITNET addresses of new discussion groups, and many up-to-date bibliographies can be found on the PACS-L. Like its brethren, the PACS-L serves to provide librarians with recent news and discipline-wide profiles of recent efforts within the group's respective area of interest. It also focuses the awareness of a large number of librarians and (in the case of PACS-L) library computer experts onto one single screen.

Following is a list of some of the bulletin boards and lists of special interest to librarians. Usually the name is sufficient to explain the interest covered; when it is not, an explanation is given. The addresses are identified as either BITNET or Internet. Lists on BITNET can be subscribed to by sending a message to LISTSERV@LOCATION, where LOCATION is the name following the "@" within the addresses listed below. In the case of PACS-L, a message is sent to LISTSERV@UHUPVM1. If you are sending the message on the Internet to a BITNET address, you must attach the suffix BITNET (ie: LISTSERV @UHUPVM1.BITNET). The message should literally read "SUBSCRIBE PACS-L John Doe". Within a day or two, the requester will begin receiving postings from the list. Lists with Internet addresses should be sent a message (to that specific address) asking to be placed on the subscribers' list. To see a compendium of lists on the BITNET send the message "LIST GLOBAL" to any LISTSERV. The following groups were gleaned from a global list current in mid-1992. Lists are coming into and going out of existence with regularity, so this compilation is constantly in flux:

Academic Librarians Forum
  BITNET: ALF-L@YORKVM1

Applied Expert Systems Research
  BITNET: AESRG-L@UMCVMB

Art Libraries Society Discussion List
  BITNET: ARLIS-L@UKCC

Artificial Intelligence, Educational Applications
  BITNET: EDUCAI-L@WVNVM

Artificial Intelligence List
  BITNET: AILIST@DBOTU111

Bibliographic Instruction Discussion List
  BITNET: BI-L@BINGVMB

BRS Software Search Retrieval Discussion Group
  BITNET: BRS-L@USCVM

Business Libraries Discussion Group
  BITNET: BUSLIB-L@IDBSU

Campus-Wide Information Systems
  BITNET: CWIS-L@WUVMD

Canadian Law Libraries List
  BITNET: CALL-L@UNBVM1

CARL Users Group
  BITNET: CARL-L@UHCCVM

CD ROM Discussion Group
  BITNET: CDROM-L@UCCVMA

CD ROM on Local Area Networks
  BITNET: CDROMLAN@IDBSU

Chemical Information Sources Discussion List
  BITNET: CHMINF-L@IUBVM

Circulation Discussion Group
  BITNET: CIRCPLUS@IDBSU

Coalition for Networked Information
  BITNET: CNI-ARCH@UCCVMA

Communication and Information Technology Discussion List
  BITNET: SCIT-L@QUCDN

Data Research ATLAS [Automatic Tabulating, Listing, and Sorting System] Users
  BITNET: ATLAS-L@TCUBVM

Education and Information Technology
  BITNET: EDUTEL@RPIECS

GEAC Users
  BITNET: ADVANCE-L@IDBSU

Geographic Information Systems Discussion List
  BITNET: GIS-L@UBVM

Government Documents
  BITNET: GOVDOC-L@PSUVM

Greek Library Automation
  BITNET: ELLASBIB@GREARN

Guttenberg
  BITNET: GUTNBERG@UIUCVMD. Interest in full text electronic format of

public domain literary classics. Aims to convert a large portion of such texts into electronically accessible files on the Matrix. Alerts subscribers to the availability of such texts, encourages individuals to "commit" to the conversion of print into electronic format, and discusses related issues.

Hypercard Discussion Group
  BITNET: HYPERCRD@PURCCVM

Information Graphics
  BITNET: INGRAFX@PSUVM. Emphasis on the use of graphics to represent information. A good source for issues in geographic information systems (GIS) and cartography in particular, but also broader concepts of two-and three-dimensional information representation.

Information Retrieval List
  BITNET: IRL@UCCVMA

Innovative Online Catalog User Group
  BITNET: INNOPAC@MAINE

Interlibrary Loan Discussion Group
  BITNET: ILL-L@UVMVM

Israel Information Retrieval Specialists Group
  BITNET: IIRS@TAUNIVM

LibNet
  Internet: LIBNET@ALISUN.UCHICAGO.EDU. Primarily aimed at librarians working in small academic libraries.

Library Administration and Management Discussion List
  BITNET: LIBADMIN@UMAB

Library and Information Science Research List
  BITNET: LIBRES@KENTVM

Library Cataloging and Authorities Discussion Group
  BITNET: AUTOCAT@UVMVM

Library Planning Discussion (Academic Libraries)
  BITNET: LIBPLN-L@QUCDN

Library Reference Issues
  BITNET: LIBREF-L@KENTVM

Medical Libraries Discussion Group
  BITNET: Medlib-L@UBVM
  Internet: Medlib@UBVM.CC.BUFFALO.EDU

MultiMedia Discussion Group
  BITNET: MMEDIA-L@VMTECMEX

Music Library Association
  BITNET: MLA-L@IUBVM

NOTIS/DOBIS Discussion Group
  BITNET: NOTIS-L@TCSVM

NOTIS Music Library List
  BITNET: NOTMUS-L@UBVM

NOTIS Rare Book Collectors
  BITNET: NOTRBCAT@INDYCMS

PARA
  Internet: PARA@CS.CMU.EDU. Emphasis on full text search and retrieval,
  free-text search strategies, retrieval software, and the development of such products. Closely allied with WAIS technology.

Public Access Computer Systems Forum
  BITNET: PACS-L@UHUPVM1

Rare Book and Special Collections Catalogers
  BITNET: NOTRBCAT@INDYCMS

Rare Books and Special Collections Forum
  BITNET: EXLIBRIS@RUTVM1

Serials Discussion Group
  BITNET: SERIALST@UVMVM

SPIRES (Stanford Public Information Retrieval System) User Group
  BITNET: SPILIB-L@SUVM

Technical Standards for Library Automation
  BITNET: TESLA@NEVRM

User Interfaces for Geographic Information Systems
  BITNET: UIGIS-L@UBVM

Women and Information Technology (EDUCOM [Educational Communications]
Group)
  BITNET: EDUCOM-L@BITNIC

On the Internet, the main source for discussion and news groups is the
USENET. The USENET is part of the Internet and usually is available
on most hosts running under UNIX. Anderson, Costales, and Henderson
(1991) describe the USENET as "a cross between a magazine and a cocktail
party full of interesting, knowledgeable people" (p. 213). Unlike the
BITNET-based discussion lists, which are mailed to subscriber mailboxes,
conferences on the USENET are accessible directly by various programs
on UNIX, such as readnews, rn, vnews, and nn, which permit the user to
read, save, and reply to messages. There is also a postnews utility, which
aids in the efficient construction of news articles. To access a complete list
of news groups, type "rn news.announce.newusers" at the UNIX prompt.
This connects to a series of announcements for new users, which can be
paged through until the "active news groups listings" is found. The same
list can also be found on the "local" host computer upon which the user
has an account under the file /usr/lib/news/newsgroups. The groups are
given topic prefixes that identify the general subject area of interest:

comp.   —Computer-related groups

news.   —Lists and news about USENET

misc.   —Miscellaneous
rec.   —Recreation, games
sci.   —Science, engineering
soc.   —Societal, political, and cultural issues
talk.   —Discussion groups

There are also important news groups listed with an "alt." prefix, indicating more informal, less restrictive editorial control.

The following list contains news groups of particular interest to librarians. They are accessed by typing "rn" followed by the name of the news group (e.g., "rn SCI.VIRTUAL-WORLDS") at the systems UNIX prompt:

ALT.HYPERTEXT

COMP.AI (artificial intelligence)

COMP.AI.NLANG-KNOW-REP (natural language)

COMP.AI.SHELLS (expert system shells)

COMP.DATABASES

COMP.INFOSYSTEMS

COMP.SYS.MAC.HYPERCARD

COMP.THEORY.INFO-RETRIEVAL

COMP.IVIDEODISC (interactive videodisc)

SCI.VIRTUAL-WORLDS (virtual reality technology)

The USENET grows each week as news groups are added across the spectrum of human interests.

Anonymous ftp

One of the more important protocols included in the TCP/IP suite are the file transfer protocols, which allow users to access any computer on the Internet and download large text files, databases, ASCII source codes, and so forth, to their local machine. Both the Internet-accessible OPAC lists described above are resident on remote computers and can be downloaded by ftp. The "anonymous" refers to the fact that most Internet hosts permit users to log on without having "authorized" accounts and passwords. The system operator, realizing that users from other parts of the Internet will want to access the "local" computer, sets up a user account whose user name is "anonymous" and password is "guest" (or some other term clearly identified by the system's prompt). This permits users without an "official" account to log on to the remote computer and use a selected number of the remote host's utilities and files. Anonymous ftp makes the Internet's global holdings of electronic journals and books, extensive bibliographies, and software available to anyone who can access a single local node.

FUTURE POSSIBILITIES

One of the major components of Internet is the NSFNET (National Science Foundation Network), a high-speed network designed to link researchers across the country to supercomputer facilities (Quarterman & Hoskins, 1986). Sometime in the early 1990's the NSFNET will become known as NREN-1 (National Research and Education Network), the first phase of a series of incremental steps taken to construct a fiber-optic-based "interstate" that eventually will link over 1 million government, academic, and business institutions (Huray & Nelson, 1990). As conceived, libraries, with their OPAC and burgeoning ancillary knowledge banks, will reside on the network as a virtual presence, "a family of decentralized centers containing information resources in various forms linked by common directories" (Cline, 1990, p. 30).

The configuration and process of implementation of the NREN is detailed in two major reports: "A Research and Development Strategy for High Performance Computing" and "The Federal High-Performance Computing Program." The Federal Coordinating Council for Science, Engineering and Technology (FCCSET) has been instrumental in developing implementation time schedules, detailed budgeting, and legislative analysis. The National High-Performance Computing Act of 1990 was put on the back burner for a year but passed in 1991. Soon the step-by-step implementation of the NREN should begin in earnest. For those interested in keeping up with the current NREN legislation and conceptualization, there are several electronic conferences to which one can subscribe. Both NREN-DISCUSS@PSI.COM and COM-PRIV@PSI.COM deal exclusively with NREN and network access issues. In the printed realm, the quarterly *EDUCOM Review* has been following developments closely, with substantial portions of recent issues (Summer 1990, Spring 1991) devoted to the NREN.

The E in the NREN stands for "education," and libraries are in the center of the configuration as central knowledge resources for national access. Cline (1990) identifies several important computerized information components already in libraries that can be expected to direct the contributions libraries initially will make to the NREN. Significant electronic attributes include OPAC, electronic acquisition systems, union OPACs, fax-based interlibrary loan systems and electronic local information bulletin boards, and other custom-crafted depositories. In addition to contributing content, libraries will be heavy users of NREN services. Although some visionaries see NREN eventually in every home throughout the United States (Weingarten, 1991), the beginning stages will be more a rationalization and ordering of current Internet options, probably with many of the attendant restrictions. In the early period, libraries, particularly public ones, might act as the community's access point to the NREN, providing a nonintrusive environment (unlike education institutions, which will integrate NREN usage into the curriculum) for individuals to pursue whatever information quests they bring to the system.

The specific parameters and access routes that will come to characterize the NREN are extremely fluid, and debate rages over the exact and even general approach to take toward creating, financing, and managing such a system. Frequently, especially on the electronic conferences devoted to NREN issues, the discussion becomes heated and even polemical, as varying Internet constituencies conceptualize competing models. One major issue is the universality of access (or lack thereof) to the NREN.

The model of the American public libraries movement of the nineteenth and early twentieth century might be instructive in developing an information philosophy of open, unrestricted, and unmonitored access. Access to the NREN as an information resource should avoid reflecting the class, economic, or educational stratifications of the society at large, or it will become a mechanism that feeds and strengthens these very divisions and the inevitable violence that results. The public library movement was always considered a means of redressing (and thereby perhaps legitimating) social and economic inequalities in American society. Embracing such a model, the NREN might also serve as an educational resource, providing universal and unconditional access to information and knowledge and the opportunities thereby derived for all members of the society.

NETWORK HELP SERVICES

A number of facilities act as directories for the Internet and BITNET. Since the Internet is a decentralized, diffuse amalgam of multiple networks, hosts, and gateways, all held together by a common communications protocol and little else, there is no one source for address and content information. Nevertheless, a number of institutions and individuals have developed files and services providing address information, online instruction, and sophisticated content search techniques:

1. *NIC.DDN.MIL.* This file contains the addresses of thousands of host computers, institutions, and individuals that can be reached through the Internet. The Whois command permits searching by name string. The coverage is wide ranging and extends beyond the military.

2. *NRI.RESTON.VA.US* 185. This is the Knowbot Information Service, which is a union list of other information directories (including NIC.DDN.MIL). Searches can be done on individuals, organizations, and institutions and limited by country.

3. *WP.PSI.COM.* The log-on is "fred"; a password is not required. This file carries personnel information on a variety of participating networks.

4. *Campus Wide Information Systems (CWIS).* Local university and academic institutes have begun mounting campus-specific information files covering their electronic resources and providing a clearinghouse of sorts for the immediate "telenvironment." Hundreds of CWIS are appearing throughout the higher educational system of the United States. There is even a BITNET mailing list on the topic of CWIS at CWIS-L@WUVMD. The three following CWIS are indicative of what can be done locally in providing a centralized access point:

Appalachian State University's Video Text System. Telnet CONRAD. APPS-TATE.EDU. Log-on as "info" and emulate VT100.

Cornell's CUINFO. Telnet CUINFO.CORNELL.EDU 300.

New Mexico State University's NMSU/INFO. Telnet INFO.NMSU.EDU

5. *Internet Resource Guide.* This book, produced by the National Science Foundation, lists many of the resources and policies of the Internet. It can be requested by sending an e-mail to NNSC@NNSC.NSF.NET. The guide can also be acquired through anonymous ftp from NNSC.NSF.NET (the directory is resource-guide). The CARL system (telnet to PAC. CARL.ORG) also has the guide online.

6. *FTP archive directory.* The Archive Server ("Archie") from McGill University contains a directory of approximately 600 ftp sites. Telnet to quiche.cs.mcgill.ca and log-in as "archie". At the archie> prompt, enter "help" or "about" to receive information concerning commands and database contents. Basically Archie serves to identify the hosts and directories in which files reside, which can be transferred through use of ftp.

7. *Bibliographies.* A bibliography on resources of information that will help readers become familiar with the concepts of internetworking is available on the USENET news group NEWS.ANNOUNCE.NEWUSER. Use the "rn" or "nn" UNIX-based news-reader programs to access the group on the USENET. The bibliography may also be procured by mailing a request to INFO-SERVER@SH.CS.NET, sending the message RE-QUEST:RFC on one line and TOPIC:RFC1175 on the next. There are approximately forty pages of books, articles, and reports cited. The bibliography is constantly being updated. Another bibliography that focuses on library-Internet/Bitnet topics is Diedre E. Stanton's *Libraries and Information Resources Networks.* This work is available via anonymous ftp from host CSUVAX1.CSU.MURDOCH.EDU.AU under the directory PUB/LIBRARY and filename STANTON.BIB.

8. *Library Resources on the Internet: Strategies for Selection and Use.* A guide to Internet resources for librarians edited by Laine Farley and published by the Reference and Adult Services Division of the American

Library Association, the document identifies main library resources on the Internet with particular emphasis on OPACs. It contains a good bibliography. It is available through anonymous ftp from DLA.UCOP.EDU (in the directory pub/internet, filename libcat-guide).

9. *Directory of Academic E-mail Conferences*, compiled by Diane Kovacs, contains five files to this list: acadlist filel, acadlist file2, acadlist file3, acadlist file4, and acadlist file5. All are available for anonymous ftp from KSUVXA.KENT.EDU.

10. *Wide Area Information Servers (WAIS)*. Perhaps most exciting, the disparate, loosely coupled nature of the Matrix has spurred the development of several "searcher" agents that can be "programmed" with a user's information need and then released into the Matrix to find the required material. Perhaps the most sophisticated project currently underway is that of the WAIS technology, being developed by Thinking Machines (Cambridge, Massachusetts). Thinking Machines engineers are developing WAIS software that will allow searching and retrieval from databases whose contents can be measured in terabytes (Kahle, 1989; Stein, 1991). (To put this in perspective, the entire full text content of the Library of Congress comes to about 25 terabytes [Stein, 1991].) WAIS technology is envisioned as being able to search quickly (ten seconds or less) through such systems as Dialog, Internet, and thousands of full text databases, looking for information in conformity with a patron's carefully defined query. Using mass parallel processing computers (such as the Connection Machine, manufactured by Thinking Machines), the user ultimately will be able to query myriad computers and files using a friendly front-end interface.

The WAIS system, described here in one of its beta incarnations, consists of hardware and software enhancements at the level of the user's personal computer that permit the system to query users about their document needs. The "Look for documents about" option is completed by the user, who then selects a variety of source servers, destinations that either possess citation and/or document files or contain the "matrix" addresses of other computers that contain such files (Stein, 1991). Examples of source servers could be specific electronic encyclopedias, almanacs, full text databases such as the *Wall Street Journal*, Dialog, news groups on the Internet, and almost any other file accessible through modem, X.25 communications, or one of the major networks (Stein, 1991, p. 164). The user is prompted by a menu of source servers, leaving nothing to the idiosyncrasies of human memory. The system almost instantly searches the delimited files for documents that meet the query's prerequisites. A list of results is posted, and from this the full text (if available) can be had by selecting the desired posting. Postings are sorted in terms of a relevancy factor (0 to 1000) and may be chosen and brought to the screen. The WAIS user interface is capable of reacting to feedback since the user can request more documents "similar to" the document chosen from the initial postings list. In this way, the initial query is given more specificity through relevance feedback. Kahle (1989) calls this method of searching "Content Navigation."

In one of the first expository articles on the WAIS technology, Stein writes, "The *similar to* function is like working with a reference librarian. First, you state the topic of your research, which the librarian translates into queries. After you examine the results of the queries, you indicate which results were on the mark; thus, the librarian gains a better understanding of your needs and can improve the search." This form of relevancy feedback is but one of many strategies employed during a reference negotiation; the extent of information that can be perused under a single interface makes the WAIS a promising technology for adoption in libraries as a kind of superpowered retrieval assistant.

For those interested in subscribing to WAIS interest groups, several conferences and news groups are available. The Internet addresses are WAIS-DISCUSSION@THINK.COM, WAIS-TALK@THINK. COM, and WAIS-INTEREST@THINK.COM. Subscription to WAIS-DISCUSSION includes the WAIS-discussion *Digest*, an electronic journal dedicated to WAIS technology and including many articles of direct relevance to librarians.

Librarians wishing to see first hand what this technology is like can telnet to QUAKE.THINK.COM. At the LOG IN, type "wais". You will be welcomed to the server and asked to identify the correct terminal emulation (most telecommunication software supports VT-100). A list of server addresses will then be scrolled with search options identified on the bottom.

INFORMATION RESOURCES

Reading some third-party literature prior to diving into the Matrix is important if the user wishes to avoid a long, difficult learning curve. Several good publications examine the mechanics, concepts, and network organization of the international Matrix. John S. Quarterman's *The Matrix: Computer Networks and Conferencing Systems Worldwide* provides a thorough, clearly written background exposition of the important international networks. Various protocols and worldwide networks are examined. An extensive country-by-country organization of networks, gateway services, and access individuals provides valuable, hard-to-find information. Extensive bibliographies and instructive network maps aid in further elucidation. A sixty-page index provides for pinpoint access to the work as a whole.

Another important directory book is *!%@ :: A Directory of Electronic Mail Addressing and Networks*, compiled by Donnalyn Frey and Rick Adams. An explanatory narrative of basic e-mail concepts and functions is provided, along with an extensive listing of networks. Each network entry has a map, facilities listing, contacts, addressing protocol, hardware/ software architecture, and future institutional plans.

The Users Directory of Computer Networks, edited by Tracy L. LaQuey (1990), is described by the author as a "road atlas of academic and research computer networks." Primarily a list of addresses, the book covers BIT-NET, DECnet, Internet, JANET, USENET, UUCP, domain structure, e-mail address tables, and a narrative description of OSI (Open Systems Interconnection).

Because the vast majority of Internet nodes run the UNIX operating system, with its powerful set of telecommunication utilities, users of the Matrix will benefit from several good books covering UNIX communications. The Waite Group's *UNIX Communications*, by Bart Anderson, Bryan Costales, and H. Henderson, offers comprehensive treatment of the mail utilities, file transfer protocol, and the USENET. Explanations are supplemented with examples, and the book is best used with a terminal. Another excellent book on UNIX is D. Scott Brandt's *Unix* and *Libraries*, which is filled with descriptions and applications of UNIX in library settings.

CONCLUSION

More than any other automation technology, the networks provide challenge and opportunity to reference librarians. The networks are the most important automation feature behind the growing connectivity of information domains. Knowledge and mastery of the rapid changes of that connectivity will become one of the most valuable and sought-after skills that reference librarians can possess.

5

Expert Systems

Expert systems are computer programs that emulate the knowledge and reasoning of some human expertise (Parsaye & Chignell, 1988, p. 1). Successful and useful implementations of such systems have been found to depend on the nature of the expertise chosen. Human expertise that is discrete, clearly understood, and frequently called upon makes the best automation candidates (Parsaye & Chignell, 1988; Frerau, 1989). During the 1980s, expert systems found homes in education, business, medicine, and manufacturing. They are no strangers to libraries either. *Library Literature* has indexed approximately 250 articles on all aspects of expert systems in the library between 1987 and 1992. In particular, expert systems have found their way into the cataloging and reference settings.

Often called knowledge-based programs or intelligent systems, expert systems provide expertise over a given knowledge domain. The MYCIN expert system, for instance, is called a medical diagnostic expert system because it is capable of diagnosing infectious diseases with the same rate of accuracy as a human expert (Buchanan & Shortliffe, 1984c, pp. 571–588). Barr and Feigenbaum (1982, chap. 7, sec. A) identify several characteristics of expert systems:

1. They seek to solve difficult problems.

2. They seek to solve such problems by applying expertise, which is represented through heuristic principles.

3. They are able to "explain" how they achieved a solution or answer.

Central to this definition is the concept of heuristics (sometimes called rules of thumb): the probabilities of X or Y being the case that allow the expert to cut through possibilities and concentrate on probabilities. A heuristic is a rule for reasoning that has a track record for being useful in applying expertise. One of the first heuristic devices commonly taught in library schools is that the initial formulation of a question does not always fully communicate the real information need of the patron. This is not always the case, but most reference librarians apply this rule of thumb when providing reference services.

Barr and Feigenbaum (1982, pp. 82, 182) also emphasize the role of explanation. A true expert system must be able to explain why it reached a certain conclusion. Since one of the attractions of expert systems is their ability to offer expertise in the absence of the human expert, they should be able to explain how a conclusion was achieved. This is of special importance when nonexperts will make further decisions based on the system's responses.

MYCIN: AN ARCHETYPICAL EXAMPLE

The first attempts to capture and represent human expertise in a computer program occurred in scientific disciplines such as medicine and chemistry during the 1960s and early 1970s. The most influential early expert system is MYCIN, a system capable of diagnosing infectious diseases.

The designers of MYCIN (Buchanan & Shortliffe, 1984d, p. 295) approached the expertise of diagnosis by breaking down the activity into two interrelated components: (1) relevant facts and rules governing clinical diagnosis and (2) the inferential reasoning that connects these facts and rules into a rational, knowledge-informed evaluation. This distinction separates what an expert knows (facts and rules) from the process of applying this knowledge to a case. In the terminology of artificial intelligence, this is referred to as the distinction between a knowledge-base and an inference engine. In one form or another, this division can be seen in many subsequent expert systems and is an important one to understand.

A knowledge base consists of a stored set of facts and principles relevant to the successful exercise of a particular expertise (Richardson, 1989, pp. 233–36). In MYCIN's case, this expertise is the diagnosis of infectious disease. The specific methods used to transfer this expertise from human to machine comprise the discipline of knowledge engineering. A knowledge engineer identifies and transfers into a knowledge base the core facts and heuristic rules governing a given human expertise (Hayes-Roth, Waterman & Lenat, 1983, p. 23). "The most difficult aspect of knowledge acquisition is the initial one of helping the expert conceptualize and structure the domain knowledge for use in problem solving" (Buchanan & Shortliffe, 1984a, p. 150). Through numerous interviews, the knowledge engineer boils down the rules of thumb and the order of their application employed in exercising the specific expertise.

Prior to translating this knowledge into the knowledge base, a decision must be made concerning how the knowledge is to be represented in the program. For MYCIN, the expertise had to do strongly with conclusions based on inferences from symptoms and symptom clusters. The designers therefore decided to represent knowledge in the form of conditional statements, the bulk of the expertise being represented in a series of if-then statements.

The if-then rule is one of the more successful means of representing expertise and knowledge in an expert system and figures prominently in reference-based expert systems. Consider the following typical if-then rule in MYCIN:

IF:	1. The stain of the organism is grampos and
	2. the morphology of the organism is coccus, and
	3. the growth conformation of the organism is chains
THEN:	There is suggestive evidence (.7) that the identity of the organism is streptococcus. (Shortliffe, 1984, p. 92)

This means that whenever these three conditions are met, there is a certainty factor of .7 that the infection involves the organism streptococcus. Certainty factors (in MYCIN, the highest certainty is 1.0) are often used in expert systems to represent the empirical, inferential nature of the reasoning processes involved. Notice that all of the antecedents are themselves conclusions of other rules that must be true if the consequent is also true. This chaining together of rules reflects the actual process taken by clinicians until a probable diagnosis can be offered.

In the rule above, how did MYCIN come to find out that the growth conformation of the organism is chains? How does MYCIN know the three antecedents are true and that a .7 chance exists that the organism is streptococcus? MYCIN has been equipped with an interface that queries the user for information concerning the infection and the results of specific tests that MYCIN presumes have been done. Van Melle calls this consultation program "the core of the system" (1984, p. 67).

Consultative activity is another dimension of expertise that must be carefully represented in the system. Not only must MYCIN ask the correct questions of the user, but the order of questions must reflect the most efficacious path by means of which a final conclusion can be drawn. During the consultation program, MYCIN asks a series of questions, some open-ended and some yes/no. Each answer is used to establish the validity of one of the hierarchically ordered if-then rules until a clinical conclusion can be reached.

While the knowledge base consists of rules, facts, and task-specific expert knowledge, the inference engine is that part of the program governing how the knowledge base is applied to a specific problem (Davis, 1984; Barr & Feigenbaum, p. 189). Traditionally the knowledge base and the inference engine have been considered two discrete interacting elements. Parsaye and Chignell (1988, p. 32) compare the distinction between knowledge base and inference engine to the distinction between knowledge and thinking or reasoning. The MYCIN rule considered above was called part of the knowledge base, and in fact the specifics of either the antecedents or the consequents are pieces of knowledge that only an expert would possess. However, the inferential procedure of applying the logical rule "if $A1$, $A2$, $A3$, . . . , then B," is valid regardless of what knowledge is represented in $A1$, $A2$, $A3$, or B. The inference engine provides the reasoning form into which the content of the knowledge is cast.

The effectiveness of expert system shells (pre-programmed inference engines that work on a user-supplied knowledge base), rests on this ability to separate expertise from the (logical) rules governing its application. In theory, rigorous adherence to such a separation makes it possible to develop new knowledge bases without having to recreate the inference engine.

Isolating the inference engine from the factual base of knowledge allowed the developers of MYCIN to produce EMYCIN, the first expert system shell:

One of the reasons for undertaking the original MYCIN experiment was to test the hypothesis that domain-specific-knowledge could successfully be kept separate from the inference procedures. . . . Specifically we believed that knowledge of a new domain, when encoded in rules, could be substituted for MYCIN's knowledge of infectious diseases and that no changes to the inference procedures were required to produce MYCIN-like consultations. (Buchanan & Shortliffe, 1984d, p. 295)

Other systems developed using the EMYCIN inference shell include SACON (Bennett & Engelmore, 1984 pp. 315–320), an expert system to assist engineers in choosing the correct methodology to use in performing a structural analysis; CLOT (pp. 320–325), a medical system that aids in the identification of certain blood clotting disorders; and PUFF (Buchanan & Shortliffe, 1984b, p. 393), a medical system dealing with pulmonary diseases. This method of using a preprogrammed multipurpose inferencing tool into which one loads the knowledge base of facts and rules has been influential in making expert systems financially feasible and available to nonprogrammers.

Commercial expert system shells lack the malleability of computer languages (Alberico, 1988a) but they are more quickly mastered by users and possess several other advantages. Although some shells provide a quasi-programming language option, most are geared for the developer who does not know how to program. In addition to being "developer friendly," they impose consistency by providing a single interface structure, an important feature for users who encounter several expert systems on the same workstation and expect them all to react the same way to inputs. A final advantage is that they have been debugged; that is, they are the products of professional programmers who have invested considerable time into making sure the shell works correctly. And since the shell provides a preprogrammed inference engine, the developer is free to concentrate solely on the rules and specific pieces of knowledge that govern his or her expertise. Once the requisite knowledge domain has been determined, the expert system shell requests that the relevant rules and facts be input using a precise syntax. Typically the rules follow the familiar if-then form. The developer also identifies the questions the end user will be required to answer when working through the system. Such answers provide the system with the "if" part of the equation. The system will then draw the consequence (then) of the rule and begin the inference process until a solution is reached. This solution is then displayed to the end user. Although the developer must be competent in the knowledge domain represented, no such facility is demanded in terms of programming.

EXPERT SYSTEMS AND THE REFERENCE DESK

Regardless of whether one uses a programming language or an expert system shell, the question remains: Exactly what areas of reference expertise allow themselves to be cast as an expert system? To provide a concrete answer to this question, some expert systems developed for the reference desk will be examined.

Pointer

Pointer (Smith, 1986) was one of the first systems to take advantage of artificial intelligence techniques for use at the reference desk. Developed at the State University of New York at Buffalo's Government Documents collection, its objective is limited "to just one step in the reference process: the step where the reference librarian chooses a reference book to satisfy the patron's information need" (p. 487). Written in LISP and later ported to BASIC, Pointer elicits information by walking the user through a series of menus that gradually focus the information request to a point where there is considerable probability that a given reference resource will satisfy the information need.

After identifying itself and the scope of its expertise ("this system will help you find reference books for U.S. documents" (Smith, 1986, p. 489), Pointer presents the user with three options: "1/a particular document for which you have a title, 2/a particular document for which you have some number such as a bill number, 3/information on some subject" (p. 490).

Since Pointer does not limit itself to a particular subject within U.S. documents, it is interesting to see how Smith deals with what might seem to be an extremely broad series of possible topic directions. This is accomplished by concentrating on the types of reference formats applicable to providing subject information in general. When searching for information on a subject (any subject), Pointer does not list a plethora of possible topics but identifies a finite series of possible reference formats: "1/Biographical information. 2/Numeric data. 3/Laws concerning your subject. 4/Regulations concerning your subject 5/Court cases concerning your subject" (Smith, 1986, p. 490). If option 4 (regulations) is chosen, Pointer provides the following reference suggestions: *CFR—Code of Federal Regulations, Federal Register, Federal Register—What It Is and How to Use It*, and the *Federal Regulatory Directory* (p. 490). Each suggestion includes the location in the U.S. Documents Collection of the Lockwood Library.

Because Pointer is written in interpreted BASIC, it must be run within the BASIC environment, no real problem for anyone using most forms of MS-DOS where GWBASIC is included. (I have not been able to run Pointer under Quick Basic.) To an extent, Pointer can also act as an expert system shell. Anyone who knows BASIC can enter new menu options and change the knowledge base of reference suggestions by changing the source code at the pertinent lines.

Pointer was one of the first attempts to bring artificial intelligence to the reference desk. It automates a complex problem and does so by tapping the expertise of professional documents librarians. Its lack of an explanation facility is not a crucial deficiency since the inferences are not lengthy; the menu series through which the user navigates is rarely more than four screens.

Answerman

At approximately the same time as Pointer's development, the staff at another special library, the National Agricultural Library, was developing a similar expert system called Answerman. One of the participants, Samuel Waters, described the initial development of Answerman in a 1986 article. The objective was to "create a microcomputer system that will guide an inquirer to a reference book likely to contain the answer to a question in a relatively narrow subfield of agriculture" (1986, p. 204). The developers decided to employ an expert system shell to minimize the time required to get the system up and running. After reviewing the literature, they decided that 1st Class from Programs in Motion promised success at a reasonable price.

Answerman, like Pointer, is menu driven and begins each session by specifying the exact scope of its expertise. First the user identifies the general area of agriculture of interest and then selects the kind of information required. The process proceeds from subject specification to format specification. After the system has received the necessary input, it displays the resources that will likely satisfy the user's information need. Displays consist of title and location information.

Unlike Pointer, Answerman can access the "external" world. After completing a session, Answerman prompts the patron for natural language sentences describing the actual query and whether the required information was found using the suggested resources. The staff uses this information to "focus, augment and improve the expert system" (Waters, 1986, p. 208). This information is also valuable to collection development efforts, in honing the collection so that it contains frequently sought information. Answerman can also access selected online databases. The configuration Waters described includes access to BRS's Superindex and the Agricola database. The communication links were written using the Crosstalk telecommunication program and require acquaintance with that software.

Having used a shell instead of pursuing the programming route, Waters is quite satisfied and remarks that the "beauty of the shell approach is that it allows librarians to create their own user-friendly system to select appropriate reference tools in any specialized field easily and quickly" (Waters, 1986, p. 208).

Plexus

Across the Atlantic, a group of researchers worked on an expert system that automated reference resource selection in the knowledge domain of gardening (Vickery, Brooks, Robinson & Vickery, 1987). Whereas Pointer's and Answerman's knowledge-base consists primarily of reference resources, Plexus supplemented printed reference resources with references to personal specialists and institutions. Programmed using the Pascal computer language, Plexus contains sophisticated algorithms for analyzing user input.

Plexus opens its session by asking questions about the user, thus creating a "simple" model of the specific patron. As distinct from menu-driven systems such as Pointer and Answerman, Plexus employs a natural language interface, which permits users to query the system with everyday English sentences. Plexus acts on the input by eliminating all stop words, stemming the remaining terms, and then comparing them to the contents of a system dictionary containing approximately 1,750 horticultural terms. Boolean strategies are employed to create precision searches or to broaden searches. The initial test knowledge base consisted of about 500 resources in the area of gardening.

Vickery and associates (1987, p. 18) list two main issues involving the Plexus interface that remain to be overcome: misspellings and ambiguous words. (Both problems plague any system designed around a natural language user interface.) The first difficulty can be partially eliminated by Plexus's stemming algorithm. Misspellings are classified as unidentified words by the system, and if the input contains a certain percentage of these "unknown terms" (those not in the system's dictionary), Plexus queries the user to determine under what category the unidentified term falls (name of an individual plant type, name of an insect, a microorganism, etc.). Ideally, the impact of the misspelling is mitigated by being linked to relevant category clusters, or the user recognizes a spelling error has been made and inputs the request again.

Remedies for word ambiguity depend on more complex steps. The word "plant," for instance, can be the stem of "planting" (an activity), "plant" (the name of an entity), or "planted" (the condition of a plant). Plexus treats such stems as possessing multiple meanings and employs a series of sentence or phrase-order rules to identify terms that precede and come after the ambiguous term (Vickery, Brooks, Robinson, & Vickery, 1987, p. 19). Depending on what types of words are in the immediate syntactic vicinity of the term, Plexus attaches a specific meaning to the term and proceeds with its search strategy, searching the knowledge base for the relevant data.

Although it is more sophisticated in its interface structure and the required syntactic and semantic sensitivities, Plexus performs the same reference role as both Pointer and Answerman: it identifies reference resources appropriate to a specific information need. Despite this restricted expertise, Plexus has begun to do something that stands at the center of reference service: question negotiation. It is a modest beginning and remains far from providing the negotiating power Taylor (1968) believes necessary for providing first-class reference service. Nevertheless, in pursuing the possible meanings of unidentified terms by querying the user, Plexus has taken the first step in computerizing the reference expertise most recalcitrant to automation: the reference interview.

ORA and REFSIM

ORA and REFSIM were developed by James Parrott at the University of Waterloo. The Online Reference Assistance (ORA) project (Parrott, 1986) emulates expertise in answering factual questions, suggesting strategies for literature searches, explaining how to find whether a specific document is in the library, and assisting in filling out an interlibrary form. Parrott and his associates also hoped that ORA might serve to train reference librarians new to a particular library. It soon became obvious, however, that a more sophisticated approach was needed. REFSIM, written in PROLOG, was constructed to "help impart the principles of both the reference interview and of search strategy prescription" (Parrott, 1988, p. 63).

REFSIM can function in three different modes. The first one is as a straight consultant and is aimed primarily at library patrons. The user queries the system, and REFSIM attempts to type-identify the question, moving through a brief dialogue with the user to determine subject area and other significant attributes of the information need. Finally REFSIM produces a set of reference tools that are ordered as a ranked series of possible sources. For instance, in response to an attempt to find a definition of the term "Mandelbrot set," REFSIM responds, "Try using the following tactics in the order given"; it then suggests the *Dictionary of Mathematics*, *Encyclopedic Dictionary of Mathematics*, the *McGraw-Hill Encyclopedia of Science and Technology*," and other sources, ending with, "Use Science Citation Index to locate an article on the subject, the article may have a definition" (Parrott, 1988, p. 65). Even in the consultation mode, REFSIM does more than just make reference suggestions; it creates a step-by-step reference strategy.

The next mode, the simulation-based coach mode, one of two ICAI (intelligent computer-aided instruction) modes, simulates an actual reference interview. REFSIM acts as coach and either as user or librarian depending on the "trainee's" selection. Trainees who choose "librarian" conduct the negotiation and are given a series of possible tactics by the coach, which they must then rank. The coach then provides the "correct" order of tactics, along with the reasoning behind the order.

The Socratic tutor mode adds a further dimension to the ICAI function by challenging the would-be librarian for the reasoning behind suggesting a reference choice—for example, "Are dictionaries/encyclopedias the first places you would look for a definition of a term?" (Parrott, 1988, p. 66). The Socratic tutor method seeks to let librarians reexamine the rules upon which reference advice is founded and to come to an explicit understanding of such rules.

REFSIM is unique in that, with its tri-part module structure, it serves as both an expert reference advisory system and an expert trainer concerning reference reasoning.

Index Expert

This expert system aids individuals in selecting an appropriate index or abstract. Developed at the University of Houston Libraries by the Intelligent Reference Systems Committee (Bailey, Fadell, Myers & Wilson, 1989), the system stands as a prototype for a more encompassing project to bring expert reference advisory systems to the university library. Evolving out of a lineage of prototypical implementations, which included the use of several expert system shells, the final Index Expert is written using the Turbo Prolog language.

The interface for Index Expert consists of menus linked to a subject classification thesaurus that contains hierarchically related subject terms. At the top level sit discipline terms (Business, Education, General, Humanities, Science, etc.). Highlighting any option in the main menu brings up a menu of relevant subcategories on another part of the screen. Selecting one of the broad terms automatically brings up an active menu containing all the subsidiary subject terms contained in the broader term. A user who selects "Humanities" must then select from Archeology, Architecture, Art, and other subcategories. Once the system's subject-tree specificity is exhausted, Index Expert presents a choice of subject aspects. For instance, the subject Art has the aspects "Business" or "Teaching." Finally, the system prompts for coverage criteria (selective versus comprehensive). After Index Expert receives this information, it processes the request and displays suitable indexes providing name, locations, subject, scope, and a brief annotation.

Most knowledge bases at the reference desk rely on the if-then rule structure to represent knowledge. Index Expert, however, uses frames to represent its knowledge (Bailey, Fadell, Myers, & Wilson, 1989, pp. 24–25). A frame can be thought of as a context of relevancy, a framework of qualities, attributes, and their interrelationships that characterize a component of knowledge. The frame paradigm is applied to the entire knowledge base itself. Frames are not discrete, unrelated environments but are hierarchically related to one another in a single overarching frame. This hierarchical structure provides for the property of inheritance, narrower frames inheriting the properties of the broader frames of which they are subspecies (Parsaye & Chignell, 1988, sec. 2.3.3).

The Intelligent Reference Systems Committee seeks to use Index Expert as the beginning step in developing a "new generation of computerized tools to help library users obtain needed information" (Bailey, Fadell, Myers, & Wilson, 1989, p. 28). During a test trial, the system was used by over 1,500 patrons. Fifty-one user surveys were returned, indicating that over 86 percent found an appropriate index, which bodes well for the reference utility of future implementations at the University of Houston.

WORK IN ONLINE SEARCH EXPERT SYSTEMS

Private and commercial online database facilities have been in existence since the early 1960s. Throughout this time, information scientists have been interested in developing software that would make searching these large information databases more user friendly. Initially, database searching was performed in a noninteractive environment. The commands were complicated, with the complexity of their syntax rivaling programming languages. Now database and interface design provide interactive opportunities and a much sleeker command interface. For a variety of reasons, however, the end user is still dependent on a skilled intermediate. Since the late 1970s, information scientists have explored the application of expert system techniques to online searching in an effort to automate the expertise of the trained intermediary. While nothing is commercially available yet, the development of expert systems as online search intermediaries has produced several noteworthy prototypes.

Early Precursors

In the 1960s, the SMART system (Salton, 1971), developed at Harvard University, was one of the first automated information retrieval systems. Used primarily to test searching algorithms and principles, it also possessed a sophisticated user interface that allowed it to accept a user-defined search strategy. SMART also permitted the user to supply weighted search concepts. Thirty years later, few would mistake the SMART interface as "friendly." Nevertheless, it was tremendously influential in setting the tone for advances in online information retrieval automation using interactive and feedback techniques.

Indebted to the SMART system is the THOMAS program (Oddy, 1977), an interactive, dialogic interface whose bibliographic domain covers medicine and biochemistry. Written in the mid-1970s by R. N. Oddy for use at the University of Newcastle-on-Tyne, THOMAS proceeds by developing an image of the user need. This image then guides the search query. As the search progresses, the user reacts to what is being found, providing feedback into the THOMAS program that contributes to image reformation. Oddy refers to Lancaster's description of a "browsing search" (Lancaster, 1968) in which a beginning search strategy is framed and implemented and initial results modified (Oddy, 1977, pp. 1–2). It is this ongoing modification of the information need itself that THOMAS accommodates.

The strength of the system resides in an ability to modify its internal image of the user's need, but this strength depends on a "hand-carved" bibliographic knowledge base: "The main component of the image used in this work is the context of the topic of enquiry, as represented by regions in the program's network knowledge base" (Oddy, 1977, p. 5). Although the bibliographic contents of the knowledge base were originally taken from the Medlars database, they have been manually reorganized into THOMAS's network structure. This limits THOMAS's dialogic approach to its specific knowledge base and makes it difficult, if not impossible, to transport its features to large online databases.

EXPERT

The EXPERT system (Marcus, 1981, 1985) interfaces with commercially available large databases such as ERIC. In a 1981 conference address, Marcus explicitly called his system an "expert system" (p. 270). EXPERT emulates the expert searcher who is helping a novice search a bibliographic retrieval system. Four functions of the intermediary are automated (1981): extrapolation of the information need, database selection, transformation of the need into a key word strategy, and strategy reformulation based on search results.

EXPERT elicits characteristics of the information need through a dialogic interface. Once the system ascertains the "major concepts" and overall subject field, it judges which databases are likely to contain relevant material and ranks them. When the user selects the database, EXPERT automatically logs on and executes the search strategy using correct software commands. The first ten hits are displayed to the user, with suggestions concerning the attached key word index terms as possible ways of broadening or narrowing the search. A modified search can be run again.

IR–NLI

Another representative search intermediary expert system from the early 1980s is IR–NLI (Information Retrieval–Natural Language Interface). Unlike EXPERT, whose dialogic interface consists of an extremely restricted series of prompts and suggestions, IR–NLI is designed to respond to a broad range of natural language input. The designers delineated three criteria any expert system must meet to function as a true online search intermediary: expertise in online searching, the ability to understand natural language, and the ability to extract from natural language dialogue the correct information need, which can then be phrased in the relevant "formal query language" (Guida & Tasso, 1983, p. 33).

IR-NLI-II (Brajnik, Guida, & Tasso, 1990) is a more advanced implementation of the original prototype. Still directed at helping the end user choose an online database (now narrowed to those in computer science), the IR-NLI-II takes advantage of a sophisticated user modeling device. The user modeling program conducts an interview and uses this information to guide its selection of appropriate databases. IR-NLI-II is capable of saving the user model for future search sessions. Among the user attributes contained in the model are educational and professional background, information request patterns, normal search requirements, subject knowledge, familiarity with databases, and information retrieval activity.

Once the user model is developed, the question is negotiated using IR-NLI-II's sophisticated natural language interface and its information retrieval expert subsystem (IRES) modules. Appropriate online databases are suggested, and, if acceptable, IR-NLI-II develops a search strategy. The natural language interface is then capable of interacting with the user to make sure the search strategy is acceptable. When the system's strategy is criticized, it provides reasons for the proposed steps. Finally, the search is conducted, and IR-NLI-II "discusses" the result with the user. Further refinement takes place (if necessary), and the search can be resubmitted.

IR-NLI-II represents state-of-the art technology in online expert system search intermediaries. The next phase in its development is to design an even more robust natural language interface (Brajnik, Guida & Tasso, 1990, p. 184).

Patent Information Assistant

The Patent Information Assistant (Ardis, 1990) mediates searches of online databases containing patent information. Unlike many of the other systems reviewed, which use either natural language or dialogic interfaces, the Patent Information Assistant depends on an elaborate interrelated menu tree. The menu-driven interface identifies the exact user goal, automatically selects and executes an online search, and provides the user with printed output. There is also a feedback option in which the user specifies what, if anything, is wrong with the output. Further refinement and online searching can then occur. Designed to run on an IBM AT, XT, or clone and using a 2400 baud modem, the system is available for patron search in the McKinney Engineering Library at the University of Austin.

CITE NLM

CITE (Doszkocs, 1983) was written to supply a friendly front end to users of NLM's OPAC and the MEDLINE database. It permits natural language input without restriction and subjects each word to a lengthy stop list, stemming the survivors. These are then relevancy weighted inverse to the frequency of appearances in the database (the assumption is that the less evenly the word is spread throughout the whole database, the more subject relevancy it provides). Searches are automatically conducted and results reviewed by the user, who can then provide feedback and make refinements. The designer, T. Doszkocs (1983, p. 369), is careful to distinguish this form of natural language facility from natural language understanding and for that reason resists characterizing CITE as possessing artificial intelligence features.

INFORMATION RESOURCES

Donald Hawkins (1988) provides more information on other expert search intermediary systems, and Ralph Alberico and Mary Micco (1990) offer a more comprehensive treatment of all types of library-related expert systems.

DEVELOPING AN EXPERT SYSTEM FOR THE REFERENCE DESK

The issues and considerations examined here are distilled from several years of developing, implementing, and maintaining expert reference advisory systems (Carande, 1989, 1990; Chan & Carande, 1991) and participating in the planning phases of others. The mistakes and failures have been just as instructive as the successes. Although some chronological approach is inevitable, these issues are best read as describing major stages and problems that should be kept in mind when embarking upon expert systems development for reference services.

Identifying the Knowledge Domain

Narrow focus on a discrete knowledge domain is an important indicator for success in the development of expert systems (Prerau, 1989; Parsaye & Chignell, 1988). Unless the knowledge domain is clearly grasped and its boundaries understood, it becomes difficult to identify the expertise involved or to go about the practical steps of implementation.

Too often designers approach the formulation of knowledge domain from a subject classification approach—for example, "The knowledge domain will be physics." Instead, a system like Answerman or IR-NLI basically performs an activity. Answerman does not "know" about reference sources in agriculture; it "suggests" reference sources in agriculture. Some systems, especially the online intermediaries, provide quite sophisticated question-negotiation dialogues. This emphasis on the performance aspect of a knowledge domain is important and should be kept clearly in mind as a guiding idea in determining how and and where expert systems are to be employed at the reference desk.

The systems already examined are based on one or more of the following performances:

1. Suggesting likely reference resources across various formats (encyclopedias, dictionaries, indexes) in response to a query.

2. Suggesting periodical indexes in response to a query.

3. Suggesting an ordered series of research steps to be taken in response to a query.

4. Conducting online search strategy, database selection, database searching, and strategy refinement.

5. Distinguishing the status (book, periodical, proceedings, etc.) of a citation.

Because librarianship is primarily an expertise of practice, the formulation of the knowledge domain must begin with identifying expert practices that take place at the reference desk. This can be accomplished by listing all the specific activities that regularly occur at the desk. An inventory based on several days is indicative of potential automation options. For large endeavors like question negotiation, the performance can be analyzed into its constituent parts.

One day, I identified the following fifteen practices that regularly occurred:

1. Answering directional questions
2. Explaining how to read a call number
3. Narrowing subject queries
4. Expanding subject queries
5. Explaining Library of Congress subject headings and how to use them
6. Explaining how to use the OPAC
7. Deciphering abbreviations and acronyms
8. Determining patron's knowledge background
9. Identifying other reference librarians with specific expertise
10. Identifying other local libraries with specific collection strengths
11. Determining a patron's query objective (writing a paper? giving a two-minute speech?)
12. Explaining the steps involved in locating a periodical in the collection
13. Explaining library circulation policy
14. Determining when a query warrants use of an online resource—and when it does not.
15. Deciphering a variety of nonverbal cues

Except for the last one, all of these practices are possible candidates for automation using common stand-alone workstations of the PC/MAC variety. Practices that appear most interesting and most efficacious in the context of the current mix of reference services are excellent candidates. Expertise that is regularly and consistently in demand should receive special attention.

Conceptualizing the System's Objective

After selecting a practical expertise, defining the total objective of the system aids in identifying the practical steps involved in implementations. There are at least six important components to consider:

1. The exact function to be automated
2. Its beginning and end (that is, exactly what stage of need is addressed and how extensive the resolution is—in other words, its place in the total context of reference service)
3. Patron access (unmediated, mediated by librarians)
4. Reference environment (will there be professional staff available nearby, or will the system be totally self-sufficient?)
5. Physical location of the system
6. The benefits the expert system will bestow upon reference services

Once these elements are clarified and understood, it becomes easier to map out the required strategy for implementation and to measure progress. Additionally, the project can be clearly communicated to others whose expertise or support is needed. At this point, "clarity" does not mean inflexibility, modifications will certainly be made before the project is fully implemented.

Identifying the Experts

People at the reference desk who possess the skills and expertise the system requires are valuable resources for the project. Even if the developer is an expert in the activity being automated, working with other experts provides feedback and differing perspectives, as well as developing support and confidence from others who may inevitably work with, or refer patrons to, the system.

Each kind of skill that goes into the activity being automated should be identified and linked to one or more specialists in that area. For instance, a reference advisory expert system such as Answerman has several distinct layers of knowledge built into it. Consider an elemental item in the knowledge base (represented here as an if-then rule):

If the subject is corn and prices,
    then go to the World Almanac.

Such specifics are based on knowing the relevance of the heuristic rule A, "For commodity prices look at a yearly almanac." And this heuristic rule is relevant only because of another rule, B, which runs something like, "Most people using this library would want only yearly average prices of commodities." If B is not the case, and most people using the library want weekly prices at specific markets, then rule A becomes irrelevant. The value of knowing that commodity prices are listed in the *World Almanac* is based on knowing that patrons usually ask for the yearly average price and typically require no more precision than that. The knowledge contained in B is different from that contained in A, and both kinds need to be coordinated. One expert may be an expert in commodity price resources (but rarely works the reference desk); another may be skilled in knowing what kinds of questions are asked (but whose subject expertise lies in physics). If both are not tapped, the proposed system will suffer.

In addition to garnering cooperation and input, communication with professionals and staff allays anxiety. Research (Bloom, 1985; Meier, 1985) has shown that the introduction of computers into the workplace can produce some anxiety. In the library context, this anxiety should not be dismissed as irrational. Attempting to bring automation to an activity as highly humanized as providing reference service seems at first glance to indicate an insensitivity to the human complexity of the endeavor. Here a precise understanding and grasp of the automation objective, particularly its place in the overall reference setting, is helpful in allaying suspicions that the developer is blinded by technology and unable or unwilling to see its limits.

Relevant Professional and Staff Groups

In conjunction with the third step, communication should be extended to those outside the expert loop as early as possible in the development of the system. Expert systems have an aura of glamour, but they need the same daily maintenance as other machines servicing the reference area. Turning the system on and off, keeping it supplied with paper, and fixing mechanical problems are responsibilities that will probably devolve onto staff. Staff need to be aware of the place the system plays in reference work so that it is not rejected as a mere encumbrance.

Many expert systems are designed to provide rudimentary reference services when professional librarians are either unavailable or off duty. At such times, staff are expected to provide directional and elementary reference advice, which requires knowledge of the major information resources available. They should possess specific, concrete knowledge of the system's subject parameters—its capabilities and limitations. At the very least, considering the proliferation of computer systems in the library, the paraprofessional staff should be aware of what an expert system is not.

Literature Resources

Some familiarity with the literature of expert systems is presupposed when determining what expertise can be automated, but a systematic review of the literature of expert systems and reference services can provide a wealth of information covering anything from epistemological issues such as knowledge representation to policy issues such as where the system ought to stand. *Library Literature* provides excellent coverage of the library journals and has a heading for expert systems going back to 1986 (prior to that, the heading "Artificial Intelligence" picks up a few early articles on the topic). *Library and Information Science Abstracts* (LISA) is another important resource when it comes to the journal literature on expert systems in library settings. LISA also focuses on core journals in information science.

While *Library Literature* and *LISA* cover the library and information science literature, there are a number of other indexes that seem far afield of reference services but are nevertheless useful. *Computer and Control Abstracts* provides comprehensive coverage of the computer literature of the world and has a section (72.10L) on library automation. Each issue usually features one or two interesting articles on expert systems and reference services. Many of these articles appear in journals outside the field of librarianship and would be missed by relying solely on *Library Literature* and *LISA*.

A further source for information on expert systems, particularly expert system shells, is *Engineering Index*. It covers the vast field of engineering literature; a great many articles are of interest to librarians concerned with developing expert systems.

Abstracts in Human-Computer Interaction, which began publication in March 1990, is a very good source for articles on expert systems design and human factors. The articles are especially important to the interface designer who must be sensitive to user psychology.

Another rich source for citations to expert systems in information work is *Information Science Abstracts*, which has a heading for expert systems and provides extensive coverage of the field of information science.

Shell versus Programming Language

Most authors (Richardson, 1989; Quinn, 1990; Alberico, 1988a; Alberico & Micco, 1990) who have discussed the shell versus custom-made issue have found advantages and disadvantages in both approaches.

Shells are relatively easy to learn, and the programs function without any crippling bugs. If a single shell is employed to produce several expert systems, then a level of consistency is introduced throughout the offerings. Also, a typical expert system shell is a commercial product produced by a reputable software house that provides some level of support.

The rapidity with which a shell can be learned is its main strength. This is a factor not only when considering time and effort spent implementing a system but also the work involved in maintaining and updating it.

The key disadvantage of an expert system shell is the opposite of its advantage: its consistency and ease of use is bought at the price of creativity. Once the shell route is taken, the designer is restricted to the shell interface, the logic and parameters governing information input, and the manner in which information is displayed to the user. Since none of the current popular shells was developed within a library setting, many of them leave much to be desired from the reference perspective when it comes to these three restrictions. The problem regarding the display of information is particularly significant. It is very frustrating for a user to navigate a system, only to be thrown by an inadequate answer display. In particular, for systems that end by suggesting reference items, if not enough room is provided for location, the user is unable to make that final, all-important physical connection with the actual resource.

An additional drawback to using an expert system shell is its initial expense. Although a few shells are available for under five hundred dollars, most hover in the thousands-of-dollars range. Furthermore, once a system is developed, it would be helpful to be able to port it to other computers in different locations at the same or another library. To do this, a run-time version of the shell must be purchased that allows the expert system to run on computers that do not have the shell software installed. The costs for run-time versions are typically high.

A directory of current expert system shells can be found in *PC AI's* annual "AI Product Guide" (the latest is July 1992) which lists several dozen manufacturers with brief nonevaluative descriptions of the shells. *Microcomputer Index* indexes evaluations of the various shells that appear in the popular PC/Apple computing literature.

Completely custom-made systems depend on the designer's ability to program using a computer language. Prolog, LISP, BASIC and Pascal have all been used within the library setting to develop expert systems. The great advantage of using a programming language is its flexibility. Interfaces, display features, the logic of information input, the kinds of questions asked the patron, the specific information processing utilized, and the mode of knowledge representation are all under the control of the programmer. Furthermore, PC-based languages are relatively inexpensive to purchase. Many permit the code to be compiled into directly executable programs, so no additional costs are incurred for run-time versions.

The disadvantages stem primarily from the amount of time needed to master the programming language. As Alberico (1988a) states about the Turbo Prolog language from Borland software, "Prolog can do a lot of things, but it has to be told how to do everything" (p. 12). Learning to tell a language how to do everything can be an expensive proposition when calculated in hours.

Input Flowcharts

The designer needs to answer two questions: What kind of advice is the system giving? What does the system need to know to give the advice? An expert system results in some decision based on input that describes a need. In the typical reference context, the need is informational. The most precise comprehensive knowledge base sits idle unless the patrons can communicate needs to a system that can understand them as meaningful. "Meaning" in this context refers to information that furthers the system's ability to make a decision.

It is important at this point to synchronize two closely related elements of the system: the knowledge base and the possible shapes the system will allow the information need to take.

Regulating the possible shapes of an information need can be achieved by menu sequences, dialogic interactions that steer the user to possible inputs acceptable to the system, or natural language interfaces capable of negotiating with the patron and determining whether the questions are "legal." The result must be an information need that the knowledge base can answer. For instance, if the knowledge base consists of reference books linked to subject and format needs (*if* agriculture and *if* statistics, *then* Almanac), the system must know something about those two dimensions to make a decision. The user's subject sophistication is unnecessary because the knowledge base is unable to use the information. Those required dimensions (subject and format) must be elicited from the user by straight natural language interaction, dialogic interaction, or menus before the system can answer with precision.

Design of the knowledge base must result in finding certain pieces of information relevant to the expert system's decision-making capacities. If the system seeks to suggest appropriate online databases for subject searches, it must possess a knowledge base that at least links subject areas with specific databases. A simple knowledge base, for example, finds information about subject interests meaningful but finds information about format interests ("I want only journals") without meaning.

The dialectical relationship between what knowledge is represented in the knowledge base and what information needs are modeled can be clarified by constructing a flowchart of the expert system. A specific transaction, narratively described, offers the basis upon which to chart—for instance; "The patron asks to find technical journals in physics, and the system tells him to check Physics Abstracts." To answer this question, the system needs to know: (1) the patron wants journal literature, (2) the patron's subject matter is physics, and (3) the content must be technical (and presumably the patron has some background in physics). Somewhere in the sequence of interactions between user and machine, the system must extract subject, format, and material sophistication requirements. This list also needs to be reflected isomorphically in the knowledge base.

Once the list of required knowledge is derived, the entire screen sequence through which the patron moves can be mapped out. The logic inherent in the structure of any information need is elicited chronologically, and menus or questions need to be designed with that logic in view. Screens that elicit from the patron the requirements listed under the information need can then be detailed and sequenced. Attention should be paid to possible answers that might be given and whether these answers will be meaningful to the knowledge base. If a response lacks meaning, how is that communicated to the user? The use of menus provides a predetermined set of possible requirements presented to the user at each step. Designing an adequate menu, however, is no easy process. Two excellent books that provide analysis of the key issues in menu (and screen) design are by Joseph Dumas (1988) and Ben Shneiderman (1987). Natural language and dialogic interactions preserve the more natural flow of reference negotiation but need to be carefully crafted if programming a custom-made system.

Since the information need is elicited through a sequence of screens or dialogue points, the information need becomes more and more focused as the session goes on. Many systems offer the patron an ongoing report of what already has been determined. This is important during longer sequences where patrons may forget what has already been resolved. It is also advantageous when the system is making a final decision and presenting an answer to let the patron know what the system thinks it has been asked. Menu systems are especially prone to a patron's inadvertently pressing the wrong key. Misunderstanding can be avoided if the system displays the information need as it understands it at any given time.

During flowcharting of the sequence of interface screens, the proposals need to be widely disseminated to other professionals who will be working at the desk. Working collectively, a reference department can assess whether the sequence provides the best possible manner of discovering what the patron wants.

Cooperative Development of the Knowledge Base

Determining the structure of a knowledge base entry, its manner of representation, is just the beginning of developing a knowledge base. It is not uncommon for one person to design and program or (in the case of some simple shells) input the knowledge base, but the best strategy in determining what goes into the system is one that maximizes the cooperation of many librarians. Cooperative efforts in developing a knowledge base offer several advantages. First, many systems cover an area that encompasses the expertise of several librarians. For instance, the Index Expert system covers a single format (periodical indexes) throughout several dozen areas of subject-bibliographic expertise. The knowledge base can be strengthened only when the appropriate subject expert provides the relevant contents. Second, the broader the participation is in developing the knowledge base, the more support and confidence the system generates among the reference librarians who will staff the desk. They trust the system's responses because in a large part they are responsible for its content.

Progress and Quality Control

Specific times should be set aside to meet with others involved in the system's development to discuss progress or review the performance of prototypes. Problems identified early in the design stage of the system are easier to rectify than when the system is performing reference work. Once a system is presented to the public, repeated deep design changes can shake user and staff confidence in the performance of the program.

Updating Schedules

Keeping expert systems updated once they are performing at the reference desk is not as glamorous as designing and prototyping them, but it is an important factor in their continued effectiveness. Unless this is clearly discussed beforehand in terms of who and when, a system in which one has invested much time can slowly become obsolete. Systems that seek to emulate the selection of reference resources quickly become outdated in terms of new additions or changed locations of old resources. The time for discussing the logistics of updating should predate the decision concerning language versus shell. If a language is chosen and one or two people are selected or volunteer to learn the language, they should also understand they will be the logical choices for "who" when it comes to keeping the system updated.

Maintenance Logistics

Finally, the time comes when the expert system is ready to perform its allotted task. In addition to determining who will perform knowledge base updates and when, a number of personnel decisions concerning the logistics of system maintenance need to have been resolved. This is when the importance of open communications with staff concerning expert system implementation bears fruit. The addition of another system that must be started and shut off daily, kept filled with paper, and involves other duties will not necessarily be greeted eagerly, particularly if the significance of the system has not been clearly communicated. Designing and implementing expert systems is only as productive as the continued patron accessibility of the final product. This accessibility is contingent on the machine's being turned on, maintained, and restarted by a specified individual or individuals.

Another important element in the logistics of continuing accessibility involves signage. It is not unusual for a reference service point to contain OPAC terminals, a plethora of CD-ROM terminals, and other information terminals. Signs are important to distinguish the system's uniqueness and as a means of advertisement. A clearly displayed sign can eliminate confusion or worse, such as when patrons leave an expert system believing they have had a disappointing session with the OPAC.

Evaluating System Effectiveness

The fact that patrons do not ask questions about a system does not mean they are being helped by it or understand it. A patron may input a request, read the information, and assume the request will be resolved if they follow the instruction—or they may misunderstand the information they are given. And when the answer sends them into the stacks, the disappointment occurs far from the reference point. In the case of expert systems at reference service points, some important capacities that need to be evaluated include response relevance (Did the system respond appropriately to the input?), response clarity (Did the patron understand the answer?), and interface sensitivity (How robust is the system's negotiating powers?).

Methods to gather evaluative evidence can be grouped into two kinds: internal and external. Internal evaluations signify efforts the system makes to evaluate its performance. This can be done through optional (or mandatory) evaluation screens within the system or through recording the user's own natural language description of the information need. External evaluations refer to questionnaires or interviews administered outside direct system-patron interaction.

Answerman is an example of a system that possesses an internal evaluative module (Waters, 1986, p. 208). Although Answerman uses an expert system shell, programmers at the National Agricultural Library linked it to a BASIC program that asks a series of evaluative questions of the patron after each completed session. Patrons are prompted to input their actual question using natural English sentences and whether they found what they were looking for in the particular tool Answerman indicated. Patrons are also asked to suggest improvements. The BASIC program saves the responses for future review.

The designers of Index Expert took an external approach (Bailey, Fadell, Myers, & Wilson, 1989). They asked patrons to fill out a questionnaire inquiring about how easy they thought the system was to learn and how satisfied they were with the effectiveness of the responses.

Regardless of what route is taken to evaluate the performance of an expert system, certain performance parameters should be included.

It is helpful to know the actual request as described by the patron using natural language sentences. Whether done internal to the system or through a questionnaire, this information should be taken with a grain of salt since it is well known that patrons are not always successful (for a variety of reasons) in initially describing their real information needs (Taylor, 1968). Nevertheless, the broad subject and format affiliations of the query are usually dependable indications of generic expectations. This type of information is important in assessing the relevance of the system's suggestions, as well as providing knowledge about patron uses and information needs.

In addition to the actual patron information need, the search strategy employed by the patron while navigating the system can aid in assessing system performance. Possible sources of patron difficulties that may be revealed include (1) misleading interface cues, such as a menu option that patrons repeatedly misinterpret or a term used in dialogue that is consistently misunderstood, (2) dialogic or menu options that do not adequately cover a specific information need even when that need falls within the requisite subject expertise (for instance, a menu-driven expert system in engineering reference resources that omits environmental engineering as an option), and (3) patron input errors.

Did the patron find the system easy to navigate? Did the patron quickly comprehend what was required, or were the directions and options murky? How tolerant does the patron find the system to error (for instance, are typos or mistaken answers easy to recover from)? While difficult to determine, it would be very helpful to find out how the patron interprets a suggestion. A reference advisory expert system covering nursing resources might be easy to use, fault tolerant, capable of eliciting a relevant and sufficient model of the user's information need, and fully perform the advisory activity at an expert level. Yet if patrons leave thinking they have been referred to all the books in the library about nursing, the expert advice is still in need of fine tuning.

Knowing whether the patron found the system's suggestions helpful is valuable, especially when the patron's actual information need and navigation strategy are also known. Knowing that a patron did not find *Index Medicus* helpful is not sufficient ground to infer anything about the system. Suppose the patron's information need concerned finding "current articles in peer-reviewed journals on speech disorders." It would be difficult to fault a system that suggested *Index Medicus* in response to such a query or to one by a person who wanted to know if there was anything in the professional medical literature on the effects of perfectly square rooms on adult nose growth. *Index Medicus* would be an adequate suggestion, but it would not be surprising if the patron failed to find information. Because the patron may not have used the resource effectively or approached with an eccentric information request, the patron's satisfaction with the expert system's performance should always be analyzed in the light of the actual information need and the navigation strategy employed.

CONCLUSION

The steps outlined highlight the significant milestones on the way to implementing an expert system at the reference desk. Depending on the specific expertise being automated, steps can be modified, expanded, or skipped. The successful implementation of expert systems can involve many staff hours; however, the paybacks are substantial. Patrons have greater access to a valuable, frequently demanded expertise, and reference librarians have greater time to devote to a more individually focused reference service. Furthermore, the cooperative approach to implementation results in both a shared sense of accomplishment and increased knowledge about the place of automation in reference services.

6

Natural Language Interfaces

In a typical reference negotiation scenario, librarian and patron spend time negotiating the query so that the actual information objective is properly conceptualized. Included in this negotiation is the process of translating the patron's information objective into the "authorized" logic of the information tool. An interface able to discuss a patron's information objective and then translate this conceptualization into an "authorized" language would need to be able to understand natural language input. Furthermore, for it to be of interest in a reference context, the interface must understand patron input in terms of the dynamics of negotiation, a discursive, sophisticated interaction typically involving a variety of linguistic and nonlinguistic communicative subtleties.

Consider a reference interview that begins with the statement, "I am looking for articles about the current theory of superstring formation." A condition for the negotiation to commence is the librarian's ability to understand the literal meaning of the sentence as offered. The reference negotiator must know the meaning of the words "articles," "theory," and "superstring." And these meanings make sense only in the context of unspoken, invisible as it were, fields such as publishing formats, science, and physics.

Behind a recognition of simple semantic components of the sentence is a further condition: the recognition of the sentence as a sentence. This recognition is based on the sentence's conforming to grammatical rules governing language usage such that a number of syntactical forms are observed: adjectives generally modify nouns, prepositions must have objects, sentences must have at least one subject and one predicate. The method of "parsing" is used to assess the parts of speech of any sentence and, derivatively, the relationships of specific parts. The sentence "Articles theory looking am about formation current I superstring of" is not immediately understandable because it lacks the grammatical structure that allows words to function as conveyers of meaning and conscious expression. Typically a natural language understanding program parses input (syntactical analysis) and then identifies meaning (semantic analysis). Functionally, this identification of meaning signifies that the system is able to translate the natural input into some internal unambiguous formalism, which can then be utilized by the program to respond correctly.

The librarian does more than simply run each word or phrase through a mental dictionary and link up the meanings. Another aspect or context of the negotiation concerns the patron's background and the various functions the information is expected to fulfill. The same series of words comprising the question about superstrings means something entirely different when uttered by someone who holds a doctorate in physics concerned with recent theoretical research than by a freshman intent on writing a three-page paper for English 101. Something like a worldview context is needed, which requires a sophisticated user model to understand fully a patron query. And so it is inevitable that a worthwhile natural language processor, if it is to provide any aid in the negotiation of reference questions, must, in addition to possessing sophisticated syntactic and semantic abilities, acknowledge how and with whom reference negotiation is conducted. Consequently, discourse- (Reichman-Adar, 1984) or script- (Schank, 1984) based models of natural language understanding in which natural language programs are initially constructed primarily to accommodate dialogue seem appropriate theoretical starting points from which natural language interfaces for reference work can be established.

According to Schank (1984) scripts are "prepackaged sets of expectations, inferences, and knowledge that are applied in common situations, like a blueprint for action without the details filled in" (p. 114). In this framework, the reference negotiation can be seen as a kind of script, with specific moves and objectives and a peculiar logic governing the discourse. Despite variations within the reference script, the interlocutionary moves exhibit persistent features that define a common set of shared expectations.

NATURAL LANGUAGE INTERFACES AND SCRIPTS

Within the reference negotiation, the discourse logic involved must be the starting point of any robust natural language interface. For this reason, the work of Roger Schank holds useful implications for developing natural language interfaces capable of conducting reference negotiations and deserves close examination. In *The Cognitive Computer* (1984), Schank seeks to determine the conceptual framework behind the complexities of human cognitive experiences: "We tend to see the world in terms of the events that take place in it. These events usually involve one or more actions, which we describe using the many verbs in our language" (p. 96). Deriving a set of primitive action relationships, such as ATRANs (change of possession) and PROPEL (application of force), Schank demonstrates how these conceptual underpinnings provide a series of cognitive expectations regarding any single instance of their expression. "John hit Bill," "Mary punched Joe," "Sam pushed the door," and "Jane struck the clay idol" are all understood as applications of force, and, because of that, certain expectations about what can and will happen are engendered. We expect the clay idol to break because we know that when fragile objects are hit, they sometimes break, and not because we know something specific about Jane or about this particular clay idol. There is a universal relationship at play that guides our perceptual expectations. Furthermore, the moment we hear "Jane hit..." a delimited finite number of possibilities arise concerning what can and will happen to the object of force, prior to knowing what specifically has been struck.

Schank believes that the specific set of primitives he has successfully worked with is not the only set obtainable. The central element in his theory is not the precise set of primitives but the insight that understanding is a conceptual representation utilizing a finite number of conceptual relationships in an identifiable and predictable way. Natural language understanding does not take place in the thick of the words but in the immediate recognition of the underlying event-archetype, which creates expectations and prepares cognition for the next discursive or narrative expression. In this sense, the primitives function as temporal structures of knowledge, providing for continuity in conscious understanding.

While primitives govern the manifest logic of a single event, a more complex knowledge structure must be evinced to explain the large-scale phenomena contained in human linguistic communication. Consider the story: "Jane hit the clay statue. It broke. The owner arrived and frowned." Anyone hearing this story understands why the owner is frowning even though the literal connection has not been expressed linguistically. Because the general significance of ownership of property and its possible expressions in a given situation (property broken, property stolen, etc.) are understood, no problem exists in understanding why the narrative describes the owner as frowning. Schank refers to these general structures that govern the progression of a complex series of linguistic expressions as scripts: "Scripts tell us what might happen next and enable us to understand the relevance of what actually does happen next; they provide connectivity between events" (p. 114).

Schankian scripts are based on consensus knowledge regarding specific scenarios. In discussions, these scenarios are shared by all participants and delimit the possible interlocution by maintaining a shared focus of expectations. The reference negotiation is especially amenable to analysis by Schankian script as a shared context-creating set of presuppositions. Consider several possible beginning to a reference negotiation. The patron asks Q1; the various possible responses (R1 . . . R*n*) follow:

Q1: Where can I find recent research on superstring theory?

R1: Are you looking for a general overview of the subject?

R2: Do you have a background in physics?

R3: How recent?

R4: Exactly what are superstrings?

R5: How do you propose to find such information?

R1 through R4 would be legitimate responses within the constraints of the reference negotiation script. R1 seeks to establish perspective, R2 a simple patron attribute, R3 a clearer concept of currency, and R4 a general discipline category. Although R4 might undermine the patron's confidence in the ultimate reference advice, it is not the type of response that would bring the reference script into question, since the role of reference librarian includes a repertoire of permissible requests for clarification. R5, however, is a question that immediately creates ambiguity regarding whether both participants share the same script because it violates the rules of the script and its subordinate roles. The patron is required to decide on a proper script to make sense of the response. The patron might reject the reference desk script and summon a broader library script, asking, "I thought this was the reference desk. Could you direct me to it?" Suppose the librarian replies, "What is a reference desk?" The patron then falls back to an even broader social script and asks whether they are even in the library. And if the librarian asks, "What's a library?" the patron begins to believe someone is playing a practical joke, and appropriate humor scripts are used to conceptualize and disambiguate the discourse.

Summoning broader and broader contexts is a process of falling back to broader and broader shared presuppositions about what is taking place in the world. Each script depends on the larger script beneath it to supply a set of meanings that need never be explicitly enunciated or agreed to verbally. Patrons rarely preface a reference interview by asking the librarian whether they know they are in the library. And a reference librarian assumes that when patrons are directed "to the folio section behind the reference collection," the patrons know they must pass the reference collection to get to the folio section.

All scripts rest upon a rich latticework of common meanings extending from the peculiar sociological and cultural interaction between human beings all the way to the general commonsense understanding of the world shared by all. This commonsense "superscript," which might be conceived as the ultimate foundation of all scripts, has been of particular interest to Douglas Lenat for many years. With a small, dedicated group of artificial intelligence scientists, Lenat has embarked on the ambitious CYC project, an attempt to create a massive and intricate knowledge base of common-sense data (Lenat, Guha, Pittman, Pratt & Shepherd, 1990). The project seeks to develop over 1 billion axioms covering all human consensus knowl-edge. CYC will provide a single knowledge base spanning "the facts and concepts that you and I know and which we each assume the other knows" (p. 33). The ultimate objective of the project is to provide a huge com-monsense knowledge base into which more focused, esoteric applications can be operationalized. Describing the best-hoped-for outcome, Lenat writes, "No one in the early twenty-first century even considers buying a machine without common sense, any more than anyone today even con-siders buying a PC that cannot run spreadsheets, word processing and networking software" (p. 34). CYC will provide the huge, sprawling axi-omatic bedrock assumed by all scripts.

CYC holds the promise of a richly textured layering of scripts, which will make for a robust interlocutor. A highly constrained script, such as the reference interview, contains broader scripts of human consensus knowledge that do not need to enter the discourse explicitly as utterances. Consequently, a successful natural language interface can be created as long as it more or less covers all possible explicit discursive moves within the given script. If the patron sticks to the prescribed role, the natural language interface (fine tuned to the reference negotiation script) will be able to accommodate and understand all input. If the interaction is allowed to stray from the delineated boundaries, then a fine-tuned natural language interface derails. Lenat refers to this phenomenon as brittleness and sees it as a serious limitation of current efforts at (non-CYC-based) artificial intelligence. Research by others (Ringle & Halstead-Nussloch, 1989; McCoy & Cheng, 1991), however, has developed a variety of techniques to ensure that such brittle human-computer conversational dialogues can impose a highly constrained focus on what can be said next, thus providing some assurance that the user will not suddenly break the required script role.

Reference librarians cannot always count on patrons knowing how to phrase an answerable question properly. One reason is that the physical organization of information creates certain conditions that govern part of the reference negotiation script. These conditions require the dialogue to include an adequate translation of the patron's need into an action that can be successfully carried out in the environment of the library. The actual layout of the library, the manner in which information is structured, indexed, and accessed, and the entire science of bibliographic control act to delimit the negotiation script. On the other side of the dialogues, the patron brings all manner of expectations and presuppositions concerning what can be asked, how something should be asked, and, behind it all, how information is organized. The patron's worldview and the methods derived from it sometimes do not correspond at all to reality. In such circumstances, the reference negotiation requires a script that is at once flexible regarding input and conversational transitions and rigid regarding the terminal point toward which the negotiation is steered. The script will then seek to be both hospitable and directive, providing reassurance regarding patron input while making maximum efforts to cast that input into an answerable query. This concept of an answerable query guides the designer of any natural language interface in determining the conditions characteristic of the negotiation's terminal point.

An answerable query means a question that can be satisfied using the reference tools at hand. In terms of a computer program, it signifies that the program possesses a knowledge base containing information concerning both the formal features of an answerable query and the capacities of specific reference tools. Formal criteria address the clarity, specificity, and completeness of the question. "I need information on physics" is not clear, specific, or complete. "I need easy-to-understand articles on the theory of superstrings" probably is, since the query identifies a level of patron competence, format, and specific subject. A natural language interface will find such a query answerable if in addition to these formal features it also knows how to answer the question satisfactorily. With the formal features as negotiation objectives, the program needs to ascertain at the earliest possible moment whether the overall type of request can be answered using the knowledge base. It makes little sense for a natural language interface whose knowledge base consists of periodical indexes to start negotiating user competence and specific subject to the query, "I am looking for books on physics."

When the minimal formal requirements of any reference negotiation (specific subject, level, and format) are melded with the characteristics of the knowledge base, a precise series of required interlocutionary steps is indicated. More than most other scripts, that of reference negotiation is singularly closed off from other scripts due to these strong formal and knowledge base restraints. And unlike other more freewheeling scripts, eager adherence to the focus and sequence of steps involved with query negotiation is characteristic of both participants in the discourse. The patron is actively concerned with traversing just those steps and providing just that information required to resolve the query and is unlikely to stray from the script by introducing extraneous factors that have nothing to do with the query resolution. Consequently, since the patron's own self-interest is involved in the resolution of the information need and since that resolution is susceptible to a specific, finite number of formal requirements (and thus elicits a finite vocabulary and syntax), the phenomenon of brittleness makes itself less apparent in the reference negotiation. It is not surprising, then, that natural language processing within the parameters of query resolution has had a strong presence for many years in the artificial intelligence community.

STATUS OF NATURAL LANGUAGE INTERFACES IN REFERENCE SERVICES

Several natural language interfaces have been developed for reference services in a variety of specialized environments. Some of these were discussed in chapter 5, most notably the systems that provide expert mediation for online searching (IR-NLI, EXPERT). Other interesting programs that have been put to work in the reference setting are described below.

ASK

ASK (A Simple Knowledgeable System) was developed in the early 1980s as a "clean engineering solution" to the challenge of implementing a knowledge base that can be queried using a limited dialect of English. Thompson and Thompson (1983) sought to create a system whose knowledge base could be created, tested, modified, extended, and queried by the end user. Information in the database is linked through a semantic net whose nodes are classes (male, female, young, old, etc.), objects (individuals, numbers, text), attributes (location, destination, size, etc.), and relations (child, cargo, author). For instance, a ship is an individual object that can fall under several different classes (Navy, freighter, tanker) and has a variety of attributes (destinations, home port, cargo loads).

One of the original objectives for ASK was to provide the end user with a system that satisfactorily answers questions 90 percent of the time. The remaining 10 percent of questions should be answered in a manner that provides the user with an understanding of how ASK arrived at the response. For instance, sometimes query sentences will contain words not in the ASK vocabulary, in which case the user is promoted for clarification. At other times, ASK will be unable to find an answer because none exists. The user then has the opportunity to add an answer—that is, to introduce more attributes into the knowledge base regarding the specific object.

In the simplest terms, ASK is capable of being educated. The types of individuals it knows and the various characteristics it attributes to these individuals are all supplied by the user. Consequently, since the user is in on the very ground floor of script construction and lexicon development, ASK can avoid the worst consequences of brittle natural language understanding.

COMODA

Whalen and Patrick (1990) have developed a system they describe as a natural language interface. While COMODA (COnversation MOdule of Database Access) is a natural language interface, Whalen and Patrick point out that it does not "understand" natural language as they define that term: "The goal is not to provide natural language understanding. A natural language understanding program would have to determine the significance of every word in the user's sentences, would have to determine the meaning of any well formed sentence, and would have to incorporate that knowledge into its database" (p. 95). Instead, COMODA recognizes phrases and words that are relevant in determining the next step in its information negotiation strategy.

The negotiation model COMODA uses is adopted from a form of discourse analysis theory developed by Brown and Yule (1983). The discursive technique can be represented by a state-transition-diagram, which consists of at least two states with a transition between them. Related to each state is some discursive text generated by the computer called an "utterance." When the user inputs text, this text is compared to a parse template, defined as "text which must match the user's response in order for that transition to be used to enter the next state" (Whalen & Patrick, 1990, p. 97). When a match takes place between user input text and parse template, there is a transition to a new state, which is again characterized by a computer utterance, and so on, until the course of a dialogue is navigated and the required information derived from the user's cumulated input.

The continuity of the discourse depends on constraining the variability of user responses to a finite number of possible parse templates. Whalen and Patrick believe there are good reasons to expect that a well-designed dialogical interface will succeed in minimizing variability. Of foremost importance is that the program begin with a state, that is, a computer utterance. This immediately delimits the scope of possible discourse to the subject-question utterance posed by the computer. According to Whalen and Patrick, "People will accept a topic of discourse imposed by the computer and not try to negotiate it" (p. 96).

COMODA was used as a dialogic interface to search databases on artificial intelligence research, AIDS, sign language, and an information file on the Division of Behavioural Research (DEBRA). A test was made of the DEBRA database using ten people who participated in 203 conversations. Fifty-nine percent of the questions were answered correctly (COMODA either retrieved the correct information or properly concluded such information was not in the DEBRA database). Thirty-seven percent were answered incorrectly (wrong information retrieved or concluding that information was not in the database when in fact it was). Whalen and Patrick hope to improve the performance of COMODA by providing more powerful templates capable of handling Boolean logic and developing a hier-archical topical structure for the databases.

GuS

There is a prototype for an information retrieval interface that employs three interrelated user models to interpret patron input (Newby, 1989). The Galileo Computer System (GuS) contains three levels of user model: stereotypical, specific experience, and intimate. "GuS is not designed spe-cifically for bibliographic IR [information retrieval], but has a related pur-pose: to identify and execute user commands, based on natural language input" (p. 72).

The stereotype level refers to the broad characterizations that can be made about most patrons, such as educational level, purpose of library use, and types of formats desired. Thus, when a PhD in philosophy asks about recent research in the epistemology of artificial intelligence, a ster-eotypical model that clusters expertise, advanced education, and technical competence allows the librarian to focus on a pertinent set of possible search options to the exclusion of strategies that would be out of character with the stereotype model. Pure stereotypes are part of GuS's initial design, and though applied to understand actual user input they are not constructed out of experience with specific users.

Newby describes the second dimension, specific experience, as "a com-bination of the outermost and the innermost" (p. 72) levels. Here GuS elaborates on stereotypes based on facts ascertained from specific patrons and their interactions. Basically, "specific experience" is simply a more refined, fact-laden type of stereotype. Whereas the pure stereotype of "college student" causes GuS to react to input from college students in a certain prescribed manner, experience with specific college students during specific interactions causes GuS to develop various distinctions concerning freshmen versus seniors or beginning versus end of semester. The pure stereotype would cause GuS to run a very wide search of the knowledge base in hopes of satisfying the information needs of an undergraduate, but a more refined stereotype would provide GuS with more focused knowl-edge concerning what this freshman or beginning-semester student might require.

Finally, the level most enriched with personal knowledge about the user is the intimate. Newby defines such intimacy as "being able to second-guess the other so well that the spoken word is only a small part of the communication" (p. 73). In an information retrieval system like GuS, such a model consists not only of general attributes concerning education and level of sophistication but specific likes and dislikes, as well as research approaches most amenable to the patron. Since GuS is capable of mean-ingfully storing the patron's name, respective queries, and all evaluations of search results, each time the patron employs the interface, GuS collects more data about the patron. GuS eventually manufactures an applicable intimate model of the patron, which is then employed to interpret that patron's natural language input.

Specialist

Controlling variability of patron input while providing for flexible response can be accomplished if the computer imposes initial topics coupled with a finite but adequate number of parse templates. This imposition reverses the usual relationship between patron and librarian in which the patron initiates and the librarian helps evoke and amplify but tries not to steer. Most of the systems already described depend on this steering to overcome the brittleness of a finite fact base and vocabulary. However, other methods of providing optimum flexibility to natural language input depend not so much on dialogical control but on formalizing large, naturally occurring semantic and syntactic data such as electronic dictionaries and thesauri and using this vast reservoir to enhance a program's capacity to understand. This effort is closely related to attempts at transforming information contained in machine-readable full-text files into computationally accessible knowledge relationships, which are then used to enhance the performance of natural language interfaces.

The flexibility of a natural language interface depends greatly on the lexicon at its disposal. A parsimonious lexicon will result in large semantic voids when it comes to ordinary English input. Large lexicons, however, are quite time-consuming and tedious to construct by hand. It has long been considered desirable by some to link natural language interfaces with existing machine-readable dictionaries, at once saving time and gaining access to a large body of definitions.

McCray and Srinivasan (1990) have used a machine-readable version of *Dorland's Illustrated Medical Dictionary* to derive semantic and limited syntactic data. Primary emphasis was placed on providing an interactive interface for definition look-up within the dictionary. Experiments were conducted to classify lexical entries syntactically. Success was achieved in identifying nouns, adjectives, and verbs. Work is underway to intermesh the lexicon with the system SPECIALIST (Specialized Interpretation of Scientific Text), which will use the domain knowledge contained in *Dorland's* to parse sentences of independent text contained in title and abstract summaries found on the Medline database (McCray, 1989).

In SPECIALIST, McCray and Srinivasan are paying special attention to the definition content of the dictionary, inferring from such definitions the specific relationships that exist between concepts. For instance, the phrase "characterized by" can be used to identify manifestations and symptoms. Other knowledge relationships might be derived from the application of phrase-sensitive algorithms to the definition contents.

LDOCE

Slator (1989) created a lexicon-constructing program that refines the machine-readable version of *Longman's Dictionary of Contemporary English* (LDOCE) into a hierarchically arranged frame-based structure. Input elicits applications of various frames. Any word might provoke the creation of several competing frames. For instance, the world "measure" might mean what any one of eight nouns, three verbs, or one adjective signify. Contextual preference is determined by an elaborate domain code, whereby each frame is provided a subject category. An overall text topic is identified by counting up the various subject categories and their superordinate clusterings within a given input. For instance, in isolation, the word "current" may possess both electrical engineering and river-flow meanings. When occurring in a context where other terms consistently provide electrical engineering or engineering meanings, the domain of the text as a whole is determined to be engineering, and the ambiguity of specific meanings is thereby resolved.

The LDOCE is part of a three-step process Slator believes will characterize significant near-term developments in natural language processing. First, machine-readable dictionaries are refined into lexical semantic knowledge bases. Second, the lexicon is used by a semantic processor to represent formally text elements found in ordinary natural language input. Finally, the semantic processor is used on short encyclopedia articles, the knowledge content being represented and manipulated through a structured semantic formalism.

INFORMATION RESOURCES

Other natural language interfaces used in reference work are described in chapter 5. For thorough reviews of natural language developments within library and information science, the *Annual Review of Information Science and Technology* (*ARIST*) provides frequent coverage. Currently found under the title "Natural Language Processing" (the older title is "Automated Language Processing), *ARIST* has published reviews and research summaries by Warner (1987), Becker (1981), Damerau (1976), Walker (1973), Kay and Jones (1971), Montgomery (1969), Salton (1968), and Bobrow, Fraser, and Quillian (1967). The annual proceedings of the American Society for Information Science (ASIS) is also a rich source for current efforts at implementing natural language interfaces in library settings.

In addition to *Library Literature* and *Library and Information Science Abstracts* (*LISA*), the *Computer and Control Abstracts* (*CCA*) provides excellent coverage in natural language research. *CCA* has an especially helpful classificatory system, which allows efficient perusal of library related work. A new resource, *Abstracts in Human-Computer Interaction* (Ergosyst Associates, Lawrence, Kansas), provides quarterly coverage to articles and books treating interface issues, including natural language understanding and processing.

FUTURE POSSIBILITIES

Natural language interfaces have only just begun to appear in the library. The complexity of the semantic sophistication and the immense number of user models involved in even the most rudimentary negotiation (not to mention the many nonverbal cues that go to make up a successful interview) contribute to the difficulty of bringing this form of artificial intelligence to the reference desk. The insight that such natural language understanding takes place in a discursive context shows much promise, however. In essence, three separate processes must take place. First, an artificial formalism must be developed capable of containing the meaning of natural language. The concern is with the literal programming code and syntax used to capture the meaningful relationships found in the user's input. LISP or Prolog is often employed to accomplish this because of their powerful list and string handling abilities, though much has been done in C and Pascal. Next, script structures must be developed that govern and inform the translation of natural language input into the artificial formalism. This is the heart of any query negotiation and is successfully accomplished only by a reference librarian. And, finally, a different set of scripts must be developed that govern and inform the translation of the formalism back out into a satisfactory natural language response. This involves not only the answer but the explanation of the reasoning process that leads to the answer. It will also include, in the case of reference resources, explanations concerning the proper use of the tool. Here, too, the reference librarian stands as the major repository of such knowledge.

Natural language understanding as an information interface promises to become a strong presence in the future. There is no escaping the fact that the reference librarians are essential to the successful implementation of natural language interfaces within the broad context of question-and-answer discourse. But more than that, much like Boolean logic and online search strategy, natural language understanding as an information interface is the type of technology that reference librarians can claim as their own if they become creatively involved in its development. This creative involvement necessitates a degree of programming literacy (see chapter 7) and participation in cooperative efforts with other librarians and information scientists (see chapter 4) to pool resources and expertise. There should be nothing controversial in the idea that natural language understanding is an integral part of library science, and an especially important object of study for reference librarians.

7

Reference Competence and Programming Languages

What is meant by computer programming, and what advantages are there in reference librarians mastering a programming language? The use of any software literally "programs" the computer even if the result is no more than ASCII text displayed on the screen in response to key strokes. Ordinarily, however, computer programming refers to the creation of code, using a symbol system capable of representing complex algorithms. (An algorithm consists of the procedural steps required to achieve a certain outcome.) The symbol systems of which this code is composed have artificial grammars and syntax and are referred to as programming languages. Code transfers the algorithm into a series of computational events, which result in whatever computer states are required to perform the algorithmic procedures.

Many pieces of commercial software come equipped with symbolic programming capacities. The symbol systems involved do not always contain sufficient powers to accommodate representation of a broad range of algorithms. The ability to create macros in popular word processors or spreadsheets is accomplished by attaining competence with a truncated symbol system too constrained and inflexible to be considered a programming language by itself. However, hypertext and hypermedia programs such as HyperCard, HyperPAD and Spinniker PlusTALK come with extremely sophisticated programming environments that must be mastered before the software can be put to optimum use. Many expert system shells also provide the option of pursuing a custom-made look by offering a complex programming language. KnowledgePro's Prolog-like language is an example of how a symbol system can be used to represent important algorithms involved in query resolution. These symbol systems, however, only elaborate on the application objectives of the product; their formative capabilities are restricted to the goals of the mother program from which they spring and on which they depend. The possession of a grammar, syntax, and symbol system sufficiently rich to make the representation of a wide variety of algorithms possible in a number of contexts (string handling, graphics, mathematical operations, etc.) is the key characteristic of a programming language. Consequently, "programming language" indicates the relatively unrestricted manipulation of the computer wherein whatever is imagined taking place on a two-dimensional surface (screen) gets actualized. All limitations on this manipulative capacity are factors of the hardware or the architecture of the central processing unit. Machine language and assembly language are, in this view, the Ur-programming languages. Starting from them, one works up through traditional languages, such as FORTRAN, C, Pascal, LISP, Prolog, and Ada, whose compilers are themselves programs written in Assembly or another high-level programming language (typically C) but whose areas of effect are still quite broad and relatively unabridged. While such programming languages have various strengths and weaknesses, all are expected to be sufficiently facile to perform complex numerical computations, string handling, graphics (here there is wide divergence), external file creation and manipulation, and device (printers, modems, etc.) driving. Functionally, especially in the context of automated reference services, all of these capacities add up to the ability to control the content and sequence of screens.

PROGRAMMING AND SCREENS

Since reference automation is primarily an interactive relationship between screen and patron, the extent to which the reference librarian controls the screen is the extent to which the reference librarian controls the interaction. Controlling a screen can be analyzed within two broad potentials: the control of screen states and the control of screen processes. States consist of screen design and the text and/or graphic content of what appears on a given screen. Processes consist of screen sequences and any changes that take place on single screens, varying from changes due to user input or other graphic representations of internal computation.

Much significant research has identified the importance of correct design of screen displays to both successful communication of information and eliciting "legal" patron responses (Dumas, 1988; Thimbleby, 1990; Shneiderman, 1987). Interface researchers such as Dumas and Schneiderman have written persuasively on the intimate relationship between a variety of visual design parameters and patron behavior. An example of interaction between screen design and patron information processing is manifest when examining the simple variation involved in an alphabetical versus nonalphabetical listing of menu options. Approaching the alphabetized screen with several terms in mind, patrons skim the menu hoping to locate their anticipated term in the relevant alphabetic order quickly. Alphabetical listing of options provides one of the conditions on which speed of use is based (assuming one of the expected terms is found). But sometimes the designer intentionally seeks to retard the search process by putting the options in nonalphabetical order. This requires the patron to move through each option visually and in the process judge the relevance of the choice to the information need. This process slows the decision but forces the patron to examine and process as many options as possible, thereby enforcing familiarity with the content of the menu screen and leading overall to a greater awareness of the possible choices.

Numerous other differences in screen design result in different effects on and patterns of patron use. In the reference setting, the different contexts in which public access computers are found will suggest different courses of overall screen design; no single configuration can be expected to fit all needs. One of the great powers of programming languages is their ability to accommodate to the fullest the subtle and complex interactions between display and behavior. Some recent library literature has intimated that knowing how to program a computer and reference librarianship are almost mutually exclusive and that programming literacy is elitist and expensive. But the screen stands more and more as the intermediate between patron and knowledge in the contemporary library. The spread of OPACs has been the key engine in the emergence of the screen interface. Since the construction of front ends placed over vendor-specific OPAC screens provides for premium intermesh between interfaces and clientele, the skills that make such a user-friendly environment possible cannot be dismissed as narrow or inappropriate. Power over screen design considerations is even more important when developing a custom-made reference resource where the alternative to programming is commercial software engineered without the library as primary market.

In a consideration of text or graphic features, the advantage of programming languages resides in their ability to control the content of whole screens. All significant programming languages compiled to run on personal computers are at least capable of placing ASCII text at any point on the screen. Depending on the type of computer, the typical language will also allow different text size and simple font variations. The native graphic abilities of some languages are considerable, and languages with meager resources are easily supplemented with relevant graphic support functions, such as those provided by Turbo C and the Borland Graphic Interface. For many custom-made reference tools, the ability to provide map information is an important part of the resource and wholly dependent on the program's graphic facilities. With regard to graphic representation, a new possibility exists of capturing images using an image scanner. A digital file of the image is created permitting direct manipulation by languages that can recognize various graphic file formats. Although sophisticated commercial software exists that can manipulate such files, here, as before, the degree of flexibility, integration, and overall design control available through application of programming languages greatly enhances the uses to which these images can be put.

Screen sequence determines the possible paths of exploration available for the user by structuring the interaction. The interaction can include such diverse processes as describing complex information needs, consulting computerized ready reference files, automatic repetitive displaying of "canned" information, or any other reference algorithm that can be encoded. Complex interactions—the kind that require patrons to describe information needs through menus, dialogue, or icon selection—are best structured as discrete incremental steps, each with its own objective and contribution to the description and resolution of the information need as a whole. The expert systems reviewed in chapter 5 were primarily reference advisory systems covering different subjects, but they all had one design feature in common: the breakdown of the information query into parts. Practically all resorted to at least a two-screen approach covering subject/topic and then format (Answerman, Pointer). Others dwelled on the subject dimension in more detail, requiring multiple screen sequences to reach the required level of completeness (Index Expert). Some of the more sophisticated systems request extensive user input to develop user models (IR-NLI). All of these implementations were devised in response to the primary strategy: "Given the objective, what does the system need to do next?"

That a specific system will be unable to reach some objectives set for it by patrons is merely another circumstance in which the primary strategy is employed. In such cases, the system needs to communicate its inability to accomplish the deed to the patron. (This is done at the reference desk whenever a referral is made to another unit within the library.) The system needs the built-in flexibility to respond to any circumstance: first, by using a CAN-DO/CANNOT-DO sort; and, second, by breaking all CAN-DO objectives into discrete, predictable interplays between system and patron. Thus, the primary strategy ("Given the objective, what does the system do next?") is applicable to an infinite number of objectives (only some of which, obviously, will be "legal"), and the screen sequences must be planned for maximum flexibility. A computer language, with its procedural sophistication and modularity, provides ample support for such a flexible structure. The procedural features inherent in programming languages permit sequence and cumulation of user input toward a fully fleshed out information need. The modularity of many languages, particularly object-oriented ones, provides the condition for successfully conceiving and coding a reference negotiation as a series of well-demarcated tasks. The overall flow and progression of the interchange between system and patron can thus be completely controlled, and the well-crafted program will have a response for every input.

Whenever custom-made reference tools are indicated, knowledge of computer languages is a truly valuable skill. There are, however, a number of issues that must be acknowledged when programming custom-made reference services. These include the length of time required to design and implement the program and the continued commitment necessary to maintain and improve the service. However, with the almost complete control such skill gives over screen design, screen/program sequencing, and input processing of information, there can be no question of declaring the reference environment innately inhospitable to such skills.

The ability to experiment with new features and new services is also enhanced when using programming languages to develop computerized reference services. Obviously not all reference librarians need to know how to program a computer, a skill that requires a tremendous investment of effort. But such knowledge can be brought into service during an entire professional life. Furthermore, mastery of programming skills reinforces a mind-set in which the computer screen becomes a deeply rooted extension of the librarian's competence rather than just the glowing side of a black box. The ability of the profession to become proactive and to develop a cutting edge in this arena depends on finding a place for such skills within the reference librarian's repertoire.

IMPORTANT COMPUTER LANGUAGES FOR LIBRARIANS

The programming languages reviewed here constitute just a small percentage of the available languages. Inclusion or exclusion is not meant as an evaluative judgment: the objective is to provide a cross-section of possible options relevant to the library environment.

Ada

Developed by the Department of Defense (DoD) to standardize the computer code used in writing software, Ada permits the modularity necessary for large-scale projects drawing simultaneously on the efforts of several programmers. Ada is a trademark of the DoD which rigorously regulates all Ada compilers to make certain they conform to standards. Thus, Ada code should be highly transportable; programs that run under one compiler should also execute under all others with minimal revision. There are several compilers available for the personal computer.

BASIC

The Beginners All-Purpose Symbolic Instruction Code, BASIC, is probably the programming language understood by more people in the world than any other. Designed by Kurtz and Kemeny in 1964, BASIC has the reputation of being an easy language to learn. Since MS-DOS comes bundled with GWBASIC, the language can be found on practically any personal computer running the MS-DOS operating system.

BASIC has been criticized as being "unstructured," though it is more accurate to say that certain versions lend themselves to unstructured programming and so-called spaghetti code. Dialects such as QuickBASIC from Microsoft, however, provide ample opportunity for a structured approach, making the source code easier to follow and improve. The fact that some form of BASIC occurs on all DOS-based machines means programs written in BASIC have a high degree of transportability. A number of significant systems have been developed using a dialect of BASIC. The final implementation of Pointer, the expert system in government documents, was written in BASIC.

C

Currently one of the most popular programming languages, C has been used to develop operating systems, word processors, spreadsheets, and other complex forms of software. It is highly transportable language, and there are numerous C compilers that run on personal computers. Some of the more prominent are Turbo-C from Borland and Quick-C from Microsoft. Recently an object-oriented form of C known as C++ has been available for programming on personal computers. Borland and Zortech have C++ compilers, and Microsoft marketed its product in 1992. Most large mainframes in academic and corporate sites have C compilers. When such computers are linked with the powers of the Internet, the C language becomes a platform for constructing executable programs accessible from any part of the world.

COBOL

COBOL thrives in the business community and on some library mainframes. Although there have been recent COBOL compilers designed for PC-based machines, it has seen limited use by librarians in this context. Brophy's *COBOL Programming: An Introduction for Librarians* provides analysis and examples of library implementations of COBOL.

PASCAL

The quintessential procedural language, Pascal has grown in popularity over the years since Niklaus Wirth introduced it to the academic community in 1971. Pascal is highly structured and therefore easy to maintain. There have been several recent updates to the language, which make it a powerful PC-based programming environment. Most notably, the recent edition of Turbo Pascal from Borland provides an object-oriented version of the language. Library applications written in Pascal include Plexus (as described in Vickery, Brooks & Robinson, 1987). (Also see Davis, Lundeen & Shaw, 1988.)

Hypertext-based Languages

Since the introduction of the program HyperCard on Apple MacIntosh computers, the HyperTalk programming language has been used to create many library reference applications. Additionally there have been a number of other hypertext programming languages, modeled on HyperTalk, that have become available. HyperPAD (BrightBill & Roberts), SuperTALK (Silicon Beach), and PlusTALK (Spinniker) are other members of this hypertext family of languages. Due to its capacity for generating crisp graphic user interfaces and its ability to accommodate hypertext structure, this family of languages has been particularly useful in programming front ends.

LISP

The Lisp language is usually identified as an artificial intelligence language because of its facility in handling and manipulating symbolic expressions such as natural language input. There are several compilers available for the personal computer. Library applications that have been programmed in Lisp include the first version of Pointer.

PL/1

In the early 1980s, Programming Language Number One (PL/1) was one of the more popular programming languages taught in library schools. Originally based on mainframes, the language's transition to microcomputer technology rendered it less effective in competing with other PC-based compilers such as Turbo Pascal (Davis, 1990). (See Fosdick, 1982, for uses of PL/1 in libraries.)

Prolog

Prolog is another language nominally grouped under the rubric "AI language." Along with LISP, it has powerful string manipulation functions. Several implementations have made it available on personal computers. Support for Borland's popular Turbo Prolog has been taken up by the Prolog Development Center in Georgia. Other companies such as Chalcedony Software and Arity Corp produce compilers that run on personal computers. The ease with which Prolog can be learned has made it a popular language among programming librarians. Such systems as CAN-SEARCH (Pollitt, 1987), REFSIM (Parrott, 1988), Index Expert (Bailey, Fadell, Myers & Wilson, 1989), and the Reference Advisory Systems Board (Carande, 1990) were programmed using some dialect of Prolog.

CONSIDERATIONS IN SELECTING A LANGUAGE

An important factor in determining whether learning a programming language is warranted is the reference objective to be realized. Unless the objective can be broadly envisioned, it may not be worth investing time in learning a programming language. If the objective consists of a single project that the reference desk wishes implemented, then all commercially available software should be exhausted before thinking of a programming language. A programming language demands considerable amounts of time to master, so unless a long-term commitment to continuous productivity in the area of custom-made reference tools is present, there can be little justification for undertaking such a task.

Once the decision is made to learn a programming language, the language and specific dialect chosen depends on the kinds of implementations envisioned. Some important features to consider when examining languages from the perspective of reference resource implementation include types of data structures, types of procedural control, graphic functions, string handling functions, external file creation and control, and modularity.

A data structure determines the kinds of data that can be stored and the various computational manipulations that can be performed on the data. A language rich in such structures permits complex relationships between data to be easily represented and managed.

A procedural control consists of the means by which the direction of program execution is determined. The if-else structure is an example common to many languages (C, BASIC, Pascal), just as the function call figures prominently in C and recursion in Prolog.

Graphic abilities vary considerably from language to language, dialect to dialect, and even version to version. For instance, the first version of Turbo Prolog had limited graphics, while the second version could take advantage of the powerful Borland Graphics Interface. BASIC is well known for its built-in graphic functions. Graphic strength is also a function of the kind of monitor and graphic board within the computer, since some graphic functions presuppose a specific hardware configuration.

Perhaps most important in the context of reference work are the string functions available in a language. "String" might loosely be defined as text, and functions that handle strings are functions that manipulate text. Most computerized offerings require some kind of string or text input from the user; menu selections, key terms, and natural language phrases all result in the program processing text. The ease with which this input can be used in creating meaningful system responses depends on the available string-handling functions. All languages provide at least the ability to write programs in which text input is divided into constituent words or searched for specified characters.

The creation of external disk-based files that can be accessed and modified by a program is also an important feature since most reference-based resources involve searching and/or updating one or more data or knowledge bases. Swapping such files or parts of them into dynamic memory and back out again is a requirement that any high-level language should be capable of meeting.

Modularity is the ability to represent important program performances in discrete sections of code. Ideally such sections contain whatever is required for them to carry out their mission without depending on other sections of code. Results are then passed onto other parts of the program, which perform their own operations on the data. Modularity guarantees two important facets of software development: rapid debugging and efficient maintenance. A great deal of programming time is spent tracking down programming errors commonly referred to as bugs. The less that sections depend upon one another, the easier it is to isolate exactly where the program goes wrong. It is very frustrating to track down errors in code that is a spider web of jumps and "go to's." Efficiency of maintenance is also enhanced when code is modular, since the entire performance of the program is easier to track. Modularity is especially advantageous when improvements and updates will be performed by individuals who did not author the initial code and will greatly benefit from a well-documented, highly structured sequence of modules, each with its own distinct function. No language resists modularity, though some, such as Pascal, Prolog, and the object-oriented languages, make modular programming easy to accomplish.

PROGRAMMING SKILLS AMONG LIBRARIANS

By the end of the 1980s the availability of classes in programming at United States and Canadian library schools had increased to 78 percent from a 1980 level of 73 percent (Davis, 1990). Although most schools provide this opportunity, only a minority require that students learn a programming language (9 percent and 17 percent in 1980 and 1986, respectively). Analyzing his research data, Davis comments "The evidence does not indicate that a significantly greater percentage of the schools required or encouraged computer programming in 1986 that did in 1980. The chi square test of independence shows that neither change is significant even at the 0.05 level" (p. 27). Davis does suggest, however, that the descriptive data may indicate a possible trend. It would be interesting to determine how many students taking such courses are public or technical services oriented, but such data have not been collected.

Davis's research has shown that the most popular language taught in library schools is the BASIC programming language. In 1986, almost half the schools (45.3 percent) offered BASIC. The secondary prominence that PL/1 enjoyed in 1980 had given way to Pascal by 1986, and a number of new language options have appeared, including C, LOGO, Prolog, and dBase.

The data collected by Davis are from 1986, restricted to library schools, and predate the plethora of new language compilers made available for the PC by major software houses. Current programming practice within the profession might reveal a different emphasis regarding the languages being used. A request on PACS-L that I posted for reports on recent, ongoing, or planned implementations in reference automation and the programming language or software platform involved resulted in the following data:

- C is being used by the UCLA Law Library to program a multimedia help station, and plans are underway to couple this station with expert system technology written in Prolog.

- At the California State University at Northridge, Pascal is used to create a log program to keep track of daily database searches and costs.

- The Clipper database programming language is used by the University of Kentucky's Medical Library to track billing and various statistics and has been used to develop a catalog of the audiovisual collection.

- UNIX, especially its Awk facility, and C++ are used at OCLC's Office of Research to facilitate records management and support.

- Bond University in Australia is using HyperCard to create online information guides.

- Librarians at the University of Toronto use AskSam's programming language to create automated reference systems.

- The Law Library at Washington and Lee provides the Pilot system for information concerning library resources, which is written in Turbo Pascal.

- San Diego State University has constructed a system of interlocking reference advisory modules using Turbo Prolog and C++.

It is impossible to extrapolate trends from such anecdotal data, but the response is indicative of the wide variety of programming tools being used in libraries.

The efficacy of programming languages has revealed itself most clearly in the provision of detailed current information concerning local resources. Increased use of programming languages to construct custom-made reference resources makes it reasonable to consider if the library profession might not need an official language to encourage resource sharing and develop a reservoir of programming expertise. One regional effort to create just such a possibility has already taken place involving the myriad hypertext-based languages that are currently available. Librarians at the California State University and the University of California have informally adopted a hypertext language approach to provide consistent user interfaces to custom-made computer-aided instruction modules (Parker, 1991). The language of choice is HyperTalk, but the emphasis is more on developing a common interface and a shared pool of expertise and CAI modules than on imposing an official language. Nevertheless, by concentrating on the HyperTalk language, a cohesive web of mutually supportive programming skills will be distributed throughout the California academic library systems.

Davis's work indicates that BASIC has become the de-facto "official" language taught in library schools, with the only significant competition coming from Pascal. Should there be an official or sanctioned language all librarians interested in programming should master? Among the candidates for such a language, C and BASIC stand out as particularly attractive options.

BASIC's strength lies in its powerful assortment of built-in functions, which include sophisticated, detailed string handling and graphics. The traditional complaints concerning BASIC as leading to unstructured and therefore difficult-to-maintain programs have been completely abrogated with the development of newer compilers, such as Microsoft's Quick-BASIC, which permit modularity and easy-to-read organization of code. The release of Visual Basic as an environment within which to program Windows's interfaces serves to maintain and reinforce BASIC's relevancy. Mention has already been made of BASIC's broad dispersal throughout the MS-DOS environment and its popularity within library schools. BASIC is also relatively easy and straightforward to learn.

C is less popular than BASIC within the library curriculum, but a growing number of practicing librarians have been attracted to the language. Certainly among professional programmers and software developers, C is the standard. This alone guarantees that there is a veritable ocean of public domain and commercial C "libraries." A "library" consists of C source code that can be readily adapted in other C programs. Typically, the libraries encode highly utilitarian functions like pop-up menus, windows, string handling, and numeric processes, all of which provide strong, bug-free enhancements to projects written in C. Perhaps the most important attribute of C is its relationship to UNIX and that system's pivotal place as an operating system within the Internet (see chapter 4).

CONCLUSION

In the future, the payback for programming competence will be even greater as interface design and control becomes less dependent on hardware and database structure and more responsive to the needs of users. The history of programming languages shows an increasing abstraction away from the hardware-oriented machine language. The transformation of "high-level" source code into machine language has become a transparent operation, occurring automatically and efficiently, neither requiring the programmer's attention nor overly restricting the programmer's freedom. And it is a persistent vision that future versions of programming languages will be equipped with high-level features distancing the programming from both data structure and hardware concerns, providing for direct, simple end user programming. Ironically, the maturation of programming language interfaces might lead to a diminished need for programming competence since such interfaces will be able to create programs extrapolated from natural language descriptions and directions provided by the librarian. Until that day, however, the profession will be well served by those who have the inclination and can find the time to master the fundamentals of programming. Hopefully, it will be a programming tradition indigenous to library science that has a strong influence on the development of mature program language interfaces, making them particularly sensitive to the needs of query negotiation and information retrieval.

8

Object Orientation

The concept of object orientation captures an important feature entwined throughout many of the most promising future computer-based information technologies. Currently employed as a paradigm and metaphor within a number of pivotal areas in information automation, object orientation reverses four thousand years of text and logic-based information structuring and manipulation by representing reality as an unmediated object. In the various contexts in which it is found, object orientation brings to the fore an important natural relationship that is characteristic of the interaction between human and environment: the epistemic and pragmatic organization of the world as a cluster of objects. Control over such a world is conceived of as control over the physical relations existing between objects. At its most radical, this conception of control is prelinguistic (or better a-linguistic), with all change and modification effected by direct physical manipulation of objects.

The early 1990s finds object orientation a central paradigm for such endeavors as computer programming, applications development, and interface design. Winblad, Edwards, and King (1990) envision a ten-year development for object-oriented approaches, which began in the early 1990s with the advent of object-oriented programming (OOP) languages and continues through object-oriented development tools, databases, operating environments, and extensive end user class libraries. Others extend the object paradigm into the virtual reality interfaces now being developed in university and corporate laboratories (Spring, 1991). Such inclusive, evolutionary models as those found in Winblad, Edwards, and King indicate that object orientation is a broader concept than object-oriented programming languages, with which it is often equated. Although object orientation in programming languages plays an important and even central role in the spread of the object orientation model as a means of representation, it is only one aspect in which the orientation has found a home.

Within the confines of information query, retrieval, and control, object orientation is an approach that seeks to transform the process of manipulating language to achieve a desired information goal into the process of manipulating objects to achieve such a goal.

The "object" concept performs differently within diverse areas of information retrieval. For the programmer, object orientation is more a metaphor and regulatory idea; coding is "object oriented" in its modularity, method of data abstraction, and the ability of one section of code to inherit properties and functional efficacy from another. Although there are pure visual-iconographic programming languages, the term "object-oriented programming" signifies a text-based programming syntax and grammar that can be used to model an interactive environment of objects. On the other hand, when it comes to user interfaces, object orientation can be taken more literally: the user masters the interface through direct manipulation of objects, usually icons, buttons, or windows. The "objects" here are literally the objects that appear on the screen (or in the case of prototypical virtual reality interfaces, the objects that appear in three-dimensional space).

Object orientation is becoming the predominant paradigm for computer coding, interface design, and models of human/computer and human/information interaction. In the future, both the reference tools ported over into the automated environment and their patrons will increasingly find themselves in an object-oriented landscape. Awareness of and familiarity with this paradigm will be required attributes of effective reference services.

OBJECT ORIENTED PROGRAMMING

Object orientation found its first expression in computer programming languages such as SmallTalk. Later, traditional procedural languages (C, Pascal) were given object-oriented extensions. Currently there are several compilers available for personal computers that can run any number of OOP languages. Interest in OOP paradigms grows unabated. While even the most ardent supporters believe object orientation is no cure-all, there is widespread agreement that OOP paradigms make programming more efficient and facilitate future modification of programming code. Yet how can a paradigm that is "objective" and essentially grounded in a physical metaphor lend itself to the organizing of a programming language that is essentially logical and analytical?

Before reviewing the more technical reasons for this efficiency, certain conceptual issues regarding the paradigm itself must be considered. Central to OOP is its application of the concept of an object to the modeling of real-world problems or tasks. An important part of its success is its ability to let people think about the world as a set of objects and relationships between objects and to facilitate the translation of that thought representation into a formal algorithm. To the extent that it is appropriate to conceive of the world as a group of objects and relationships between objects, OOP permits the modeling of such a world in code.

Although there are several visual programming languages that are literally composed of geometric shapes (Chang, 1990a, 1990b), most OOP languages provide syntax and grammars through which objects can be represented in text-based code. In theory, the OOP language lets the programmer envision the task or problem as an aggregate of objects by mediating the transference of this aggregate into a codified structure. Consequently, leaving aside the technical strengths of any given OOP, one of the most important conditions making OOP a significant paradigm is the relevance of the object modeling approach as an appropriate means of thinking about a task.

Within certain prevalent epistemologies, the concept of as object is used over and against the concept of a subject. In commonsense usage, "object" implies a certain passivity, a turgid "thingness" that is inactive. The original sense of the Latin word meant "barrier," a thing thrown in the way. The OOP conception of an object is in variance with this traditional definition. The OOP object both acts and is acted upon. Technically it is defined as possessing both data and methods or processes. Objects, then, are capable of modeling the world as an aggregation of discrete entities, both affecting and being affected by one another.

Attributes of an object-based paradigm include clearly delineated entities that control both their own internal states and their actions in regard to other entities. Objects can model relations of dependency in which one object rests upon or within a larger object. They can even resemble one another or be attached to one another so they share the same sides. Parts of objects can be "inherited" by other objects, which are subsequently called into action.

Central concepts involved in OOP include "objects, messages and methods, classes and instances, and inheritance" (Winblad, Edwards, and King, 1990, p. 28). Various OOP languages have differing terminologies to refer to these important categories, but the basic underlying cluster of capacities remains the same.

Objects are the discrete modules out of which a program is constructed. Unlike most traditional procedural languages, which rigorously separate data manipulation procedures from the data, an OOP language encapsulates both within the confines of the object. Consequently, an object possesses specific capacities to act and produce programmatically relevant results. It is the constant locale in which the program performs.

Object activation is accomplished by directing a message toward it. Typically, one object directs a message requesting another object to perform some task. For instance, an object named Subject Determination is sent a message to determine a given subject. The potentials to perform such activities are inherent within the object and are called methods (SmallTalk) or member functions (Turbo C++).

On a more abstract level lies class structure. A class consists of a number of similar objects. More specifically, a class is composed of a series of methodologies common to a number of objects. The codes upholding these methods reside in the class structure and are summoned into object existence whenever a relevant message is received by the class requesting the activation of the methodology. For instance, the parent class Reference Negotiation contains the method Determine Subject. During the course of a program, user input is analyzed for subject details on several occasions. On each occasion, the program sends a message to the parent class Reference Negotiation, prompting it to activate the Determine Subject methodology.

The structure of inheritance is where OOP stands out as unique. According to Khoshafian and Abnous (1990), the concept of inheritance permits object orientation to model real-world applications and achieve software reusability and extensibility (p. 79). Winblad, Edwards, and King (1990) succinctly define the concept as follows: "Inheritance is the mechanism for automatically sharing methods and data among classes, subclasses and objects" (p. 34). At the highest level, classes consist of the methods participated in by all objects of a specific kind. For instance, the class Reference Question contains the methods Subject Specification, User Background Modeling, and Format Specification. A subordinate class, Science Reference Question, inherits all the methods from Reference Question to add to its own method, Identify-Scientific-Discipline. This relationship reflects the actual versatility contained in the real-world skill of being able to conduct a reference negotiation in a number of different disciplinary contexts. On the programming side, it dramatically curtails the need to recode the same activity again and again to cover shifting contexts.

How appropriate is the OOP's paradigm for establishing computer simulations of library functions? Under the object orientation perspective, the library can be represented as an organization of physical objects taken in the widest sense to comprise not only books and shelves but also reference service points, circulation points, acquisitions, networks, OPACs, printed records, computers, offices, librarians, bureaucratic responsibilities, officials, and behaviors. Librarians exert and maintain control over the library by regulating the interactions of these various objects. Furthermore, upon examination, each one of these objects contains subaltern objects: the catalog consists of bibliographic objects, authority objects, circulation objects; the reference negotiation consists of determine-the-specific-subject object, determine-the-format-object, determine-the-patron's-background object, and so forth. Losee (1990) believes the object-oriented paradigm actually reflects the way the library is organized so there is less distortion in the way various roles are simulated: "OOP has the natural ability for correlating . . . [the] . . . objects occurring in an information center with objects and classes in the systems design and programs" (p. 78). It can thus draw upon the librarian's own way of thinking about the library.

Losee (1990) has also suggested OOP modeling for the development of catalog structures, and there are many object-oriented databases on the market that provide a rich set of objects capable of holding a variety of formats (text, graphics, pictures, illustrations). The simulation of the reference interview modeled as a series of interlocking objects has been suggested by a number of paradigms, particularly expert systems or question/ answer models that carefully separate different reference negotiation goals (identify subject, identify format, identify currency) that must be combined to create the questions that a knowledge base, external to the goal sequence, can answer. Such prescribed goals easily lend themselves to modeling as objects, with the OOP provision that the knowledge base for each object be resident within the object and that the entire sequence itself be a single encompassing object in which the others rest.

The pseudo-code that follows incorporates the negotiation scenario as a set of objects that resolve reference questions by posing a series of questions to the patron. The interaction always takes place within the confines of an object. The actual source code using Turbo C+ + can be found in the appendix to this chapter.

1.0 Create Assess-the-format-level-currency OBJECT
    (series of interactive questions about the format, level and currency of information requested).

2.0 Create Assess-science-discipline OBJECT
    2.1 Identify science discipline
    2.2 Inherit from Assess-the-format-level-currency OBJECT

3.0 Create Assess-social-science-discipline OBJECT
    3.1 Identify social science discipline
    3.2 Inherit from Assess-the-format-level-currency OBJECT

4.0 Create Assess-humanities-discipline OBJECT
    4.1 Identify humanities discipline
    4.2 Inherit from Assess-the-format-level-currency OBJECT

*5.0 Query user about discipline

*6.0 Activate relevant Assess-AREA-discipline OBJECT

The asterik denotes an interaction between programs and patron. The code should be read as two parts. The first part creates both a set of objects that will respond in a certain way whenever activated and a set of very simple relations between them; basically, the assess-AREA-discipline OBJECT inherits the inner structure of the assess-the-format-level-currency OBJECT. The second part is the actual implementation of the OBJECTs in response to patron answers.

The session begins with the program's asking the user to identify the broad discipline domain, in this case, science, social science, or the humanities. This activates one of the relevant assess-AREA-discipline OBJECTs. Each assess-AREA-discipline OBJECT does two things. First, it assesses the specific subdiscipline within the broader domain—physics, astronomy, sociology, anthropology, philosophy, and rhetoric. After this is done, the particular assess-AREA-discipline OBJECT "inherits" all the internal structures found in assess-format-level-currency OBJECT.

The assess-format-level-currency OBJECT was created to gather together all those queries that pertain to any reference question regardless of discipline:

1. What type of format (books, journals, etc.)?
2. What level of sophistication?
3. How current the information?

In the example code in the chapter appendix, these questions are rigidly posed with no possibility for refining answers. Also, no response objects have been developed; the program terminates after all questions have been answered. This deviation from the requirements of a true reference negotiation is done to highlight the object structuring of the program and would have to be supplemented to cover a useful set of possible patron responses and appropriate librarian answers. The significant point from the object perspective is that all the assess-AREA-discipline OBJECTs inherit the same code. Numerous assess-AREA-discipline OBJECTs could be constructed, and as long as the assumption concerning the broad applicability of the queries contained in assess-format-level-currency OBJECT is correct, each new object could fruitfully use the same code as its own. Subobjects within the assess-AREA-discipline OBJECT could be added by creating subdiscipline OBJECTs, which could inherit most of their parental code.

The example illustrates the applicability of algorithmically representing reference negotiation as a process of discrete objects that inherit and pass messages to one another. Anyone compiling the Turbo C+ + code will find the resulting interface to be a simple menu question/answer–driven affair. Object orientation does imply more than just a programming paradigm, however. Its significance is also felt in the design of interface displays, particularly when the object orientation is built into the programming language used to code the interfaces. The results on possible display designs can be enormous.

OBJECT-ORIENTED LANGUAGES AND INTERFACE DESIGN

Object-oriented programming technique need not always result in a user interface that is object oriented in the sense of being a graphical user interface (GUI). Frequently, however, because OOP lends itself so dramatically to such interface development (objects on screen linked to "objects" in the code), the ensuing interface is primarily centered on object (graphics) controls.

There are several recent examples of OOP's being employed in the development of GUIs. Grady Booch (1991) applies OOP languages to specific applications, and several of the involved interfaces are graphically based. SmallTalk is used to develop a home heating system controlled by a button and lever scheme (Booch, 1991). Mary Mock (1990) uses Object Pascal coupled with the Macintosh's windowing environment (MACApp) to create a user interface to data visualization called Double Vision: "Some techniques demonstrated in Double Vision are multiple views of the same data, pseudo color encoding of data values, palette manipulation techniques, selection techniques for continuous data" (p. 139). Rapid manipulation of data from a variety of perspectives and in a variety of representational format (graphs, color schema, overview, detailed) aids the user in quick comprehension of complex data and data patterns. Booch also uses Object Pascal to create a geometrical optics construction kit that supports a screen-based optical workbench in which optical principles can be demonstrated. Another project of interest is the detailed graphic interface with map overlays successfully developed using Objective C for the SITMAP system (Knolle, Fong & Lang, 1990). Such a system provides real-time graphic representation for military assessment.

The benefits of using OOP for rapid prototyping of visual interfaces are discussed by C. Thomas Wu (1990a, 1990b). Wu posits six interface design principles central to any successful interface: (1) ability to augment initial information offering, (2) error recovery, (3) multiple ways of performing the same function, (4) similar operations should be performed in a consistent manner, (5) different pieces of information should be displayable at the same time, and (6) the same piece of information should be displayable from a variety of different aspects. Wu develops a visual information interface called Graphics Language for Database (GLAD), for accessing data records. Implemented in the OOP language ACTOR, the GLAD interface successfully instantiates all six principles, indicating the suitability of OOP for interface design.

Other applications of OOPs to GUI can be found in Pinson and Wiener (1990a). An excellent introduction to the concept of object orientation as a programming paradigm and the construction of user interfaces, particularly on the MAC, is Khoshafian and Abnous's *Object Orientation: Concepts, Languages, Databases, User Interfaces*. In *Object Oriented Design with Applications*, Booch combines analysis of the conceptual foundations of object orientation with several hands-on applications. Sample interfaces using SmallTalk, Object Pascal, C + +, Common LISP, and Ada are provided with detailed source code of the principle algorithms. The *Journal of Object Oriented Programming* also contains articles on the application of OOP to the programming of interfaces.

OBJECT-ORIENTED USER INTERFACES

Graphic user interfaces are object oriented in two different senses. Many GUIs are written in an object-oriented language. This permits a corresponding relationship between screen object and embedded code object, which Khoshafian and Abnous refer to as a "physical metaphor" (1990, p. 390). Indeed, the whole enterprise lends itself to a GUI where commands, files, and processes are objects to be manipulated. On a nontechnical level, apart from the relation of the GUI to the underlying code and in terms of the relationship between interface and user, GUIs are object oriented because they permit the user to accomplish some information task through the manipulation of objects (typically icons). Put another way, there are two distinct levels at which object orientation can come into play when talking about GUI: programming GUI and using GUI. It is this latter level of object orientation in the use of GUI as an information tool that is of interest in discussing GUIs. At this level, "object" is meant in a less metaphorical, more literal sense. Bars, buttons, levers, and windows are literally objects-to-hand that determine the activity of the system depending upon how they are manipulated by the user.

GUIs were first developed at the Xerox Palo Alto Research Center (PARC). Unlike text command-driven interfaces, which proceed on the basis of text input, a GUI activates program functions through user manipulation of iconic and graphic features such as pop down/up menus, scroll bars, buttons, and switches. Typically, though not necessarily, an external pointing device other than the keyboard is used to manipulate such graphic controls. The most common device is the mouse, but others include the roller ball, light pens, and even joy sticks. And recently direct-touch screens have come under serious scrutiny by library and information scientists (Sears, Plaisant & Shneiderman, 1990).

The LISA computer from Apple was one of the earliest commercial applications of a GUI. Later, this same interface was updated and placed on the Macintosh, where it has since had a great influence on the design of other software interfaces. The NeXT computer adopted the GUI interface, and the IBM family and clones have seen the GUI platform of Windows 3.0 grow in popularity. The surge in GUI-based word processors and the resultant decline in command-driven processor interfaces now place this form of user control at the center of the most significant type of commercial software. The extent to which linguistic elements are not directly on the screen but resident within windows (a kind of object) that lay on top and overlap one another is an indication of the presentational primacy of the object. Even when the window is expanded to fill the entire screen so that momentarily it is indistinguishable from a single screen interface, the window remains a manipulatable active object providing a medium for user-imposed determinations that the single screen cannot and does not possess.

The purest "object-oriented" GUIs are the totally iconographic interfaces, where shape and visual template take on the burden of communicating meaning and facilitating user action. Such "direct manipulation" interfaces have many advantages. When well designed, icons accelerate recognition. The relevant icon is more quickly distinguished from its compatriots faster than a text term is from other text terms. Huang (1990, p. 73) elaborates on two aspects that underlie the functional efficacy of such directness: "distance," which refers to the cognitive efforts required to comprehend how to make the user interface work, and "engagement," which refers to the immediacy the user attains when dealing directly with objects as opposed to linguistic entities that represent and stand as substitutes for the objects: "The interface is itself a world where the user can act and that changes state in response to actions" (p. 75).

Most applications, however, are not totally iconographic but instead combine elements from both icon and button-enshrouded text approaches. The presence of text does not, by itself, mitigate the purity of the object orientation so long as it is ensconced in an object that can be handled. When text is presented through the medium of object elements, such as windows or "marked" blocks that can be directly acted upon, it attains an easy pliability by being attached to such malleable elements. Windows, for example, being spatiotemporal entities, can be rapidly resized, selected, multiplied (with each containing access to different text places within a single document), and linked to one another.

Noteworthy GUI developed for use in reference services and taking advantage of direct manipulation include several hypertext-based information services, geographic information systems (GIS), and a variety of other multimedia systems. Usually such interfaces reside on Macintosh or NeXT computers, although with the advent of various windowing programs on the PC, direct-manipulation GUI will begin appearing on that platform in greater number.

Tschanz (1991) describes use of a HyperCard-based program "designed to provide computer-assisted reference service" at the University of Denver. A Mac SE is used to house the Guide to Business Information along with instruction on using the local OPAC and CARL Uncover. Three hundred thirty cards were used to create the entire system; all can be navigated by clicking on buttons. In addition to straight linear navigational buttons, graphic devices are used to aid entry to dialogue boxes (from whence the OPAC can be searched by key word). The Map device is a flowchart overview of session progress that permits direct jumping to other available options. Hypertext, with myriads of possible navigation routes, is easy to get lost in, so the map aid is frequently called upon by patrons. The map is a good example of button-enshrouded text where the graphic box is selectable and the diagramatic overviews and linkages render additional information content beyond what pure text could provide.

A similar system that depends upon a HyperCard-based interface is the Company Research Advisor written by Catherine Friedman and programmed by Merle Vogel. Available in the general reference section at San Diego State University Library, the Advisor uses both icons and button-enshrouded text to elicit a detailed description of the kind of information a patron needs about a company. The Helper then makes suitable suggestions from a list of directories and other resources. Navigation through the system and access to help screens are based upon direct manipulation by mouse of the various HyperCard objects.

The InfoStation (Lee, 1990) uses the NeXT computer as a platform for its multimedia access approach to information retrieval. Produced by VTLS Inc., the InfoStation incorporates expert systems design, natural language interface, and powerful "direct manipulation graphical techniques" by mouse. Activation of graphic icons initiates voice instruction and/or gets the relevant media. Media consist of sound, image, and text, all of which can be managed by a combination of screen-based buttons and levers. In late 1990 the InfoStation was being beta-tested at Virginia Tech's Newton Library.

The AGILE (An Information Graphics Interface for Libraries) prototype is a more ambitious undertaking (Rodriguez, 1987). Using an icon-based graphics approach, AGILE supports Boolean searching of bibliographic databases. After an initial alphanumeric input screen ascertains the Boolean search strategy, a series of digitized icon menus provide possible characterization of the search strategy. Selected icons are identified by placing a light pen on a digitizer tablet. The early prototype of AGILE was a "proof-of-concept" application and was not fully implemented because it was too costly.

On a more theoretical level, object orientation permits the "visualization of hierarchical information structures" (Johnson & Shneiderman, 1991). Work at the Human-Computer Interaction Laboratory at the University of Maryland has focused on the portrayal of hierarchically structured information. Tree mapping was proposed as a means of visually tracing such information structures onto a two-dimensional screen so that the relationships between components within a hierarchy could be quickly ascertained. "Visual display properties such as color (hue, saturation, brightness), texture, shape, border blinking" (p. 6) are some of the elements used to represent both structure and component content. Users can navigate the large, complex hierarchy rapidly by zooming and selecting a single section from the display. This methodology and the related display algorithms have been used to represent highly convoluted directory and file structures visually. By transforming logical and semantic relations into visual objects through the method of tree mapping, advantage can be taken of geometry, both to represent complexity as well as to manipulate it.

OBJECT-ORIENTED DATABASES

Some of the first commercial manifestations of the object-oriented paradigm were in the field of database management systems (DBMS), with several systems already on the market.

The meaning of "object oriented" here signifies a database that holds objects instead of data: "The difference between objects and data is that while data contains just information in a particular structure, objects contain information encapsulated with their associated behavior" (Datapro Research Group, 1991). Object-oriented database management systems (OODBMS) are versatile in accommodating structure and flexible in modification. Adding new fields for certain records requires not recalibrating the entire data template but only adding a subclass that "inherits" all the fields of the record class, combined with the idiosyncratic features of the subclass.

Losee (1990) examines how an object-oriented database might be implemented using the University of Chicago's database structure as a platform. Using a "quadraplanar" structure, the University of Chicago splits all records into four hierarchical bibliographical planes: universal, collection, institutional, and specific copy. An object-oriented model creates four bibliographic objects, each inheriting the information from the objects above it. Thus, the object that identifies information pertaining to the specific copy contains all the information above it, such as authorized subject headings, standard numbers, and call numbers. Suppose we wish to add a piece of information to the entire database. Instead of entering it separately for all records, we merely modify the universal object. And if a specific copy has a notable attribute specific to it alone, there is no need to modify the structure of the database as a whole to provide an extra field or space. Simply modify the given object or create a subobject that inherits all the information "above" it.

Although the object-oriented database is a new paradigm, there are already some established commercial database products with impressive track records:

Objectivity/DB
    Objectivity Inc.
    800 El Camino Real, 4th Floor
    Menlo Park, CA 94025
    415–688–8000

ObjectStore
    Object Design
    One New England Industrial Park
    Burlington, MA 01803
    617–270–9797

Ontos
    Ontologic, Inc.
    Three Burlington Woods
    Burlington, MA 01803
    617–272–7110

GemStone
    Servio Logic Corporation
    1420 Harbor Bay Parkway, Suite 100
    Alameda, CA 94501
    510–748–6200

Versant
    Versant Object Technology
    4500 Bohannon Dr.
    Menlo Park, CA 94025
    415–329–7500

CONCLUSION

Object orientation cuts across several reference automation processes integral to applied library science. The construction of direct manipulation interfaces and the underlying formal representation of reference negotiation as a sequence of discrete objects (each with its own resolution to achieve) are the two primary impacts on reference automation. Interface design issues will probably initially have the greater influence as the profession seeks to provide more flexible and resilient tools by which to search and display information. But the conversion of many traditional procedural languages to object orientation continues unabated. In the future, the formal algorithms that librarians depend upon and that will constitute a central part of librarianship will be developed through object orientation. Just as the procedural languages pulse beneath current OPAC, online searching, and network technology, so in the near future the object-oriented languages will create primary, formal conditions for information technology.

Appendix: Turbo C++ Source Code for Simple Reference Negotiation When Entered in the Borland C++ Editor, This Source Code Compiles into a Simple Reference Negotiation Program.

```
#include <stdio.h>
#include <string.h>
#include <conio.h>
#include <ctype.h>

class QuestionNegotiation
  {
   public:
     char Format[80], Level[80], Years[80];

     virtual void AskQuestion(void);

     };

class ScienceQuestionNegotiation : public QuestionNegotiation
  {
public:
 char Discipline[80];
 virtual void AskQuestion(void);

  };

class SocSciQuestionNegotiation : public QuestionNegotiation
  {
 public:
   char Discipline[80];
   virtual void AskQuestion(void);
  };

class HumanitiesQuestionNegotiation : public QuestionNegotiation
  {
 public:
   char Discipline[80];
   virtual void AskQuestion(void);
  };
```

Appendix (continued)

```cpp
QuestionNegotiation *Process[20];
  int I;


 void QuestionNegotiation::AskQuestion(void)
    {
     printf("\n\n");
     printf("What   format   of   information   are   you   looking   for
(magazines,\n");
     printf("books etc): ");
     scanf("%s",Format);
     printf("What level of sophistication? ");
     scanf("%s",Level);
     printf("How many years back to you wish to search? ");
     scanf("%s",Years);
       }

 void ScienceQuestionNegotiation::AskQuestion(void)
    {
     QuestionNegotiation::AskQuestion();
     printf("Specifically, in what scientific discipline are you
iinterested? \n");
     scanf("%s",Discipline);
     }

 void SocSciQuestionNegotiation::AskQuestion(void)
    {
     QuestionNegotiation::AskQuestion();
     printf("In   what   particular   social   science   are   you
interested?\n");
     scanf("%s",Discipline);
     }

  void HumanitiesQuestionNegotiation::AskQuestion(void)
     {
     QuestionNegotiation::AskQuestion();
     printf("In what humanities area are you interested?\n");
     scanf("%s",Discipline);
     }
```

Appendix (continued)

```c
int main(int,char *)

{
 char choice, anykey[1]; clrscr();
 printf("In what area does your subject fall:\n\n");
 printf("  A: Science\n");
 printf("  B: Social Science\n");
 printf("  C: Humanities\n\n");
 printf("  Select: ");
 choice = tolower(getch());

 switch (choice)
 {
 case 'a': Process[I] = new ScienceQuestionNegotiation;break;
 case 'b': Process[I] = new SocSciQuestionNegotiation;break;
 case 'c': Process[I] = new HumanitiesQuestionNegotiation;break;
 case 'x': clrscr();break;
 default : printf("\n"),
    printf(" Wrong choice.  Execute program again");
    gets(anykey);break;
 }
 Process[I]-> AskQuestion();


}
```

9

Virtual Reality

A virtual reality (VR) is a computer-manufactured three-dimensional matrix that the user can experience and manipulate as a surrounding environment. Of all technologies examined in this book, virtual reality lies furthest away in the future of reference services. Currently, research is underway at dozens of academic and corporate research laboratories developing and applying this technology to areas such as entertainment, computer-aided design, medical imaging, and information representation.

The roots of such a vision go back to a brief but influential symposium paper written in 1965 by I. E. Sutherland. In the paper, "The Ultimate Display," Sutherland (1965) speculated about the efficacy of a three-dimensional information display produced by two CRTs (cathode ray tubes) mounted in a helmet to produce stereopsis (depth perception). More recently, the novels of William Gibson have provided an exciting narrative dimension to the concept of a virtually real data matrix. Called Cyberspace, such a matrix is a "consensual hallucination experienced daily by billions. ... A graphic representation of data abstracted from the banks of every computer in the human system. Unthinkable complexity. Lines of light ranged in the nonspace of the mind, clusters and constellations of data. Like city lights, receding" (Gibson, 1984, p. 51).

Gibson's characters "jack" directly into cyberspace through cranial implantations; current technology, however, is far from such organic union with VR. The contemporary configuration of a VR system includes, in addition to the software and computer, at least a pair of stereoscopic goggles and a manipulation device, typically a glove. Upon donning the goggles, the user is within the virtual environment and can "move" objects around by moving the glove, which is virtually present in the space.

Sophisticated avionic systems produced by the Department of Defense and the National Aeronautics and Space Administration provide for heads-up-all-around displays in which the pilot can simultaneously monitor gauges and the sky. Such displays project the instrument information onto the windshield or on a face plate built into the helmet. Heads-up displays are used for training pilots and astronauts (although the heads-up display features have long been incorporated into actual jet fighter avionics). The various VR visualization techniques and apparatus developed by NASA's Ames Research Laboratory in the 1980s have had tremendous influence on the fledgling VR community. Such techniques and instruments draw on the impressive powers of mainframe and super computers. NASA systems also include earphones and body suits for total virtual envelopment.

Virtual realities need not be isolated one-person events. A number of prototypical systems provide simultaneous access for numbers of people, resulting in a VR where each person can see the virtual body of the other (Blanchard et al., 1990; Walser, 1990a, 1990b, 1990c). Multiple accessibility will make it possible to enter into a VR and "see," "hear," and "touch" a person whose physical being is thousands of miles away.

COMMERCIAL SYSTEMS

Leaders in the manufacturing field for commercially available VR systems are VPL Research Inc. and Autodesk. The VR industry is very young, and the economics of scale have yet to be felt. However, the potential for this alternative reality encompasses information storage and retrieval, scientific visualization, medical imaging, virtual exploration of remote terrain, and training, not to mention the vast market for entertainment.

VPL

Currently VPL has the most sophisticated VR commercially available. The Reality Built for Two (RB2) system provides access to VR for two people simultaneously. The system consists of an EyePhone head-mounted stereo display system, a DataGlove, a spatial tracking system attached to the head mount, and several pieces of software that control the data communication between components and permit programming of virtual worlds. The system uses a Macintosh for "world design" based on RB2 Swivel software. Four supermicrocomputer graphic workstations are required to render "worlds with approximately 1400 simultaneously visible polygons" (Blanchard et al., 1990, p. 36). Those who have experienced

RB2 liken its virtual quality to that of an animated cartoon—except that this animation is a three-dimensional environment through which the user moves.

VPL-based worlds that have been reviewed or mentioned in the popular literature include various three-dimensional architectural renderings, city skylines, the bondings between molecules, a patient's brain (through which physicians wearing goggles and head-trackers can walk), and a variety of physical activity games (Brand, 1990). On a more imaginary note, experiments at VPL involving full body suits (which provide the user with complete virtual body presence in the VR) have been able to "transform" users into lobsters, gazelles, and winged angels. In addition to these presentational worlds, Janot Lanier, the founder of VPL, has described several RB2 representational worlds that move around information storage and retrieval issues: "We're doing some work with actuaries. They can fly over an abstract forest that represents various insurance statistics. It helps them notice patterns in the data more easily than they could on even a very large computer screen" (Brand, 1990, p. 114). Programmers are described as being able to view programs from afar as large spatial structures, which can be efficiently manipulated.

AutoDesk's Cyberspace Project

Another important player in the fledgling VR industry is Autodesk, whose Autocad has become the standard software package in CAD-CAM (computer-aided design/computer-aided manufacturing). John Walker's paper "Through the Looking Glass" (1988) is credited with turning corporate interest at AutoDesk toward what has become known as the "Cyberspace Project," the creation of a VR software capable of running on 25 and 33 megahertz PC 386s.

Walker elucidates the history of computers in terms of "modalities of operation" (p. 1). The first generation of interfaces consisted of plugboards and knobs. The ENIAC computer is an example of such an interface. Next came the batch control process using punch cards. Eventually the logic of batch processing led to the realization of time-sharing systems that provided interaction between computer and user. This kind of "conversational computing" is at the foundation of such languages as BASIC and current operating systems like MS-DOS and UNIX. With the advent of fast alphanumeric terminals capable of presenting the user with 1,000 characters per second, programmers designed software to incorporate full-screen menus, thus opening up the interaction to noncomputer specialists. This fourth generation of menu-driven computers, like the third, is still present.

As the price of computer memory fell, interface designers began to take advantage of graphics. This fifth generation of operation modality permitted the user to manipulate the computer directly by manipulating the graphic representation. "Pointing" devices such as mouses or light pens bypassed the keyboard altogether and set the stage for the forthcoming modality in which "direct manipulation" would be taken to its logical end: "Now we're at the threshold of the next revolution in user-computer interaction: a technology which will take the user through the screen into the world inside the computer—a world in which the user can interact with three-dimensional objects whose fidelity will grow as computing power increases and display technology progresses" (Walker, 1988, p. 6). For Walker, Cyberspace is that modality where representation ceases and the user stands among the data. As such it is presented as the elimination of interface.

Since Walker's initial paper, AutoDesk has been working on a product that will be released in 1992 or 1993. (Other papers that elaborate on the design and possible applications of Cyberspace include Walser, 1990a, 1990b, 1990c; Foltz, 1990; and Tollander, 1990.)

Walker's antirepresentational bias is consistent with AutoDesk's product line and Cyberspace's proposed place in it as sophisticated CAD. However, there is no reason that Cyberspace could not contain the three-dimensional representation of information and act as an interface to that information. Any sign or representational element, including text, has an irreducible material presence, which, stripped of its symbolic function, reverts to pure presentational immediacy. The reverse is also true: all presentational or self-referential elements can be made to bear the weight of representation. What is knot in string for one is navigational information for another.

POTENTIAL INFORMATION APPLICATIONS

There are two conceptual models behind cyberspace: representational and presentational. The representational model is purely an informational one; cyberspace is the three-dimensional graphic representation of stored information. As such, the graphic features are signs for both data and the organization of data within the cyberspace. The presentational model, on the other hand, proposes that cyberspace be a world of virtual objects in its own right, without reference to any representational function. The objects themselves are environmental features. These two models of cyberspace, representation of information and presentation of (virtual) reality, can be seen in much of the work being done in this area.

Information and Sign

The possibility of using graphical three-dimensional representations of data in a VR environment rests upon the distinction between information and sign. A sign is the material conveyer of information. This "material" may be graphical, phonic, textual, or gestural. "Three pounds of corn,"

"3 lbs of corn," the vocal declaration "Drei Pfund Mais!" and three upraised fingers on the hand of a farmer weighing corn are four different signs communicating the same piece of information. Each sign succeeds in conveying the information due to a long, complex history of conventions, in the course of which such sign systems became required cultural skills. A number of factors conjoined to make written text (including numbers) the sign system of choice during the last millennium. The transformation of poetry from an oral to a textual format and the commitment of ever-increasing parts of human memory to written text are two examples of the centrality of this text tradition.

A recurrent challenge with text sign systems is their ability to accommodate information change. The sign "The book X is due back on 3–18–91" cursively written on a ledger containing the alphabetically arranged title listings of circulating books needs to be physically changed when the book is renewed and the information changes. For a single item, an erasure or a cross-out suffices. But suppose there are 1,000 books due back on March 18, 1991, that are renewed for irregular periods (one is due the next day, another three weeks hence). Fortunately, quick and efficient remedies to the challenge of massive information alteration have come from computers. The computer stores information using a binary (on/off) sign system, which permits rapid updating and global alterations in the body of information. The text sign system, however, is still primary since the interface that initiates alterations in the binary sign system is typically the alphanumeric keyboard. While binary signs store the meaning, the manipulation and cognition of such meaning takes place via the text-based sign system.

Representing relationships between items in a database has been more difficult to achieve using symbolic architectures whose manipulation interface involves the primacy of the text sign system. One solution involves giving common "type" terms to items whose commonality is expressed in the meaning of the term. Thus, records are organized internally using the same template whose fields are identified by authorized terms. Each record, for example, has a location field, and each location field can be east, west, south, or north. All items related to one another by being located in the north can then be gathered together. Another solution, particularly helpful in libraries where the relevant relationship between items involves topic content, lies in the various subject heading systems. Items sharing the same content are given the same subject term expressing the meaning of what is shared. Another side of this approach are the subject classification schemes such as the Dewey, Library of Congress, or colon method.

Commonality, Generalization, and Individuality

A fundamental disadvantage of subject or classification schema is that within a commonality, there can be no further distinction. Commonality determines membership but not individuality. For instance, a search on the subject heading C (Computer Language) finds seventy-five references. But which of these seventy-five books are closer to which, in terms of content, is not available. Boolean logic applied to a hierarchically organized system of authority terms goes as far in resolving this problem as a text-sign-system will allow. Thus, by ANDing the set of seventy-five C (Computer Language) items to the subject terms GRAPHICS, we receive a subset of five, indicating that among the initial seventy-five, five were closely related to one another in terms of applying the C programming language to graphics. Within that subaltern set, though, no further delineations can be made.

Several conditions make computerized text-based search strategies possible. System-wise, a programming algorithm must be activated that string-matches input to selected record field content. Conceptually, such record field content must exhibit the knowledge relationships sought. By using subject terms to capture these relationships, classification schemas inevitably cast such content in terms of generalized nouns. The common features shared by A and B are searchable in terms of the common subject terms they possess in the relevant record field. This commonality means that idiosyncratic features of items, degrees of commonality, and the unique ways individual items share in the common concept cannot be entertained. Items adhere to common concepts through a process of generalization in which aspects of individuality are left unrepresented. Current VR interface technology provides a number of nontext knowledge representation avenues that completely eliminate this need for generalization in the representation of commonality.

Speculative Examples of VR Interface Applications for Information Retrieval

Visual representation force-feedback and visual display techniques (Iwata, 1990; Minsky, Ouh-young, Steele, Brooks, Behensky, 1990) provide the platform for information retrieval interfaces that can represent commonality without losing individuality. Both derive this possibility through literal three-dimensional object representation of documents.

Visual VR interfaces for information retrieval and relevancy representation would consist of a three-dimensional Euclidean space viewable through visors, a geometric object set capable of representing documents, and some keyboard-based search input language. The Euclidean space would be swept clean after each search. As a universe whose members are the sum total of all possible search strategies throughout time, the space could be said to contain the entire database. However, each "state space," existing as the result of a given search strategy, displays only those object documents that pertain to the search strategy. Visual displays using this configuration could represent retrieval results in the following way: The search topic becomes the Euclidean space state containing all object documents capable of existing in such a space. The specific arrangement of the object documents is determined by some second factor, which creates clustering. Thus, a set of object documents, A, meeting the search criteria is capable of exhibiting clustering internal to set A. For example, not only do documents 1–20 contain evaluations of Cy Twombly, but documents 4, 7, and 8 are clustered together less than a few virtual feet apart, indicating similarity in, say, applied principles of aesthetics or perhaps use of color reproductions (or whatever other aspect is chosen).

The VR might also represent a simple three-dimensional environment within which significant characteristics of information were sculpturally manifest. Citation patterns within a whole section of physics might be rendered using such forms, or the presence of certain theoretical beliefs informing the same literature might be a focus. The historical development of the influence of an idea could be tracked through the literature and communicated three-dimensionally.

In force-feedback interfaces, a simple joystick (Minsky, Ouh-young, Steele, Brooks, & Behensky, 1990) or a more sophisticated "master manipulator" (Iwata, 1990) is used to create the experience of force when moving objects in a three-dimensional artificial reality. Such systems have been used to represent chemical bonding between molecules (Brand, 1990; Brooks, Ouh-young, Batter & Kilpatrick, 1990), the kinesthetic qualities involved in holding a virtual camera (analyzed during preproduction design work), and the realistic choreography of three-dimensional virtual dancers (Iwata, 1990, p. 165). Force feedback could also function effectively to represent knowledge relationships between documents or between documents and a search query.

A VR interface for information retrieval with force-feedback component would consist of a finite three-dimensional Euclidean space accessible through visors, some kind of force-feedback controller capable of virtual representation of the user's arm, plus a geometric object set capable of representing documents, concepts, and conceptual relations. Felt force could represent retrieval factors in the following ways:

1. The relevance of a concept to a small set of documents present as a circle of fist-sized spheres arranged around the concept represented as another, larger sphere. The relative significance of the concept to each of the documents is measured in terms of the amount of resistance encountered when trying to move a document away from the concept. The spheres could also represent sets of documents resulting from competing search strategies, resistance lending itself to an evaluation of search terms, and logic.

2. The relative "closeness" of documents to one another within a small object set in terms of a given concept. The arrangement involves document pairs equi-

distant from one another whose likeness to each other regarding the concept in question is measured by the amount of force required to move them apart.

3. Fluctuations in relevance of a given document to a series of incremental changes within a concept. The document is a sphere held in the palm of a virtual hand and becomes progressively heavier in proportion to the relevance it possesses to a specific subject variability. The subject might be something like World War I, with the document heavier during the final years than during the initial years.

Both force feedback and visual display are VR interfaces that passively reveal the state of a database in response to some user input. Using a VR to search, update, and otherwise directly manipulate the database is also possible. For instance, the entire database might be represented as a pole. Suppose a remote computer named Z signals that it needs the contents of the database. Instead of accessing telecommunications software and fussing with a-semantic commands organized around nonintuitive syntax, simply dawn goggles and place a garland of laurel leaves (Z's symbol) around the pole. A copy of the database is instantly transmitted to the Z computer.

CURRENT STATE OF VR INFORMATION AND KNOWLEDGE REPRESENTATION

Given the enthusiasm with which librarians and information scientists have greeted VR, are there practical uses to which this interest can be currently applied? If the question assumes "virtual reality" to be an environmental interface that includes the viewer "within it," then the current literature on applications will disappoint. Practically all the literature describing research, development, and application of VR to information representation works within the confines of representing a three-dimensional matrix on a two-dimensional computer screen (McKinney, 1991; Henderson, 1991; Huntley & Partridge, 1991). This work has genuine value as a relatively inexpensive way of experimenting with three-dimensional shapes as information representations. Many significant elements and rules regarding such representations can be tested and evaluated through such a process. On the other hand, the advantages of direct physical interaction and manipulation derived from an environmental interface as well as other hitherto unknown opportunities available with all-around representing are lost when the two-dimensional screen remains the real mode of operation.

The Virtual Interface Environment Workstation (VIEW) developed at NASA's Ames Research Center is an example of a current environmentally based virtual reality "dataspace" (Fisher, 1990, 1991). Creation of three-dimensional environments is accomplished by using a "wide angle stereoscopic display unit glove-like devices for multiple degree-of-freedom tactile input, connected speech recognition technology, gesture tracking devices, 3-D auditory display and speech synthesis technology, and computer graphic and video image generation equipment" (Fisher, 1991, p. 105). One of the chief objectives of the VIEW technology is to provide a virtual workspace for controlling and manipulating the information complexities of the proposed space station. With over 3,000 different control elements monitoring and potentially affecting all aspects of the station, VIEW designers have opted to represent such mechanisms virtually, permitting rapid deployment of whatever control elements are relevant within a small, easily accessible space. Users verbally summon the subset of controls necessary, physically arrange them for ergonomic and access efficiency, and perform the tasks required by the station. The first task accomplished, the control panels for the next can be quickly summoned into the same convenient space. Being able to summon and dismiss data and information panels through a combination of gesture and voice, the VIEW technology is the most advanced implementation of virtual reality within an information retrieval context to be found in the literature.

During a recent American Society for Information Science conference session on virtual reality uses in information representation a librarian asked whether adding a spatial-environmental dimension to the information interface provided new opportunities for information and knowledge representation absent from more traditional two-dimensional displays. If there are new representational forms, are they worth the expense to manufacture and maintain? In fact, there are many reasons to expect that three-dimensional representation will deliver new options for information access and conceptualization; some of these have already been suggested. A more immediate pragmatic significance lies precisely in this relationship between two-dimensional screen-based representation and VR representation. Thinking about information as represented in a three-dimensional VR might make certain aspects of information access more obvious—aspects that could be translated back into the available two-dimensional screen and text-based representational structures.

Virtual reality "thought experiments" concerning information features to be represented through VR interface and data displays become the ground for an ever-increasing flexibility and sensitivity of contemporary representation and database design techniques. For instance, the VR concept of force feedback as felt datum might itself be represented in some precise numeric equation that is attached to the document record and called into play when a particular concept is linked to the document as a relevancy factor. A sorting algorithm could display the "hits" in conformity to the concept being measured. This would involve some knowledge engineering and a rich hierarchical thesaurus of concepts, with each document mapped to every concept in the thesaurus in terms of relevance. Or, some type of formula might generate numeric factors that permit exhaustive ranking of a finite number of document pairs sorted by the likeness of each document in the pair to its mate in terms of a specified concept. This "pairing" could be generalized into a "set" wherein the similarity of one document to any other document in the set, with respect to a concept or idea, could be variously represented as a clustering on a two-dimensional surface or as a derived relevancy number attached to the document representations.

The VR model of interaction as a direct user manipulation of the environment in three dimensions might also be used as a paradigm in the development of graphical user interfaces, especially in rethinking the function of the cursor, which is now only able to traverse the two-dimensional screen. Instead of using two-dimensional clustering and/or ordering of icons, a third dimension could be added that might be explored using a cursor with the ability to go forward and backward. The cursor might be programmed to provide perspective so that the back or sides of an icon might be explored in greater detail. Icons themselves might be composed of logically subordinate icons (e.g., the icon for the geology of India placed on the lower righthand side of the India icon) visible to closer scrutiny and capable of being selected in their own right.

INFORMATION RESOURCES

To keep abreast of developments in virtual reality, the best source is the USENET discussion list SCI.VIRTUAL-WORLDS. Issues from all aspects of virtual reality are discussed, and the news group is a goldmine for relevant bibliographic references, conference announcements, and descriptions of meetings. One of the early moderators of the SCI.VIRTUAL-WORLDS, Howard Rheingold, has published an important book on the subject. *Virtual Reality* (1991) focuses on theoretic issues and practical implementations of the technology to information visualization and representation and is an excellent source or the fundamentals of this new science.

Articles on virtual reality have appeared in many magazines and journals, including *Omni, Science, Scientific American, BYTE,* and *Newsweek.* However, for regular, frequent coverage, *Computer Graphics* (a publication of ACM SIGGRAPH) is best, particularly issues containing conference proceedings with several sections devoted to virtual reality. Starting in 1991, the SIGGRAPH Conference issue (typically the fourth issue of the volume or year) has a list of ongoing VR research projects and provides addresses, objectives, and current status. *Presence*, a peer-reviewed journal devoted exclusively to virtual reality and telepresence issues, began publication in March 1992 by MIT Press.

CONCLUSION

Virtual reality is a technology that is a decade or two away from the reference scene. Probably its first appearance in the library will be in the media room or children's library, where it will provide access to worlds both imaginary and historical. Pre-made worlds will become part of the materials budget, to be evaluated in terms of the overall collection development goals of the institution. At some point, however, end user world construction will enable individuals (unversed in the intricacies of graphics programming and geometry) to create and maintain virtual realities. That is when the real opportunity of virtual reality as an information representation will challenge reference librarians.

Appendix: Index to Recent Computer-Based Reference Services

The following index is a subject organization to articles and books describing the implementation of computer systems for reference services. All of the items describe actual implementations of computers in the performance of important reference services. In most cases, the computers involved are the personal computers found on many librarians' desks, although some particularly interesting uses of minicomputers and mainframe are also identified.

Voluminous topics that have been extensively and repeatedly chronicled in other books, such as CD-ROM, online computer searching, and OPACs, will be linked to a few significant bibliographic resources but without attempting here to provide numerous items. When innovative applications are reported (such as CD-ROM LANs, expert system online intermediaries, or locally mounted databases) they will be included.

The subject list is organized alphabetically and identifies the primary author and date. For authors with more than one source in a given year, lowercase letters will be used to discriminate between articles (e.g.: Smith 1990a). Occasionally it is necessary to abbreviate a word in the subject phrase to adequately convey the thrust of the coverage. Such words will be alphabetically sorted as if fully spelled. Some frequently encountered abbreviations are "es" for "expert systems" and "ref" for reference.

Although some subject phrases may seem unrelated to computers (e.g., "call numbers—locating in stacks"), everything in the list describes an actual automation application.

References

Ackerman, Katherine. (1987). The subject is: business; an update on electronic information sources. *American Libraries, 18*, 378.

Adkins, R. T. (1989). Online data bases. In R. T. Adkins (Ed.), Information sources in polymers and plastics (pp. 100–108). London and New York: Bowker-Saur.

Ahtola, A. Anneli. (1989). In-house databases: An opportunity for progressive libraries. *RQ, 29*, 36–47.

Akeroyd, John. (1991). CD-ROM networks. *Electronic Library, 9*(1), 21–25.

Alberico, Ralph. (1988a). Software for expert systems: Languages versus shells. *Small Computers in Libraries, 8*(7), 4–12.

Alberico, Ralph. (1988b). User-supported artificial intelligence. *Small Computers in Libraries, 8*(2), 4–9.

Alberico, Ralph. (1988c). Using public domain software to develop an expert system: A business reference sources knowledge base. *Library Software Review, 7*, 190–191.

Alberico, Ralph, & Micco, Mary. (1990). *Expert systems for reference and information retrieval.* Westport, CT: Meckler.

Albrecht, M. A., & Egret, D. (Eds.). (1991). *Databases and on-line data in astronomy.* Boston: Kluwer Academic Publishers.

Ali, S. Nazim. (1990). Databases on optical disks and their potential in developing countries. *Journal of the American Society for Information Science, 41*, 238–244.

Allen, Ferne, C., & Ferrel, Wanda R. (1989). Numeric databases in science and technology: An overview. *Database, 12*(3), 50–58.

Alston, Patricia Gayle. (1991). Environment online: The greening of databases. Part 2. Scientific and technical databases. *Database, 14*(5), 34–52.

Anders, Vicki, & Jackson, Kathy M. (1988). Online vs CD-ROM—the impact of CD-ROM databases upon a large online searching program. *Online, 12*(6), 24–32.

Anderson, Bart, Costales, Bryan, & Henderson, H. (1991). *UNIX Communications*, Carmel, IN: SAMS.

Anderson, Charles. (1986). Getting SAVVY: A database for reference use. *Wilson Library Bulletin, 61*(1), 41–43, 95.

Anderson, V. N. (1987). Searching the engineering databases. *Database, 10*(2), 23–27.

Anick, P. G., Brennan, J. D., Flynn, R. A., & Hanssen, D. R. (1990). A direct manipulation interface for Boolean information retrieval via natural language query. In *Proceedings of the 13th International Conference on Research and Development in Information Retrieval* (pp. 135–150). New York: ACM Press.

Ardis, Susan B. (1990). Online patent searching: Guided by an expert system. *Online, 14*(2), 56–62.

Arms, Caroline R. (1990a). A new information infrastructure. *Online, 14*(5), 15–22.

Arms, Caroline R. (1990b). Using the national networks: Bitnet and the Internet. *Online, 14*(5), 24–29.

Arnold, Stephen E. (1987). End users: Dreams or dollars. *Online, 11*(1), 71–81.

Atkinson, Steven D., & Hudson, Judith. (1990). *Women online*. Binghamton, NY: Haworth Press.

Aubry, John W. (1972). Timing study of the manual searching of catalogs. *Library Quarterly, 42*, 399–415.

Bailey, Charles W. (1990). Intelligent multimedia computer systems: Emerging information resources in the network environment. *Library Hi Tech, 8*(1), 29–41.

Bailey, Charles W., Fadell, J., Myers, J. E., & Wilson, T. C. (1989). The Index Expert system: A knowledge-based system to assist users in index selection. *RSR, 17*(4), 19–28.

Bailey, Charles W., & Gunning, Kathleen. (1990). The intelligent reference information system. *CD ROM Librarian, 5*(8), 10–19.

Baker, Christine A. (1981). Piggy in the middle: Observations on the role of the intermediary. In *5th International Online Information Meeting Proceedings* (pp. 23–24). Medford, NJ: Learned Information.

Bakowski, Vicki B., & Moeckel, Lisa E. (1990). The impact of local tape databases on the library: The M(I)DAS touch. *Online, 14*(4), 38–42.

Balas, Janet. (1989). Through the gateway with Easynet. *Computers in Libraries, 9*(10), 22–24.

Ball, Sarah. (1989). *Directory of international sources of business information*. Philadelphia: Trans-Atlantic Publications.

Banwell, L. (1990). User modelling in library-based information systems: The use and evaluation of user models in multidisciplinary fields of knowledge. In Keven P. Jones (Ed.), *Prospects for Intelligent Information Retrieval. Informatics 10. Proceedings of a Conference* (pp. 303–308). London: ASLIB.

Barnard, John M. (1989). Chemical retrieval systems. In Charles Oppenheim, Charles Citroen, & Jose-Marie Griffiths (Eds.), *Perspectives in information management 1* (pp. 133–168). London and Boston: Butterworths.

Barr, Avron, & Feigenbaum, Edward A. (1982). *The handbook of artificial intelligence. Vol 2.* Los Altos, CA: William Kaufmann.

Bates, Marcia J. (1989). The design of browsing and berrypicking techniques for the online search interface. *Online Review, 13,* 407–424.

Batt, Fred. (1988). *Online searching for end users.* Phoenix: Oryx Press.

Becker, David. (1981). Automated language processing. In Martha E. Williams (Ed.). *Annual Review of Information Science and Technology, 16* (pp. 113–138). White Plains, NY: Knowledge Industry Publications.

Bell, Steven J., & Halperin, Michael. (1991). M&A moves abroad: Databases for researching cross-border deals. *Database, 14*(5), 20–32.

Bellamy, Lois M. (1991). Of mice and Macs: Integration of the Macintosh into the operations and services of the University of Tennessee, Memphis Health Science Library. In Edward J. Valauskas & Bill Vaccaro (Eds.), *Macintoshed Libraries 4* (pp. 1–11). Cupertino, CA: Apple Library Users Group.

Bellamy, Lois M., Silver, John T., & Givens, Mary K. (1991). Remote access to electronic library services through a campus network. *Bulletin of the Medical Library Association, 79,* 53–62.

Benefiel, Candace R. (1989). Microcomputer software for bibliographic instruction statistics. *College & Research Libraries News, 50,* 801–805.

Bennett, James S., & Englemore, Robert S. (1984). Experience using EMYCIN. In B. G. Buchanan & E. H. Shortliffe (Eds.), *Rule based expert systems* (pp. 314–328). Reading, MA: Addison-Wesley.

Bernal, N. E., & Renner, Iris A. (1990). CD-ROM Medline's impact on mediated online searches when patron cost is not a variable. *Laserdisk Professional, 3*(2), 25–27.

Binkley, David. (1990). Getting the most from downloaded data: A dBase parsing routine. *Library Software Review, 9,* 271–276.

Bivins, Kathleen T., & Eriksson, Lennart. (1982). REFLINK: A microcomputer information retrieval and evaluation system. *Information Processing and Management, 18*(3), 111–116.

Bjorklund, L., Orlander, B., & Smith, L. C. (1989). The personal hypercatalog. In J. Katzer & G. B. Newby (Eds.), *Asis 89, Proceedings of the 52nd ASIS Annual Meeting* (pp. 115–120). Medford, NJ: Learned Information.

Black, K. (1990). The development of IWS—an integrated workstation for librarians. *Program, 24*(1), 49–58.

Blanchard, C., Burgess, S., Harvill, Y., Lanier, J., Lasko, A., Oberman, M., & Teitel, M. (1990). Reality built for two: A virtual reality tool. *Computer Graphics, 24*(2), 35–36.

Block, Eleanor S., & Bracken, James K. (1991). *Communication and the mass media: A guide to the reference literature.* Englewood, CO: Libraries Unlimited.

Bloom, A. J. (1985). An anxiety management approach to computerphobia. *Training and Development Journal, 39*(1), 90–92.

Bobay, J., Stockey, E., & Popp, M. P. (1990). Library services for remote users with Linkway. *RSR, 18*(3), 53–57.

Bobrow, D. G., Fraser, J. B., & Quillian, M. R. (1967). Automated language processing. In Carlos A. Cuadra (Ed.), *Annual Review of Information Science and Technology, 2* (pp. 161–186). New York: John Wiley & Sons.

Bodtke-Roberts, Alice. (1983). Faculty end user searching of BIOSIS. In Martha E. Williams & Thomas H. Hogan (Eds.), *National Online Meeting Proceedings—1983* (pp. 45–46). Medford, NJ: Learned Information.

Booch, Grady. (1991). *Object oriented design with applications.* Redwood City, CA: Benjamin/Cummings Publishing Company.

Borgman, Christine L., Bower, J., Auth, Michael J., & Krieger, David. (1989). From hands-on science to hands-on information retrieval. In J. Katzer & G. B. Newby (Eds.), *Asis 89, Proceedings of the 52nd ASIS Annual Meeting* (pp. 96–103). Medford, NJ: Learned Information.

Brahmi, Frances A. (1989). The effect of CD-ROM MEDLINE on online end user and mediated searching. *Medical Reference Services Quarterly, 7*(4), 47–56.

Brajnik, Giorgio, Guida, G., & Tasso, C. (1990). User modeling in expert man-machine interfaces: A case study in intelligent information retrieval. *IEEE Transactions on Systems, Man and Cybernetics, 20*, 166–185.

Brand, Stewart. (1991). Interview: Jaron Lanier. *Omni 13*(1), 44–46, 113–117.

Brandt, D. Scott. (1991). *Unix and libraries.* Westport, CT: Meckler Publishing.

Breeding, Marshall. (1988). Enhancing a mainframe library system through microcomputer technology. *Library Software Review, 7*, 331–339.

Britten, William A. (1990). BITNET and the Internet: Scholarship networks for librarians. *College and Research Libraries News, 51*, 103–107.

Brooks, Frederick P., Ouh-young, M., Batter, James J., & Kilpatrick, P. Jerome. (1990). Project GROPE—Haptic displays for scientific visualization. *Computer Graphics, 24*(4), 177–185.

Brophy, Peter. (1976). *COBOL programming: An introduction for librarians.* Hamden, CT: Linnet Books.

Brown, Gillian, & Yule, George. (1983). *Discourse analysis.* Cambridge and New York: Cambridge University Press.

Buchanan, Bruce G., & Shortliffe, Edward H. (1984a). Knowledge engineering. In B. G. Buchanan & E. H. Shortliffe (Eds.), *Rule based expert systems* (pp. 149–158). Reading, MA: Addison-Wesley.

Buchanan, Bruce G., & Shortliffe, Edward H. (1984b). Other representation frameworks. In B. G. Buchanan & E. H. Shortliffe (Eds.), *Rule based expert systems* (pp. 391–396). Reading, MA: Addison-Wesley.

Buchanan, Bruce G., & Shortliffe, Edward H. (1984c). The problem of evaluation. In B. G. Buchanan & E. H. Shortliffe (Eds.), *Rule based expert systems* (pp. 571–588). Reading, MA: Addison-Wesley.

Buchanan, Bruce G., & Shortliffe, Edward H. (1984d). Use of the MYCIN inference engine. In B. G. Buchanan & E. H. Shortliffe (Eds.), *Rule based expert systems* (pp. 295–301). Reading, MA: Addison-Wesley.

Burge, Cecil D. (1989). SABRE—a novel software tool for bibliographic post-processing. *Electronic Library, 7*, 220–223.

Butkovich, Nancy J., Browning, Marilyn M., & Taylor, Kathryn L. (1991). The reference expert: A computerized database utilizing INMAGIC and a WORM drive. *Database, 14*(6), 35–38.

Butkovich, Nancy J., Taylor, Kathryn L., Dent, Sharon H., & Moore, Ann S.

(1989). An expert system at the reference desk: Impressions from users. *Reference Librarian, 23,* 61–74.

Buttlar, Lois. (1989). *Education: A guide to reference and information sources.* Englewood, CO: Libraries Unlimited.

Byskov, Lene, & Albretsen, Jorgen. (1991). Business sense: Using the Macintosh in a business school library. In Edward J. Valauskas & Bill Vaccaro (Eds.), *Macintoshed Libraries 4* (pp. 33–37). Cupertino, CA: Apple Library Users Group.

Carande, Robert J. (1989). Reference advisory systems (RAS): Some practical issues. *RSR, 17*(3), 87–90.

Carande, Robert J. (1990). Reference advisory systems board. *Information Technology and Libraries, 9,* 180–184.

Carey, Joan, & Massey-Burzio, Virginia (1989). Installing a local area compact disk network. *College and Research Libraries News, 50,* 988–991.

Carrington, Bessie M. (1990). Expert systems: Power to the experts. *Database, 13*(2), 47–50.

Case, Donald Owen, & Borgman, Christine L. (1989). BIBLIOMAC: A Macintosh Hypercard interface for an online catalog. In J. Katzer & G. B. Newby (Eds.), *Asis 89, Proceedings of the 52nd ASIS Annual Meeting* (pp. 111–114). Medford, NJ: Learned Information.

Cerf, V., & Kann, R. (1990). Selected ARPANET maps 1969–1990. *Computer Communication Review, 20*(5), 81–110.

Chadwick, Terry B. (1990a). International trade information: Other business databases online. *Database, 13*(4), 26–31.

Chadwick, Terry B. (1990b). Trade information services online. *Database, 13*(3), 38–49.

Chan, Lillian L., & Carande, Robert J. (1991). Public health—in search of a knowledge domain and expert reference advisory system. *Bulletin of the Medical Library Association, 79,* 178–181.

Chang, Sheau-hwang, & Tu, Shu-chen. (1990). Automating the production of subject bibliographies. *OCLC Micro, 6*(5), 18–21.

Chang, Shi-kuo (Ed.). (1990a). *Principles of visual programming systems.* Englewood Cliffs, NJ: Prentice-Hall.

Chang, Shi-kuo (Ed.). (1990b). *Visual languages and visual programming.* New York: Plenum Publishing.

Chen, Ching-chih. (1991). *Optical discs in libraries: Use and trends.* Medford, NJ: Learned Information.

Cherry, Joan M., Turner, James, & Clinton, Marshall. (1990). Online public access catalogues (OPACs): Design of instructional software for user training. In Diane Henderson (Ed.), *ASIS '90, Proceedings of the 53rd ASIS Annual Meeting* (pp. 143–150). Medford, NJ: Learned Information.

Chignell, Mark H., Jaffe, L., Smith, Philip J., Krawczak, D., & Shute, Stephen J. (1990). Knowledge-based search intermediaries for online information retrieval. In Rao Aluri & D. E. Riggs (Eds.), *Expert systems in libraries* (pp. 170–191). Norwood, NJ: Ablex Publishing.

Chu, C. (1991). A HyperCard map information system. *Computers in Libraries, 11*(3), 34–38.

Clausen, Helge. (1991). Electronic mail as a tool for the information professional. *Electronic Library, 9*(2), 73–83.

Cline, Nancy. (1990). Information resources and the national network. *EDUCOM Review, 25*(2), 30–34.

Combs, Richard, & Moorhead, John. (1990). Competitive intelligence: Finding the clues online. *Database, 13*(5), 15–18.

Computer-readable databases: A directory and data sourcebook (semiannual). Detroit: Gale Research.

Cooper, Michael D., & DeWath, Nancy A. (1977). The effect of user fees on the cost of on-line searching in libraries. *Journal of Library Automation, 10*, 304–319.

Corbett, Patti K. (1984). Automating reference department functions via an electronic spreadsheet. *Medical Reference Services Quarterly, 3*(3), 85–88.

Cornick, Donna. (1988). Microcomputer scheduling of reference desk staff. *RQ, 28*, 46–53.

Cornick, Donna. (1989). Being an end-user is not for everyone. *Online, 13*(2), 49–54.

Cornwell, D. W. (1991). Downloading from Dialog into dBASE III Plus. *Online, 15*(3), 91–93.

Crispell, Diane. (1987). The world of demographic data. *Database, 10*(2), 36–43.

Cropley, Jacqueline. (1989). Business information online. In Charles Oppenheim, Charles Citroen, & Jose-Marie Griffiths (Eds.), *Perspectives in information management 1* (pp. 273–302). London and Boston: Butterworths.

Dale, Doris C. (1989). Subject access in online catalogs: An overview bibliography. *Cataloging and Classification Quarterly, 10*(1–2), 225–251.

Damerau, Fred. J. (1976). Automated language processing. In Martha E. Williams (Ed.), *Annual Review of Information Science and Technology, 11* (pp. 107–161). Washington, DC: American Society for Information Science.

Datapro Research Group. (1991). Interview with David A. Taylor, PhD, on object-oriented databases. *Datapro reports on microcomputers*, CM–45–010–204.

Davidson, Lloyd, & Schneider, Peter. (1990). Expert systems for library applications. *Database, 13*(1), 80–83.

Davis, Charles H. (1990). Programming languages taught in library schools, 1980 versus 1986. *Journal of Education for Library and Information Science, 31*(1), 25–32.

Davis, Charles H., Lundeen, Gerald W., & Shaw, Debra. (1988). *Pascal programming for libraries: Illustrative examples for information specialists*. Westport, CT: Greenwood Press.

Davis, Elisabeth B. (1987). *Guide to information sources in the botanical sciences*. Littleton, CO: Libraries Unlimited.

Davis, Randall. (1984). Interactive transfer of expertise. In B. G. Buchanan & E. H. Shortliffe (Eds.), *Rule based expert systems* (pp. 171–205). Reading, MA: Addison-Wesley.

Delfino, Erik. (1990). E-mail connections: It's still a jungle out there . . . but it is getting better. *Online, 14*(5), 31–35.

D'Elia, Stephen J. (1989). How a school librarian looked at a gnawing problem (and saw how the Mac and HyperCard might solve it). In Bill Vaccaro and

References

171

Edward J. Valauskas (Eds.), *Macintoshed Libraries 2.0* (pp. 21–23). Cupertino, CA: Apple Library Users Group.

DeMiller, Anna L. (1991). *Linguistics: A guide to the reference literature*. Englewood, CO: Libraries Unlimited.

Desmarais, Norman. (1991a). *CD-ROMS in print. 1991: An international guide*. Westport, CT: Meckler Publishing.

Desmarais, Norman. (1991b). *CD-ROM local area networks: A user's guide*. Westport, CT: Meckler Publishing.

Dickinson, Gail K. (1990). CD-ROMs in the school library: One district's experience. In Linda Stewart, Katherine S. Chiang, & Bill Coons (Eds.), *Public Access CD-ROMs in libraries: Case studies* (pp. 147–156). Westport, CT: Meckler Corporation.

Dillon, A., McKnight, C., & Richardson, J. (1988). Reading from paper versus reading from screen. *Computer Journal, 31*, 457–464.

Diodata, Virgil. (1986). Eliminating fees for online search services in a university library. *Online, 10*(6), 44–50.

Directory of online databases (updates three times a year). Santa Monica, CA: Cuadra/Elsevier.

Doszkocs, Tamas E. (1983). CITE NLM: Natural-language searching in an online catalog. *Information Technology and Libraries, 2*, 364–380.

Doszkocs, Tamas E., & Weinberg, Bella Hass. (1988). Natural language interfaces for information retrieval. In J. A. Benson & B. H. Weinberg (Eds.), *Gateway software and natural language interfaces* (pp. 123–133). Ann Arbor, MI: Pierian Press.

Drabenstott, Karen Markey. (1990). Online assistance in online catalogs. In Denise Kaplan (Ed.), *Online user assistance: A symposium* (pp. 72–74). *Library Hi-Tech, 8*(1).

Dubester, Henry. (1964). Studies related to catalog problems. *Library Quarterly, 34*, 97–105.

Dueltgen, Ronald R. (1990). Ceramics! *Database, 13*(6), 103–104.

Dueltgen, Ronald R. (1991). Access to Japanese technical information. *Database, 14*(2), 105–107.

Dumas, Joseph S. (1988). *Designing user interfaces for software*. Englewood Cliffs, NJ: Prentice-Hall.

Duncan, E. B. (1989). A concept-map thesaurus as a knowledge-based hypertext interface to a bibliographic database. In Kevin P. Jones (Ed.), *Prospects for Intelligent Information Retrieval. Informatics 10. Proceedings of a Conference* (pp. 43–52). London: ASLIB.

DuPont, G., & Dutcher, G. A. (1990). AIDS information from the National Library of Medicine. *Medical Reference Services Quarterly, 9*(2), 1–19.

D'Urso, Lawrence A. (1981). The application of microcomputers to new I&R files: A beginner's experience. *RQ, 21*, 143–146.

Eaton, Nancy L., MacDonald, Linda B., & Saule, Mara R. (1989). *CD-ROM and other optical information systems*. Phoenix: Oryx Press.

Efthimiadis, Efthimios N. (1990a). Online searching aids: A review of front ends, gateways and other interfaces. *Journal of Documentation, 46*, 218–262.

Efthimiadis, Efthimios N. (1990b). The growth of the OPAC literature. *Journal of the American Society for Information, 41*, 342–347.

Elias, Arthus W., Vaupel, Nancy, & Lingwood, David. (1980). End-user education: A design study. *Online Review, 4*, 153–162.

Elsbernd, Mary Ellen Rutledge, Campbell, Nancy F., & Wesley, Theresa L. (1990). The best of OPAC instruction: A selected guide for the beginner. *Research Strategies, 8*(1), 28–36.

Evers, Hans. (1989). Patent information. In Charles Oppenheim, Charles Citroen, & Jose-Marie Griffiths (Eds.), *Perspectives in information management 1* (pp. 219–255). London and Boston: Butterworths.

Fadell, Jeff, & Myers, Judy E. (1989). The information machine: A microcomputer-based reference service. *Reference Librarian, 23*, 75–112.

Faibisoff, Sylvia, & Hurych, Jitka. (1981). Is there a future for the end user in online bibliographic searching? *Special Libraries, 72*, 347–355.

Farber, Evan I. (1989). On or off campus: The prospects for bibliographic instruction. In Barton M. Lessin (Eds.), *Off-campus Library Services Conference Proceedings* (pp. 91–100). Mount Pleasant, MI: Central Michigan University Press.

Fidel, Raya. (1990). The selection of search keys. In Rao Aluri & D. E. Riggs (Eds.), *Expert systems in libraries* (pp. 155–169). Norwood, NJ: Ablex Publishing.

Fisher, Scott S. (1990). Virtual interface environments. In Brenda Laurel (Ed.), *The art of human-computer interface design* (pp. 423–438). Reading, MA: Addison-Wesley Publishing.

Fisher, Scott S. (1991). Virtual environments: Personal simulations and telepresence. In Sandra K. Helsel & Judith Paris Roth (Eds.), *Virtual reality: Theory, practice, and promise* (pp. 101–110). Westport, CT: Meckler Publishing.

Fjallbrant, N., Kihlen, E., & Malmgren, M. (1983). End-user training in the use of a small Swedish database. *College and Research Libraries, 44*, 161–167.

Flanders, Bruce. (1990). Computerized orientation systems: The Franklin Institute Model. *Computers in Libraries, 10*(11), 36–38.

Foltz, Gary. (1990). *Cyberspace: The magic theater for all of us.* Available from Autodesk Inc., Sausolito, CA.

Forcier, Richard C. (1990). Information technology program initiated. *PNLA Quarterly, 54*(2), 29–30.

Fosdick, Howard. (1982). *Structured PL/1 programming: For textual and library processing.* Littleton, CO: Libraries Unlimited.

Frank, Robyn C. (1987). Agricultural information systems and services. In Martha E. Williams (Ed.), *Annual review of information science and technology, 22* (pp. 293–334). New York: Elsevier Science Publishers.

Freed, Melvyn N., Diodato, Virgil P., & Rouse, David A. (1991). *Business information desk reference: Where to find answers to business questions.* New York: Macmillan.

Freed, Melvyn N., Hess, Robert K. & Ryan, Joseph M. (1989). *The educator's desk reference (EDR): A sourcebook of education information and research.* New York: Macmillan.

Frey, Donnalyn, & Adams, Rick. (1990). *!%@:: A directory of electronic mail addressing and networks.* Sebastopol, CA: O'Reilly and Associates.

Friend, Linda. (1990). Online searcher education and training: Options and opportunities. *Reference Librarian, 30*, 119–132.

Fritze, Ronald H., Coutts, Brian E., & Vyhnanek, Louis A. (1990). *Reference Sources in History*. Santa Barbara, CA: ABC-CLIO.

Fulton, Alan R. (1990). The use of WORM optical disk storage for newspaper cuttings in a public library. *Electronic Library, 8*(3), 167–171.

Galneder, Mary. (1989). Computer applications for map libraries. *Bulletin of the Special Libraries Association Geography and Map Division, 157*, 33–36.

Gibson, William. (1984). *Neuromancer*. New York: Ace Books.

Gilbert, Pamela, & Hamilton, Chris J. (1990). *Entomology—A guide to information sources*. 2d Ed. London and New York: Mansell.

Glitz, Beryl, & Yokote, Gail A. (1990). CD-ROM technology in a biomedical library. In Linda Stewart, Katherine S. Chiang, & Bill Coons (Eds.), *Public access CD-ROMs in libraries: Case studies* (pp. 267–278). Westport, CT: Meckler Corporation.

Godin, Robert, Pichet, C. & Gecsei, J. (1989). Design of a browsing interface for information retrieval. In *International ACMSIGIR Conference on Research and Development in Information Retrieval* (pp. 32–39). New York: ACM Press.

Gordon, Dena W. (1983). *Online training for the end user or information consumer*. ERIC Document ED 245–697.

Gouke, Mary N., & Pease, Sue. (1982). Title searches in an online catalog and a card catalog: A comparative study of patron success in two libraries. *Journal of Academic Librarianship, 8*, 137–143.

Griffin, Marjorie. (1962). The library of tomorrow. *Library Journal, 87*, 1555–1557.

Grignetti, Mario. (1963). *Computer aids to literature searches*. Report No. 1074, submitted to Council on Library Resources. Cambridge, MA: Bolt, Beranek and Newman.

Grosch, A. N. (1991). The University of Minnesota Libraries' electronic bulletin board. *OCLC Micro, 7*(1), 24–25.

Guerena, Salvador. (1990). *Latino librarianship: A handbook for professionals*. Jefferson, NC: McFarland & Co.

Guida, Giovanni, & Tasso, C. (1983). IR-NLI: An expert natural language interface to online databases. In *Conference on Applied Natural Language Processing* (pp. 31–38). Menlo Park, CA: Association for Computational Linguistics.

Guy, Robin F., & Large, J. A. (1989). Business information. *Education for Information, 7*, 313–371.

Harley, Bruce L., & Knobloch, Patricia J. (1991). Government documents reference aid: An expert system development project. *Government Publications Review, 18*, 15–33.

Hartely, Richard J., Keen, E. M., Large, J. A., & Tedd, L. A. (1990). *Online searching: Principles and practice*. London and New York: Bowker-Saur.

Haselbauer, Kathleen J. (1987). *A research guide to the health sciences: Medical, nutritional and environmental*. Westport, CT: Greenwood Press.

Hawkins, Donald T. (1988). Applications of artificial intelligence (AI) and expert systems for online searching. *Online, 12*(1), 31–43.

Hawkins, Donald T. (1990). Information delivery—paper and e-mail. *Online, 14*(2), 100–103.

Hayes-Roth, F., Waterman, D. A., & Lenat, D. B. (1983). An overview of expert systems. In Frederick Hayes-Roth, Donald A. Waterman, & D. B. Lenat (Eds.), *Building expert systems* (pp. 3–29). Reading, MA: Addison-Wesley.

Heilprin, L. B. (1961). On the information problem ahead. *American Documentation, 12*(1), 6–14.

Henderson, Joseph. (1991). Designing realities: Interactive media, virtual realities and cyberspace. In Sandra K. Helsel & Judith Paris Roth (Eds.), *Virtual reality: Theory, practice, and promise* (pp. 65–73). Westport, CT: Meckler Publishing.

Herzog, Kate. (1990). Collection development for the electronic library. *Computers in Libraries, 10*(10), 9–13.

Hetzer, A. (1990). Microcomputer applications in manuscript and rare book collections. In Ahmed H. Helal & Joachim W. Weiss (Eds.), *Developments in Microcomputing—Discovering New Opportunities for Libraries in the 1990s. 12th International Essen Symposium* (pp. 41–56). Essen, Germany: Universitatsbibliothek Essen.

Hightower, Christy & Schwarzwalder, Robert. (1991). A comprehensive look at materials science databases. *Database, 14*(2), 42–53.

Hildreth, Charles R. (1985). Online public access catalogs. In Martha E. Williams (Ed.), *Annual review of information science and technology* (pp. 233–285). White Plains, NY: Knowledge Industry Publications.

Hildreth, Charles R. (1990). Online user assistance for information retrieval systems. In Denise Kaplan (Ed.), *Online User Assistance: A Symposium* (pp. 74–78), in *Library Hi-Tech, 8*(1).

Hitchingham, E., Titus, E., & Pettengill, R. (1984). A survey of database use at the reference desk. *Online, 8*(2), 44–50.

Hodges, Pauline R. (1989). Reference in the age of automation: Changes in reference services at Chemical Abstracts Library. *Special Libraries, 80*, 251–257.

Hollnagel, Erik. (1989). Evaluation of expert systems. In G. Guida & C. Tasso (Eds.), *Topics in expert systems design* (pp. 377–415. North Holland: Elsevier Science Publishers B.V.

Hoppe, H. U., Ammersbach, K., Lutes-Schaab, B., & Zinssmeister, G. (1990). EXPRESS: An experimental interface for factual information retrieval. *Proceedings of the 13th International Conference on Research and Development in Information Retrieval* (pp. 63–82). New York: ACM Press.

Hopson, Jean B., & Yeung, Jimmy T. (1989). Using dBASE III for self help information services. *Electronic Library, 7*, 12–19.

Horton, Forest W. (1991). InfoMapping. *Electronic Library, 9*, 17–19.

Howard, Ellen H., & Jankowski, Terry A. (1986). Reference services via electronic mail. *Bulletin of the Medical Library Association, 74*, 41–44.

Hu, Chengren. (1989). Microcomputers in online services. *Library Software Review, 8*, 73–78.

Huang, Kuan-tsae. (1990). Visual interface design systems. In Shi-kuo Chang (Ed.), *Principles of visual programming systems* (pp. 60–143). Englewood Cliffs, NJ: Prentice-Hall.

Hunter, J. A. (1983). What did you say the end-user was going to do and how much is it going to cost? In Martha E. Williams & Thomas H. Hogan (Eds.),

National Online Meetings Proceedings—1983 (pp. 223–229). Medford, NJ: Learned Information.

Huntley, Joan S., & Partridge, Michael. (1991). Fluxbase: A virtual exhibit. In Sandra K. Helsel & Judith Paris Roth (Eds.), *Virtual reality: Theory, practice, and promise* (pp. 75–93). Westport, CT: Meckler Publishing.

Huray, Paul G., & Nelson, David B. (1990). The federal high-performance computing program. *EDUCOM Review, 25*(2), 17–24.

Hurt, C. D. (1983). Intermediaries, self-searching and satisfaction. In Martha E. Williams & Thomas H. Hogan (Eds.), *National Online Meeting Proceedings—1983* (pp. 231–238). Medford, NJ: Learned Information.

Hutchins, G., Anders, V., & Jaros, J. (1987). End user perceptions of teaching methods. In Martha E. Williams & Thomas H. Hogan (Eds.), *National Online Meeting Proceedings—1987* (pp. 183–190). Medford, NJ: Learned Information.

Iwata, Hiroo. (1990). Artificial reality with force-feedback: Development of desktop virtual space with compact master manipulator. *Computer Graphics, 24*(4), 165–170.

Jackson, K. M. (1990). Loading Wilson Indexes locally—the Texas A&M experience. *Online, 14*(4), 42–45.

Jacobs, P. S., & Rau, L. F. (1990). SCISOR: Extracting information from on-line news. *Communications of the ACM, 33*(11), 88–97.

Jamison, Wesley, & Lewis, C. Michael. (1988). Use of menu and command modes in a hybrid interface. In C. L. Borgman & Edward Y. H. Pai (Eds.), *ASIS '88: Proceedings of the 51st ASIS Annual Meeting* (pp. 127–131). Medford, NJ: Learned Information.

Janke, Richard V. (1984). Online after six: End user searching comes of age. *Online, 8*(6), 15–29.

Jensen, Eric. (1990). Knowledge gateway project: Increasing access for everyone. In Bill Vaccaro & Edward J. Valauskas (Eds.), *Macintoshed Libraries 3.0* (pp. 32–37). Cupertino, CA: Apple Library Users Group.

Johnson, Brian, & Shneiderman, Ben. (1991). *Tree-maps: A space filling approach to the visualization of hierarchical information structures*. Report numbers CAR-TR–552 and CS-TR–2657. College Park, MD: Human-Computer Interaction Laboratory, Center for Automation Research, University of Maryland.

Johnston, Mark, & Weckert, John. (1990). Selection advisor: An expert system for collection development. *Information Technology and Libraries, 9*, 219–225.

Kahle, Brewster. (1989). *Wide area information server concepts*. Version 4. Cambridge, MA: Thinking Machines.

Kahle, Brewster, & Medlar, Art. (1991). An information system for corporate users: Wide area information servers. *Online, 15*(5), 56–60.

Kane, William P. (1989). A HyperCard call number directory: Using stacks to find stacks. *College and Research Libraries News, 50*, 576–577.

Karch, Linda S. (1990). Serials information on CD-ROM: A reference perspective. *RSR, 18*(2), 81–86.

Kay, Martin, & Jones, Karen Sparck (1971). Automated language processing. In

Carlos A. Cuadra (Ed.), *Annual Review of Information Science and Technology, 6* (pp. 141–166). Chicago: Encyclopedia Britannica, Inc.

Kehoe, Cynthia A. (1985). Interfaces and expert systems for online retrieval. *Online Review, 9,* 489–505.

Kelly, Noreen. (1991). Searching the online globe: Best files for country profiles. *Database, 14*(3), 40–47.

Kelly, Sarah A. (1988). Retrieving information on the neurophysiology of speech. *Medical Reference Services Quarterly, 7*(4), 31–45.

Khoshafian, Setraj, & Abnous, Razmik. (1990). *Object orientation: Concepts, languages, databases, user interfaces.* New York: John Wiley & Sons.

Kibbee, Josephine Z. (1991). *Cultural Anthropology: A guide to reference and information sources.* Englewood, CO: Libraries Unlimited.

Kilgour, Frederick G. (1970). Concept of an on-line computerized library catalog. *Journal of Library Automation, 3,* 1–11.

Kilgour, Frederick G. (1972). Objectives and activities of the Ohio College Library Center. In Lois L. Yoakam (Ed.), *Collected papers of Frederick G. Kilgour: OCLC years,* Vol. 2 (pp. 217–221). Dublin, OH: OCLC Online Computer Library Center.

Kimball, J., Thorin, S., & Arret, L. (1990). Providing preference assistance for machine-readable materials: The Library of Congress completes a one-year pilot. *Reference Librarian, 31,* 31–38.

King, Alan. (1991). Let your fingers do the walking: A guide to information sources about CD-ROM. *Database, 14*(4), 97–99.

Kinnell, Susan K., & Richards, Tyde. (1989). An online interface within a hypertext system: Project Jefferson's electronic notebook. *Online, 13*(4), 33–38.

Kinyon, William R., Clark, Katherine E., Loomis, Rosemary, & Martin, Susan J. (1990). Producing in-house indexes at Texas A&M. *RQ, 30,* 51–59.

Kittle, Paul W. (1985). Putting the medical library online: Electronic bulletin boards . . . and beyond. *Online, 9*(3), 25–30.

Knolle, Nancy T., Fong, Martin W., & Lang, Ruth E. (1990). SITMAP: A command and control application. In Lewis J. Pinson & Richard S. Wiener (Eds.), *Applications of object-oriented programming* (pp. 28–65). Reading, MA: Addison-Wesley Publishing.

Kosmin, L. J. (1991). Electronic reference desk: Multimedia integration opportunities. In Martha E. Williams & Thomas H. Hogan (Eds.), *National Online Meeting Proceedings—1991* (pp. 197–199). Medford, NJ: Learned Information.

Krulee, Gilbert, K., & Vrenios, Alexander. (1989). An expert system model of a reference librarian. *Library Software Review, 8,* 13–15.

Lamb, Connie. (1981). Searching in academia: Nearly 50 libraries tell what they're doing. *Online, 5*(2), 78–81.

Lambert, Nancy. (1991). After the grant: Online searching of legal status information for U.S. patents. *Database, 14*(4), 42–48.

Lancaster, Frederick W. (1968). *Information retrieval systems: Characteristics, testing and evaluation.* New York: Wiley.

LaQuey, Tracy L. (1990). *The user's directory of computer networks.* Bedford, MA: Digital Press.

Lathrop, Ann. (1989). *Online and CD-ROM databases in school libraries*. Engle-
    wood, CO: Libraries Unlimited.
Lawson, V. Lonnie. (1989). Using a computer-assisted-instruction program to re-
    place the traditional library tour: An experimental study. RQ, 29, 71–79.
Lazinger, Susan S. (1990). Producing an LCSH authority list for special libraries
    with dBase. *Electronic Library, 8*(1), 8–14.
Le Bas, M. J., & Durham, J. (1989). Scientific communication of geochemical data
    and the use of computer databases. *Journal of Documentation, 45*, 124–138.
Lee, Newton S. (1990). InfoStation: A multimedia access system for library au-
    tomation. *Electronic Library, 8*, 415–421.
Lenat, Douglas B., Guha, Ramanathan V., Pittman, K., Pratt, D., & Shepherd,
    Mary. (1990). CYC: Toward programs with common sense. *Communications
    of the ACM, 33*(8), 30–49.
Li. Tze-chung. (1990). *Social science reference sources: A practical guide*. Westport,
    CT: Greenwood Press.
Licklider, J.C.R. (1965). *Libraries of the future*. Cambridge, MA: MIT Press.
Linder, Gloria A., et al. (1986). Training the end user: The Stanford Medical
    Center Experience. In M. Sandra Wood, Ellen Brassil Horak, & Bonnie
    Snow (Eds.), *End user searching in the health sciences* (pp. 113–126). New
    York: Haworth Press.
Lirov, Yuval, & Lirov, Viktor. (1990). Online search + logic programming =
    subject bibliography: An expert systems approach to bibliographic process-
    ing. *Online Review, 14*, 3–12.
Losee, Robert M. (1990). The object-oriented paradigm for library systems de-
    velopment. *Information Technology and Libraries, 9*, 74–79.
Lucia, Joseph, & Roysdon, Christine. (1984). Online searching as an educational
    technology: Teaching computer-wise end users. In Martha E. Williams &
    Thomas H. Hogan (Eds.), *National Online Meeting Proceedings—1984*
    (pp. 187–193). Medford, NJ: Learned Information.
Lundy, Frank A. (1964). Reference vs. Catalog: A basic dilemma. In Arthur R.
    Rowland (Ed.), *Reference services* (pp. 112–117). Hamden, CT: Shoe String
    Press.
Lynch, Anne, & Lord, Hazel. (1989). The USC College Library—a Macintoshed
    system. In Bill Vaccaro and Edward J. Valauskas (Eds.), *Macintoshed Li-
    braries 2.0* (pp. 35–38). Cupertino, CA: Apple Library Users Group.
MacDonald, M., Maskell, C., & Auer, J. (1990). CD-ROM at Brock University:
    Introduction, integration, adaptation. In Linda Stewart, Katherine S.
    Chiang, & Bill Coons (Eds.), *Public access CD-ROMs in libraries: Case
    studies* (pp. 23–38). Westport, CT: Meckler Corporation.
Machalow, Robert. (1989). Using Lotus 123 for schedules. *Computers in Libraries,
    9*(6), 23–25.
Machalow, Robert. (1990). Using Lotus and Excel for a reference file. *Computers
    in Libraries, 10*(2), 44–47.
Mahon, B. Meinkohn, F., & Lella, G. (1990). Tootsi: Creating a toolkit for building
    user interfaces to business information services. *Online Review, 14*, 378–
    388.
Marcus, Richard S. (1981). An automated expert assistant for information retrieval.
    In L. F. Lunin, M. Henderson, & H. Wooster (Eds.), *The Information*

Community: An Alliance for Progress. Proceedings of the 44th ASIS Annual Meeting (pp. 270–273). White Plains, NY: Knowledge Industry Publications.

Marcus, Richard S. (1985). Development and testing of expert systems for retrieval assistance. In C. A. Parkhurst (Ed.), *ASIS 85. Proceedings of the 48th ASIS Annual Meeting* (pp. 289–292). White Plains, NY: Knowledge Industry Publications.

Marcus, Richard S. (1988). Expert retrieval assistance development and experimentation. In C. L. Borgman & Edward Y. H. Pai (Eds.), *ASIS '88: Proceedings of the 51st ASIS Annual Meeting* (pp. 115–119). Medford, NJ: Learned Information.

Marill, J. L., & Graves, J. B. (1991). The ACCESS project: New directions in user interface for the Library of Congress. In Martha E. Williams & Thomas H. Hogan (Eds.), *National Online Meeting Proceedings—1991* (pp. 245–248). Medford, NJ: Learned Information.

Marmion, Dan. (1988). Library applications of database management systems. *Small Computers in Libraries, 8*(2), 14–17.

Marmion, Dan. (1990). How do you manage those projects? *Computers in Libraries, 10*(2), 29–31.

Masek, Doris B. (1989). Microcomputers in the small elementary school media center. *Illinois Librarian, 71*, 273–276.

Mates, Barbara T. (1990). CD-ROM: A new light for the blind and visually impaired. *Computers in Libraries, 10*(3), 17–20.

Matthews, Joseph R., Lawrence, Gary S., & Ferguson, Douglas K. (Eds.). (1983). *Using online catalogs: A nationwide survey.* New York: Neal-Schuman.

McCleary, Hunter, & Mayer, William J. (1988). Expert systems the old fashioned way: Person to person. *Online, 12*(4), 15–24.

McCoy, Kathleen F., & Cheng, Jeannette. (1991). Focus of attention: Constraining what can be said next. In Cecile L. Paris, William R. Swartout, & William C. Mann (Eds.), *Natural language generation in artificial intelligence and computational linguistics* (pp. 103–124). Boston: Kluwer Academic Publishers.

McCray, Alexa T. (1989). Parsing, analyzing, and accessing biomedical text. In J. Katzer & G. B. Newby (Eds.), *ASIS '89: Proceedings of the 52nd ASIS Annual Meeting* (pp. 192–197). Medford, NJ: Learned Information.

McCray, Alexa T., & Srinivasan, S. (1990). Automated access to a large medical dictionary: Online assistance for research and application in natural language processing. *Computer and Biomedical Research, 23*, 179–198.

McGlamery, Patrick. (1990). Parallax: Cartographic information in transition. *RSR, 18*(2), 89–92.

McKay, Duncan J., & O'Donoghue, Michael. (1989). Computerized information services and geologic databases/databanks. In David N. Wood, Joan E. Hardy, & Anthony P. Harvey (Eds.), *Information sources in the earth sciences*, 2d Ed. (pp. 78–133). London and New York: Bowker-Saur.

McKinney, G., & Mosby, A. P. (1986). Online in academia: A survey of online searching in US colleges and universities. *Online Review, 10*, 107–124.

McKinney, Bret C. (1991). The virtual world of HDTV. In Sandra K. Helsel & Judith Paris Roth (Eds.), *Virtual reality: Theory, practice, and promise* (pp. 41–49). Westport, CT: Meckler Publishing.

Meglio, Delores. (1987). Full text online delivery. In Bernard F. Pasqualini (Ed.), *Dollars and sense: Implications of the new online technology for managing the library* (pp. 88–96). Chicago: American Library Association.

Meier, S. T. (1985), Computer aversion. *Computers in Human Behavior, 1*(2), 171–179.

Miller, N., Kirby, M., & Templeton, E. (1988). Medline on CD-ROM: End user searching in a medical school library. *Medical Reference Service Quarterly, 7*(3), 1–13.

Minsky, M., Ouh-young, M., Steele, O., Brooks, F., & Behensky, M. (1990). Feeling and seeing: Issues in force display. *Computer Graphics, 24*(2), 235–243.

Mischo, William H. (1989). Expert system interface software in microcomputer workstations. *Bookmark, 47,* 207–212.

Mock, Mary. (1990). DoubleVision: A foundation for scientific visualization. In Lewis J. Pinson & Richard S. Wiener (Eds.), *Applications of object-oriented programming* (pp. 139–163). Reading, MA: Addison-Wesley Publishing.

Monk, J. Thomas, Landis, Kenneth M., & Monk, Susan S. (1988a). *The Dow Jones-Irwin banker's guide to online databases.* Homewood, IL: R. D. Irwin.

Monk, J Thomas, Landis, Kenneth M., & Monk, Susan S. (1988b). *The Dow Jones-Irwin investor's guide to online databases.* Homewood, IL: R. D. Irwin.

Montgomery, C. A. (1969). Automated language processing. In Carlos A. Cuadra (Ed.), *Annual Review of Information Science and Technology, 4* (pp. 145–174). Chicago: Encyclopedia Britannica, Inc.

Moon, Y. S. (1989). An expert/information system—EISIP. *Microcomputers for Information Management, 6,* 187–195.

Moore, May M. (1990). Compact disk indexing and its effects on activities in an academic library. *Journal of Academic Librarianship, 16,* 291–295.

Morris, Sandra K., & Zimmerman, Paula S. (1989). DVI and its applications. In Sally Oberlin & Joyce Cox (Eds.), *Microsoft CD-ROM yearbook* (pp. 72–79). Redmond, WA: Microsoft Press.

Morrow, Blaine V. (1990). Do-it-yourself CD-ROM LANS: A review of LAN-tastic and CD–Connection. *CD-ROM Librarian, 5*(10), 12–24.

Myaeng, Sung H., & Korfhage, Robert R. (1990). Integration of user profiles: Models and experiments in information retrieval. *Information Processing and Management, 26,* 719–738.

Nagle, Ellen. Date varies. Sci tech online. *Science and Technology Libraries.* Issues vary. Regular column.

Newby, Gregory B. (1989). User models in information retrieval: Applying knowledge about human communication to computer interface design. In J. Katzer & G. B. Newby (Eds.), *ASIS '89: Proceedings of the 52nd Annual Meeting* (pp. 71–74). Medford, NJ: Learned Information.

Nickerson, Gord. (1990). A mouse-based OPAC interface. *Computers in Libraries, 10*(8), 33–34.

Nickerson, Gord. (1991a). Implementing the common command language on a micro. *Online, 15*(2), 44–46.

Nickerson, Gord. (1991b). Networked resources: The Internet. *Computers in Libraries, 11*(8), 25–29.

Nielsen, Brian. (1987). Do user fees affect searcher behavior? In Bernard F. Pasqualini (Ed.), *Dollars and sense: Implications of the new online technology for managing the library* (pp. 29–37). Chicago: American Library Association.

Nixon, J. M. (1989). Online searching for human nutrition: An evaluation of databases. *Medical Reference Service Quarterly, 8*(3), 27–35.

Nolte, James. (1990). The electronic library workstation—today. *Computers in Libraries, 10*(9), 17–20.

Nute, Donald. (1990). Scholar: A scholarship identification system in Prolog. In Rao Aluri & Donald E. Riggs (Eds.), *Expert systems in libraries* (pp. 98–108). Norwood, NJ: Ablex Publishing Company.

O'Brien, A. (1990). Relevance as an aid to evaluation in OPACs. *Journal of Information Science, Principles and Practice, 16*, 265–271.

Oddy, R. N. (1977). Information retrieval through man-machine dialogue. *Journal of Documentation, 33*, 1–14.

Ohio State University Libraries. Office of Library User Education. (1990). *The Ohio State University Libraries present the Gateway to Information*. Columbus, OH: Ohio State University Libraries.

Ojala, Marydee. (1991a). Business credit reports online. *Online, 15*(4), 83–86.

Ojala, Marydee. (1991b). Communing with Eastern European Business Information. *Online, 15*(1), 67–69.

Ojala, Marydee. (1991c). Driving data: The automotive industry online. *Database, 14*(5), 76–79.

Ojala, Marydee. (1990a). Finding information on the travel/tourism industry. *Database, 13*(3), 80–83.

Ojala, Marydee. (1990b). Information sources for the Pacific century. *Database, 13*(2), 81–84.

Ojala, Marydee. (1990c). Insurance industry information onlinc. *Online, 14*(1), 71–74.

Ojala, Marydee. (1990d). Real estate: A new online frontier. *Database, 13*(1), 73–75.

Ojala, Marydee. (1990e). The seas of change: New sources for company information. *Online, 14*(2), 74–77.

Ojala, Marydee. (1990f). The winds of change in corporate directory databases. Online, 14(3), 76–79.

O'Leary, Mick. (1990a). Local online: The genie is out of the bottle, part I. *Online, 14*(1), 15–18.

O'Leary, Mick. (1990b). Local online: The genie is out of the bottle, part II. *Online, 14*(2), 27–33.

Pagell, Ruth A. (1990). What's for dinar: Foreign exchange rate data sources. *Database, 13*(6), 46–51.

Parker, Joan. (1990). Macintosh computers at Cal State, Long Beach Library: A brief history. In Bill Vaccaro & Edward J. Valauskas (Eds.), *Macintoshed Libraries 3.0* (pp. 69–73). Cupertino, CA: Apple Library Users Group.

Parker, Joan. (1991). The HyperCard Library Instruction Project. In Edward J. Valauskas & Bill Vaccaro (Eds.), *Macintoshed Libraries 4* (pp. 60–63). Cupertino, CA: Apple Library Users Group.

Parrott, James R. (1986). Expert systems for reference work. *Microcomputers for Information Management, 3*, 155–171.

Parrott, James R. (1988). REFSIM: A bimodel knowledge-based reference training and consultation system. *RSR, 16*(1–2), 61–68.

Parsaye, K., & Chignell, M. (1988). *Expert systems for experts*. New York: John Wiley & Sons.

Pask, Judith M. (1990). *User education for online systems in libraries: A selective bibliography, 1970–88*. Metuchen, NJ: Scarecrow Press.

Pasqualini, Bernard F. (1987). Online reference services: Funding methods, Appendix A. In Bernard F. Pasqualini (Ed.), *Dollars and sense: Implications of the new online technology for managing the library* (pp. 105–109). Chicago: American Library Association.

Peischl, Thomas M., & Montgomery, Marilyn. (1986). Back to the warehouse or some implications on end user searching in libraries. In Martha A. Williams and Thomas H. Hogan (Eds.), *National Online Meetings Proceedings—1986* (pp. 347–352). Medford, NJ: Learned Information.

Pejtersen, A. M., & Goodstein, L. P. (1988). Beyond the desk top metaphor: Information retrieval with an icon based interface. In P. Gorny & M. J. Tauber (Eds.), *Visualization in Human Computer Interaction. 7th Interdisciplinary Workshop on Informatic and Psychology. Selected Contributions* (pp. 149–182). Berlin: Springer Verlag.

Perez, E. (1990). Low-budget, cost-effective OCR: Optical character recognition for MS-DOS micros. *Library Software Review, 9*, 209–217.

Peterkin, Karen, & Black, Donald V. (1989). *Directory of Online Healthcare Databases*. Los Altos, CA: Medical Data Exchange.

Pickering, W. R. (1990). *Information sources in pharmaceuticals*. London and New York: Bowker-Saur.

Pinson, Lewis J., & Wiener, Richard S. (1990a). *Applications of object-oriented programming*. Reading, MA: Addison-Wesley Publishing.

Pinson, Lewis J., & Wiener, Richard S. (1990b). Object-oriented design of a branch path analyzer for C-language software systems. In Lewis J. Pinson & Richard S. Wiener (Eds.), *Applications of object-oriented programming* (pp. 164–208). Reading, MA: Addison-Wesley Publishing.

Plutchak, T. Scott. (1990). New approaches to access: CD-ROM at the St. Louis University Medical Center Library. In Linda Stewart, Katherine S. Chiang, & Bill Coons (Eds.), *Public Access CD-ROMs in libraries: Case studies* (pp. 109–122). Westport, CT: Meckler Corporation.

Pollitt, A. S. (1987). CANSEARCH: An expert systems approach to document retrieval. *Information Processing and Management, 23*(2), 119–138.

Pollitt, A. S. (1990). Intelligent interfaces to online databases. *Expert Systems for Information Management, 3*(1), 49–69.

Prerau, David S. (1989). Choosing an expert system domain. In G. Guida & C. Tasso (Eds.), *Topics in expert systems design* (pp. 27–43). Amsterdam: Elsevier Science Publishers.

Quarterman, John S. (1990). *The Matrix: Computer networks and conferencing systems worldwide*. Bedford, MA: Digital Press.

Quarterman, John S., & Hoskins, Josiah C. (1986). Notable computer networks. *Communications of the ACM, 29*, 932–971.

Quinn, Kenneth. (1990). Expert system shells: What to look for. *RSR, 18*(1), 83–86.

Quint, Barbara. (1987). Setting our priorities. In Bernard F. Pasqualini (Ed.), *Dollars and sense: Implications of the new online technology for managing the library* (pp. 1–8). Chicago: American Library Association.

Raeder, Aggi W., & Andrews, Karen L. (1990). Searching library catalogs on the Internet: A survey. *Database Searcher, 6*(7), 16–31.

Raimondo, Paula G. (1990). CD-ROM teaching techniques: Instructing PsycLIT users in a health sciences library. In Linda Stewart, Katherine S. Chiang, & Bill Coons (Eds.), *Public access CD-ROMs in libraries: Case studies* (pp. 135–146). Westport, CT: Meckler Corporation.

Ranade, Sanjay. (1990). Archive storage media alternatives. *Optical Information Systems, 10*(1), 7–13.

Rapaport, Matthew J. (1991). Computer conferencing, bulletin boards, and information professionals. *Online, 15*(3), 33–37.

Rapp, Barbara A., Siegel, Elliot R., Woodsmall, Rose Marie, & Lyon-Hartmann, Becky. (1990). Evaluating MEDLINE on CD-ROM: An overview of field tests in library and clinical settings. *Online Review, 14*, 172–186.

Reese, Jean. (1990). CD-ROM technology in libraries: Implications and considerations. *Electronic Library, 8*(1), 26–35.

Reichman-Adar, Rachel. (1984). Extended person-machine interface. *Artificial Intelligence, 22*, 157–218.

Rheingold, Howard. (1991). *Virtual reality.* New York: Summit Books.

Richardson, John. (1989). Toward an expert system for reference service: A research agenda for the 1990's. *College and Research Libraries, 50*, 231–248.

Riechel, Rosemarie. (1989). Online information retrieval in the public library: Staff selection and development for quality service. *Reference Librarian, 25/26*, 617–629.

Ringle, Martin D., & Halstead-Nussloch, Richard. (1989). Shaping user input: A strategy for natural language dialogue design. *Interacting with Computers, 1*, 227–244.

Roberts, Justine T., & Jensen, Lydia. (1986). Self-service at the information supermarket: Report on an enduser's online shopping trip. *Reference Librarian, 16*, 153–175.

Robinson, Mark L. (1990). Dialog business databases: An informal survey of prices. *Online Review, 14*, 318–326.

Rodriguez, Walter E. (1987). Computer graphic tools and the design of microcomputer graphics user-interface to improve the information systems dialogue. *Microcomputers for Information Management, 4*, 283–301.

Rosen, Linda. (1990). CD-ROM user interfaces: Consistency or confusion? *Database, 13*(2), 101–103.

Rosenberg, Victor. (1989). Desktop research and software connectivity. *Library Hi Tech, 7*(4), 85–88.

Rosenberg, Victor. (1990). Desktop research: Information management for the scholar. In *Proceedings of the 5th Jerusalem Conference on Information Technology. Next Decade in Information Technology* (pp. 639–642). Los Alamitos, CA: IEEE Computer Society.

Roysdon, Christine M., & Elliot, Laura Lee. (1988). Electronic integration of library services through a campuswide network. *RQ, 28*, 82–93.

Salomon, Kristine. (1988). The impact of CD-ROM on reference departments. *RQ, 28*, 203–215.

Salton, Gerald. (1968). Automated language processing. In Carlos A. Cuadra (Ed.), *Annual Review of Information Science and Technology, 3* (pp. 169–199). Chicago: Encyclopedia Britannica, Inc.

Salton, Gerald (Ed.). (1971). *The SMART retrieval system: Experiments in automatic document processing.* Englewood Cliffs, NJ: Prentice–Hall.

Sano, Hikomaro. (1988). Online databases as sources of linguistic information. *Online Review, 12*, 15–23.

Sarangapani, Chet. (1990). Development and evaluation of a reference expert system in chemistry. In Martha E. Williams (Ed.), *National Online Meeting. Proceedings 1990* (pp. 355–362). Medford, NJ: Learned Information.

Scanlan, Jean M., de Stricker, Ulla, & Fernald, Anne C. (1989). *Business online: The professional's guide to electronic information sources.* New York: John Wiley & Sons.

Scanlan, Jean M. (1990). Comparison shopping of tax research databases. *Database, 13*(1), 13–17.

Schank, Roger C., with Childers, Peter G. (1984). *The cognitive computer: On language, learning, and artificial intelligence.* Reading, MA: Addison-Wesley Publishing.

Schleifer, Neal. (1989). Use of the Macintosh in the reference section. In Bill Vaccaro & Edward J. Valauskas (Eds.), *Macintoshed Libraries 2.0* (pp. 71–73). Cupertino, CA: Apple Library Users Group.

Schloman, Barbara F., Gatten, Jeffrey N., & Byerly, Greg. (1990). Fee-based CD-ROMs at Kent State University. In Linda Stewart, Katherine S. Chiang, & Bill Coons (Eds.), *Public access CD-ROMs in libraries: Case studies* (pp. 207–216). Westport, CT: Meckler Corporation.

Schneider, M., & Trepied, C. (1990). Graphical description and query interface for databases. In G. Cockton (Ed.), *Engineering for Human Computer Interaction. Proceedings of the IFIP TC2/WG 2.7 Working Conference* (pp. 63–86). Amsterdam: North-Holland.

Schuyler, Michael. (1991). Systems librarian and automation review. *Computers in Libraries, 11*(8), 35–40.

Schwarzwalder, Robert. (1991). Online protein sequence data searching. *Database, 14*(5), 106–108.

Sears, A., Plaisant, C., & Shneiderman, B. (1990). *A new era for touchscreen applications: High precision, dragging icons, and refined feedback.* Report numbers CAR-TR–506 and CS-TR–2487. College Park, MD: Human-Computer Interaction Laboratory, Department of Computer Science, University of Maryland.

Shneiderman, Ben. (1987). *Designing the user interface: Strategies for effective human-computer interaction.* Reading, MA: Addison-Wesley Publishing.

Shneiderman, Ben. (1991). *Tree visualization with tree-maps: A 2-d space-filling approach.* Report numbers CAR-TR–548 and CS-TR–2645. College Park, MD: Human-Computer Interaction Laboratory, Center for Automation Research, University of Maryland.

Shockley, J. S. (Ed.). (1988). *Information sources for nursing*. New York: National League for Nursing.

Shortliffe, Edward H. (1984). Details of the consultation system. In B. G. Buchanan & E. H. Shortliffe (Eds.), *Rule based expert systems* (pp. 78–132). Reading, MA: Addison-Wesley.

Shroder, Emelie J. (1981). Community information in the 80's: Towards automation of information and referral files. *RQ, 21*, 135–155.

Silver, Howard, & Dennis, Sharon. (1990). Monitoring patron use of CD-ROM databases using SignIn-Stat. *Bulletin of the Medical Libraries Association, 78*, 252–257.

Silverstein, Steven H. (1990). An index model of query formulation. *Legal Reference Services Quarterly, 10*(3), 115–124.

Simon, Marjorie. (1986). The BRS/After Dark search service in a health sciences library. In M. Sandra Wood, Ellen Brassil Horak, & Bonnie Snow (Eds.), *End user searching in the health sciences* (pp. 163–178). New York: Haworth Press.

Slator, Brian M. (1989). Extracting lexical knowledge from dictionary text. *Knowledge Acquisition, 1*, 89–112.

Slavens, Thomas P. (1989). *Retrieval of information in the humanities and social sciences: Problems as aids to learning*. New York: Marcel Dekker.

Slonim, J., & Bauer, M. A. (1990). The role of workstations in the information utility: A model for user oriented information systems. In H. Berghel, E. Unger, & R. Rankin (Eds.), *Proceedings of the 1990 ACM SIGSMALL/ PC Symposium on Small Systems* (pp. 228–237). New York: ACM Press.

Smith, Dana E. (1989). Reference expert systems: Humanizing depersonalized service. *Reference Librarian, 23*, 177–190.

Smith, Karen F. (1986). Robot at the reference desk? *College and Research Libraries, 47*, 486–490.

Smith, Karen F. (1990). POINTER: The microcomputer reference program for federal documents. In Rao Aluri & Donald E. Riggs (Eds.), *Expert systems in libraries* (pp. 41–50). Norwood, NJ: Ablex Publishing Company.

Snow, Bonnie. (1989a). Patents in non-patent databases: Food, agriculture and environment files. *Database, 12*(6), 115–119.

Snow, Bonnie. (1989b). When hospitals mean business: Online sources for health care marketing information. *Online, 13*(6), 112–116.

Spring, Michael B. (1991). *Being there or models for virtual reality*. Unpubished manuscript. Pittsburgh, PA: Information Science, University of Pittsburgh.

Stahl, J. Natalia. (1990). Using the Internet to access CARL and other electronic information systems. *Science and Technology Libraries, 11*(1), 19–30.

Starr, Karen. (1990). The byte of electronic information at Oregon State University: The CD-ROM Reference Center at the Kerr Library. In Linda Stewart, Katherine S. Chiang, & Bill Coons (Eds.), *Public access CD-ROMs in libraries: Case studies* (pp. 193–206). Westport, CT: Meckler Corporation.

Steffen, Susan Swords. (1986). College faculty goes online: Training faculty end users. *Journal of Academic Librarianship, 12*, 147–151.

Steffey, Ramona J., & Meyer, Nicki. (1989). Evaluating user access and satisfaction with CD-ROM. *Laserdisk Professional, 2*(5), 35–45.

Stein, Richard M. (1991). Browsing through terabytes. *BYTE, 16*(5), 157–164.

Stern, D., Mischo, W. S., & Cole, T. W. (1990). Customizing searcher workstations: Development of communication and software for online searching. *Database Searcher, 6*(3), 16–22.

Stern, David. (1991). Physics and astronomy databases: Inspec and Phys compared. *Database, 14*(5), 55–66.

Stern, H. David. (1990). Artificial intelligence databases: A survey and comparison. *Database, 13*(4), 19–24.

Stewart, Linda. (1990). An overview of public access issues. In L. Stewart, Katherine S. Chiang, & Bill Coons (Eds.), *Public access CD-ROMs in libraries: Case studies* (pp. 1–22). Westport, CT: Meckler Corporation.

Stewart, L., Chiang, Katherine S., & Coons, Bill (Eds.). (1990). *Public access CD-ROMs in libraries: Case studies*. Westport, CT: Meckler Publishing.

Stewart, Linda, & Olsen, Jan. (1988). Compact disk databases: Are they good for users? *Online, 12*(3), 48–52.

Stone, Peter. (1991). JANET: An overview for libraries. *Electronic Library, 9*(3), 174–175.

Stoss, Frederick, W. (1991). Environment online: The greening of databases. Part 1. General interest databases. *Database, 14*(4), 13–27.

Stout, Robert J., & Peterson, Dennis R. (1989). E-mailing downloaded search and SDI results using a DEC VAX and ALL-IN-1 Software. *Special Libraries, 80*, 164–168.

Sutherland, I. E. (1965). The ultimate display. In Wayne A. Kalenich (Ed.), *Proceedings of the IPIP Congress 65, Vol. 2* (pp. 506–508). Washington, DC: Spartan Books.

Sutter, Eric. (1989). Standards information retrieval. In Charles Oppenheim, Charles Citroen, & Jose-Marie Griffiths (Eds.), *Perspectives in information management 1* (pp. 119–132). London and Boston: Butterworths.

Swanson, Don R. (1964). Dialogues with a catalog. *Library Quarterly, 34*, 113–125.

Talbot, Dawn E. (1991). *Japan's high technology: An annotated guide to English-language information sources*. Phoenix: Oryx Press.

Tatalias, Jean. (1985). Attitudes and expectations of potential end user online searchers. In Martha E. Williams & Thomas H. Hogan (Eds.), *National Online Meeting Proceedings—1985* (pp. 457–462). Medford, NJ: Learned Information.

Taylor, Robert S. (1968). Question negotiating and information seeking in libraries. *College and Research Libraries, 29*, 178–194.

Thimbleby, Harold. (1990). *User interface design*. New York: ACM Press.

Thompson, Bozena H., & Thompson, Frederick, B. (1983). Introducing ASK, a simple knowledgeable system. In *Proceedings of the Conference on Applied Natural Language Processing* (pp. 17–24). Menlo Park, CA: Association for Computational Linguistics.

Tinsley, G. Lynn. (1989). An electronic bulletin board: Library. *Special Libraries, 80*(3), 188–192.

Tollander, Carl. (1990). *Collaborative engines for multi-participant cyberspace*. Available from Autodesk, Inc. Sausalito, CA.

Tschanz, Virginia. (1991). Assessment of a HyperCard program at Penrose Library, the University of Denver. *RSR, 19*(1), 39–47.

Uehara, K. (1989). An intelligent on-line help system: ASSIST. *Future Generations Computer Systems, 5*(1), 11–20.

Van Camp, Ann J. (1990). Strategies and codes for finding cancer information online. *Online, 14*(5), 114–116.

Van Melle, William. (1984). The structure of the MYCIN system. In B. G. Buchanan & E. H. Shortliffe (Eds.), *Rule based expert systems* (pp. 67–77). Reading, MA: Addison-Wesley.

Vedder, Richard G., Fortin, Maurice G., Lemmermann, Scott A., & Johnson, Ralph N. (1989). Five PC-based expert systems for business reference: An evaluation. *Information Technology and Libraries, 8*, 42–54.

Vickery, Alina, Brooks, H., Robinson, B., & Vickery, B. (1987). A reference and referral system using expert system techniques. *Journal of Documentation, 43*, 1–23.

Waiblinger, John. (1991). USCInfo: A development platform for tomorrow's information rich environment. In Edward J. Valauskas & Bill Vaccaro (Eds.), *Macintoshed Libraries 4* (pp. 74–80). Cupertino, CA: Apple Library Users Group.

Walker, Donald E. (1973). Automated language processing. In Carlos A. Cuadra (Ed.), *Annual Review of Information Science and Technology, 8* (pp. 69–119). Washington, DC: American Society for Information Science.

Walker, Geraldene. (1990). Searching the humanities: Subject overlap and search vocabulary. *Database, 13*(5), 37–46.

Walker, John. (1988). *Through the looking glass: Beyond user interfaces.* Sausalito, CA: Autodesk.

Wall, C., Haney, R., & Griffin, J. (1990). Hard copy versus online services: Results of a survey. *College and Research Libraries, 51*, 267–276.

Walser, Randal. (1990a). Doing it directly—the experiential design of cyberspace. In John O. Merritt & Scott S. Fisher (Eds.), *Proceedings of 1990 SPIE—International Society for Optical Engineering, Volume 1256. Stereoscopic Displays and Applications* (pp. 147–153). Bellingham, WA: Society of Photo-optical Instrumentation Engineers.

Walser, Randal. (1990b). Elements of a cyberspace playhouse. In *Proceedings of National Computer Graphics Association '90.* (pp. 403–411). Fairfax, VA: National Computer Graphics Association.

Walser, Randal. (1990c). *The emerging technology of cyberspace.* Sausalito, CA: Cyberspace Project, Advanced Technology Department, Autodesk.

Walsh, B. P., et al. (1987). *Online information: A comprehensive business user's guide.* Cambridge, MA: Blackwell Press.

Warner, Amy J. (1987). National language processing. In Martha E. Williams (Ed.), *Annual Review of Information Science and Technology, 22* (pp. 79–108). New York: Elsevier Science Publishers.

Wasserman, Paul, Koehler, Barbara, & Lev, Yvonne. (Eds.). (1987). *Encyclopedia of senior citizen information sources.* Detroit: Gale Research.

Waters, Samuel T. (1986). Answerman, the expert information specialist: An expert system for retrieval of information from library reference books. *Information Technology and Libraries, 5*, 204–212.

Weckert, John, & Cooper, Clara. (1990). Artificial intelligence, expert systems and librarianship: A review of the literature. *Australian Library Review, 7,* 281–299.

Weingarten, Fred. (1991). Five steps to NREN enlightenment. *EDUCOM Review, 26*(1), 26–30.

Weintraub, I. (1986). Computerized information systems in American agriculture. *Quarterly Bulletin. International Association of Agricultural Librarians and Documentalists, 31*(3), 119–125.

Whalen, Thomas E., & Patrick, Andrew S. (1990). COMODA: A conversation model for database access. *Behavior and Information Technology, 9*(2), 93–110.

Whitaker, Cathy Seitz. (1990). Pile-up at the reference desk: Teaching users to use CD-ROMs. *Laserdisk Professional, 3*(2), 30–40.

White, Frank. (1990). Scripting: Automate your library's PC telecommunications. *Online, 14*(6), 49–51.

White, Howard D., & Woodward, Diana. (1990). A model of reference librarian's expertise: Reviving research on a microcomputer. In Rao Aluri & Donald E. Riggs (Eds.), *Expert systems in libraries* (pp. 51–63). Norwood, NJ: Ablex Publishing Company.

Wiggins, Gary. (1990). *Chemical information sources*. New York: McGraw-Hill.

Whillhite, Sherry, & Nickelson-Dearie, T. (1990). RoboRef at the University of California, San Diego. In Bill Vaccaro & Edward J. Valauskas (Eds.), *Macintoshed libraries 3.0*. (pp. 77–81). Cupertino, CA: Apple Library Users Group.

Winblad, Ann L., Edwards, Samuel D., & King, David R. (1990). *Object-oriented software*. Reading, MA: Addison-Wesley Publishing Company.

Wirick, Terry. (1991). GET reference after dark. *Computers in Libraries, 11*(3), 22.

Woggon, Michele. (1987). Economic statistical data online: A primer. *Database, 10*(5), 70–74.

Woods, L. B., & Walker, Jon. (1989). Automation of community information and referral services. *Information Technology and Libraries, 8,* 393–399.

Wu, C. Thomas. (1990a). Benefits of object-oriented programming in implementing visual database interface. *Journal of Object Oriented Programming, 2*(6), 8–16.

Wu, C. Thomas. (1990b). Development of a visual database interface: An object-oriented approach. In Lewis J. Pinson & Richard S. Wiener (Eds.), *Applications of object-oriented programming* (pp. 101–138). Reading, MA: Addison-Wesley Publishing.

Yee, Martha M. (1991). System design and cataloging meet the user: User interfaces to online public access catalogs. *Journal of the American Society for Information Science, 42,* 78–98.

Young, Robert J. (1990). Artificial intelligence and school library media centers. *School Library Media Quarterly, 18,* 150–157.

Youngkin, Mary E., McCloskey, Kathleen M., Dougherty, Nina E., & Peay, Wayne J. (1990). CD-ROM utilization in a health sciences setting. In Linda Stewart, Katherine S. Chiang, & Bill Coons (Eds.), *Public access CD-ROMs in libraries: Case studies* (pp. 123–134). Westport, CT: Meckler Corporation.

Index

About the Author

ROBERT CARANDE is Head of the Science Division in the University Library of San Diego State University. He specializes in expert systems and computer applications in reference services.